PAINTING

WITH

NUMBERS

**Presenting Financials and Other Numbers
So People Will Understand You**

PAINTING

WITH

NUMBERS

RANDALL BOLTEN

WILEY

WILEY

John Wiley & Sons, Inc.

Published by John Wiley & Sons, Inc., Hoboken, New Jersey.

Published simultaneously in Canada.

For general information on our other products and services or for technical support, please contact our Customer Care Department within the United States at (800) 762-2974, outside the United States at (317) 572-3993 or fax (317) 572-4002.

Wiley also publishes its books in a variety of electronic formats. Some content that appears in print may not be available in electronic books. For more information about Wiley products, visit our web site at www.wiley.com.

Library of Congress Cataloging-in-Publication Data:

Bolten, Randall,
Painting with numbers: presenting financials and other numbers so people will understand you/Randall Bolten.
　　p. cm.
　　Includes index.
　　ISBN 978-1-118-17257-5 (book); 978-1-118-22789-3 (ebk); 978-1-118-23996-4 (ebk); 978-1-118-25782-1 (ebk)
　　1. Business mathematics.
　　2. Microsoft Excel (Computer file) I. Title.
　　HF5691.B675 2012
　　650.0285′554—dc23

　　　　　　　　　　　　　　　　　　　　　　　　　　　　　　　　2011042678

Printed in the United States of America

10　9　8　7　6　5　4　3　2　1

For Rachel and Molly,
my favorite girls
and my two favorite writers

Contents

Foreword

I first met Randall Bolten in early 2009, as I was beginning my run for California statewide office. He was my contact for a dinner speech I was giving, and I sent him some economic data to be turned into slides and a handout. What came back was not just a correct and accurate presentation of the data, but one that was clear, concise, and comprehensible. Based on that experience, I retained Randall to prepare the economic and fiscal policy handouts that I used throughout the campaign. My data and graphical presentations became a mainstay of how I presented my public policy suggestions. I feel strongly that clearly and honestly presented data is essential to an informed electorate, and Randall made it possible for me to put that belief into practice.

Looking back on my terms in the U.S. Congress, in the California State Senate, and as Director of Finance for California, I am struck by how often arguments are won on the basis of how the numbers are presented. I am also struck by how great the temptation is for shading numerical data. Some of that temptation comes simply from the presenter's lack of skill at presenting numbers. But some of that temptation also comes from the view—which, sadly, is all too often correct—that the audience will not speak up when they do not understand or are skeptical of the information put in front of them, and will, instead, be swayed simply by the amount, or exclamatory nature, of the data presented.

As Director of Finance for the State of California, I had to reconcile many different ways of presenting similar data from different departments of the state government. In that position, it was obvious that how clearly and coherently information is presented has a huge impact on how effective the presentation is. It was also obvious that a consistent approach to presenting the underlying numbers—in essence, creating a "common language"—is critical in a complex organization like the government of the State of California to making intelligent decisions, and to fostering a team approach to problem solving.

As a Dean in both public and private universities, I was introduced to new ways of presenting similar data, and my ability to comprehend the information was strongly affected by the way the data were presented.

In all of my roles, the ability to explain decisions to a larger audience—voters, students, faculty, trustees, legislature, press—demanded a need for simplicity, clarity, and transparent honesty. In the best-functioning organizations I have been associated with, the key players have had this ability when presenting statistics, financial data, and other numbers, and their audience has expected and demanded no less.

I'm delighted that a book like *Painting with Numbers* is available. I am confident that the lessons Randall Bolten sets forth in this book, a first of its kind, will have a hugely positive effect on the level of public debate, and thus, the quality of the choices we make in our public and private lives.

Tom Campbell

Preface

Everybody talks about the weather, but nobody does anything about it.

—Mark Twain

The concept for *Painting with Numbers* was one of those ideas that just emerged slowly over time. During my nearly 20 years as chief financial officer of high-technology companies in Silicon Valley, I saw small changes in documents containing numbers make a huge difference in how well they were understood. This happened over and over. In the case of financial documents, poorly understood reports could lead to mass confusion or even mistakes costing millions of dollars. But the right presentation of that same information could make an audience think *aha!* and motivate outstanding performance.

I also couldn't help observing that the people generating these reports—extremely competent and intelligent people—often overlooked the nuances of these small changes and the effect they had on their audiences. When we reviewed the results afterward, though, they readily saw the connection. It became increasingly clear to me that presenting numerical information is a *communication* skill, and not some sort of black art practiced only by the "numbers guys." I've stated that premise in hundreds of conversations since I began writing this book—with people ranging from accounting students and administrative assistants to CEOs and corporate directors—and the response has always been enthusiastic agreement. At the same time, though, very few of the people I spoke with had any sense of what that *meant* for how they should lay out numbers on a page, or a computer monitor, or a projection screen.

Think about it. A significant portion of our school years, especially in elementary and middle school, is devoted to training us to write and speak correctly, clearly, succinctly, and eloquently. We are taught grammar, vocabulary, diction, sentence structure, and paragraph organization. Even beyond our basic education, we are expected to continue to improve our grasp of the nuances of effective writing and speaking—*about* a particular subject, *to* a particular audience, *with* a particular purpose in mind. Bookstore shelves are loaded with books intended to sharpen those skills, with titles including *The Elements of Style*; *Eats,*

Shoots & Leaves; *The Careful Writer*; *The Business Letter Handbook*; *How to Write a Million-Dollar Memo*; and *Public Speaking: An Audience-Centered Approach*.

Still, mathematics for the most part continues to be taught as a computation skill, not as a language for describing complex problems and situations. And although there are plenty of books about how to *understand* numbers, about the underlying mathematics, and even about how people try to fool you with numbers, there are *no* books focused solely on how to make yourself understood when you are presenting numbers.

Because the need to present numbers is critical in so many places in our society, I'm grateful and flattered that Tom Campbell agreed to write the Foreword for *Painting with Numbers*. His remarkable career has included public service as an elected legislator (U.S. Representative and State Senator) and executive branch appointee (California Budget Director when the state last reported a budget surplus); a Ph.D. economist, lawyer, and law professor; and a dean of both a business school (U.C. Berkeley, Haas School of Business) and a law school (Chapman University School of Law). Perhaps more important, he speaks and writes with precision, grace, humor, and a respect for his audience.

My goal with *Painting with Numbers* is to enable you to become as skilled at presenting numbers to an audience as the most articulate among us are at writing for and speaking to an audience. Whether you are an accounting, finance, or engineering professional who presents numbers as an essential part of your job; or you are a corporate law, litigation, human resources, marketing, investor relations, fundraising, or other professional who presents numbers less frequently (but when you do the stakes are high); or you are a government official or elected representative responsible for understanding and explaining important issues of fiscal management, taxation, healthcare, or other areas of public policy; or you are a senior manager or board member who must make complex decisions under time pressure based on the information presented *to you*—this book is for you. Enjoy!

Randall Bolten
Glenbrook, Nevada
February, 2012

Acknowledgments

First, my sincerest thanks go to Taylor Ray, editor extraordinaire, who understood what *Painting with Numbers* was about from the very beginning and stuck with the project through all its stops and starts. She was both immensely supportive and unfailingly candid, and worked tirelessly to make sure I honored my compact with the reader.

A few played special roles in the creation of this book. Joel Orr helped me get organized, explained the ins and outs of the publishing business, and offered wisdom that was rabbinical in the best sense of the word. John Cardozo demonstrated that a friend is someone who reads every word you've written even when he has more important things to do. And Tom Campbell not only agreed to apply its lessons to the electorate and lend his name to this book, he was the most punctilious, yet most insightful, witty, and supportive of readers—and this while running for statewide office in California.

Many people read parts of this book and made invaluable comments, including Stephen Few, Shomit Ghose, Dana Hendrickson, Karl May, Barbara McMurray, Larry Moseley, Ethan Thorman, Linda Wilson, and Donna Winslow. The finance team at Fortinet (Robert Lerner, Tim Emanuelson, Keith Andre, Jim Bray, Daneya Denson, Doug May, Scott Robinson, and Simran Singh) met with me frequently as a group to offer their from-the-trenches perspectives. To readers I somehow failed to mention, my apologies and my thanks.

My professional colleagues in the Silicon Valley chapter of Financial Executives International deserve special thanks as a group. Many made contributions to the content of this book, whether they knew it or not, and all indulged me patiently as I talked through my ideas.

I thank current math faculty at St. Albans School—Messrs. Kelley, Hansen, and Eagles—for their feedback on the book and for introducing its lessons to high school students. I also salute some of the teachers from my days as a student there, who made it clear that expressing yourself in your own language and style was not just tolerated, but a sacred obligation—especially Messrs. Means, Saltzman, Ruge, and McCune.

Many folks at Wiley deserve mention. Tim Burgard, Stacey Rivera, Andrew Wheeler, and Helen Cho were a real help to a first-time author and led me to intelligent choices. Natasha Andrews-Noel shepherded this book and a demanding author through a production process that was much more complex than I could possibly imagine. And my thanks go to Anne Ficklen for the introduction, and to Michael Rutkowski for just nailing the jacket design.

Some people less directly involved with the book itself deserve mention. A few comments made years ago still stick with me and helped spur me to this project: my appreciation goes to Jeff Walker, Woody Rea, Nort Rappaport, and Van Van Auken. I thank Claude and Sue and Leland, who offered excellent company and an indulgent ear, not to mention good food in the dead of winter. Family members Joshua, Susanna, Dede, and Jimmy provided feedback and cheerleading, and have assured me they will generate thousands of orders for this book.

One person was essential to this book in many, many small, and a few big ways. Well done, Petunia!

Even a book about expressing yourself with clarity, precision, and accuracy will inevitably have errors. For these I accept responsibility. I hope you will let me know about them. I also hope that you have gotten value from this book.

quantation (kwŏn-tā´-shən) *n.* [English, c. 2008; from QUANTitative + communicATION.] The act of presenting numbers, such as financial results, electronically or in written form for the purpose of informing an audience.

INTRODUCTION

This Book is *Not* About Numbers—Honest!

The way you present says a lot about the way you think.

—Irwin Federman, venture capitalist

This book is not about numbers. This book is about *presenting* numbers, and doing it clearly, concisely, elegantly, and, most of all, *effectively*. This distinction between numbers and presenting numbers is critical, and to give you a glimpse of what's to come, let me ask you some questions. When doing *quantation*,[1] have you ever experienced the following:

- Your audience simply didn't "get it"?
- You spent too much time just explaining how to read and understand your tables, charts, or slides, instead of discussing the actual contents of your reports?
- You depended on people to read your materials *before* the meeting or presentation, and when they didn't do it, you couldn't achieve what you wanted?
- You caught some dumb mistakes, but only after it was too late to fix them? Or even worse, *your audience* caught your dumb mistakes?
- Your report/presentation had too much detail for your audience to zero in on the really important stuff? Or even worse, they simply gave up trying to understand?

If your answer is *yes* to any of these questions, then you've felt the agony and frustration of poor quantation. If you've been one of the "victims" in the audience,[2] then you've known the sinking feeling of watching a presenter's time and credibility painfully slip away.

Being "Literate"

Presenting numbers is the same as presenting any other information. If your audience can't follow what you are presenting well enough to understand it, then *you* haven't communicated. It doesn't matter if your numbers are well-researched, organized with great effort, and *correct*. If no one understands what you're trying to say, the problem is yours to fix.

Put another way, to do effective quantation you need to "be literate." And I don't just mean the more conventionally known definition of "being able to read." Being literate means much more than that. Being literate is not merely about understanding *words*, but about comprehending *any* information presented to you—images, numbers, charts. It's not just about *comprehending* information, but about *how you present it*. And it's not just about what you *know*, but about *people's perceptions* of what you know. In other words, being literate is about your knowledge, and your ability to present it so others perceive you as knowledgeable.

It's What *They* Think That Matters

The previous point deserves some extra emphasis. An important part of being literate comes from other people's perceptions of what you know. To help you understand how this works in real life, consider these questions:

- When you see someone confuse *its* and *it's*, do you form a general conclusion about the writer's literacy or even about his or her intellect?
- Do you (like many other people) routinely reject job applicants who have even one typo in their résumé or cover letter?
- Do you form distracting and negative conclusions about people from their unintentionally hilarious errors?

Perception is important, and *based on little things, people form global, and sometimes harsh, conclusions about you*—about your intelligence, your literacy, your grasp of the subject matter, your professionalism, your ethical standards, and your respect for your audience (to name a few traits you probably value).

There's one more thing about these little errors and embarrassments: the more important and influential people are, the more likely they are to form these snap judgments, and form them quickly. Not only are these people very busy, but they're the kind of people who take pride in their speed and decisiveness. And the saddest part about the harshest conclusions is that *people will rarely tell you*. It's like that little piece of spinach stuck between your teeth all evening at the annual company holiday party. No one mentioned it to *you*, but it sure was amusing conversation the next day in the hallways and the break room.[3]

So how do you avoid these negative perceptions and make sure that you are received as professionally as possible? If you're communicating in *words*, you have lots of tools to guide you that you spent years learning: there's vocabulary, grammar, diction, sentence structure, and paragraph organization. And if you use these tools well, your audience will consider you to be thoughtful and careful. But what about *quantation*? Are there rules and guidelines for presenting numbers? Of course there are, and that's what this book is about.

What You Were Never Taught

The rules and practices that help you present numbers are similar to the rules and practices that make people effective writers and speakers. Unfortunately, very little of your education was probably devoted to developing these skills of quantation. This is especially unfortunate because typically when numbers are presented, significant decisions need to be made. These presentation skills are important even if you don't present numbers often, because when you *do* have to present numbers, it's likely that the stakes are going to be especially high.

Moreover, much of the value you reap from presenting numbers does not result from the time you spend compiling and generating the information, but rather from the time you take designing, organizing, and laying out the information you worked so hard to collect. The time that it takes to design, organize, and lay out your reports typically only takes 20% (or less) of your time. But then there's that "80/20 Rule" that every MBA learns: 80% of the impact of any effort comes from only 20% of the time you spend on that effort. In a nutshell, this book is about spending that 20% of your time to your best advantage so you can become a better communicator of numbers, *and therefore a better communicator in general.*

Let's recap the key points so far:

1. When you present numbers, you are responsible for making sure your audience comprehends the information. Your audience will certainly hold you responsible.

2. If your audience fails to understand the information, your professional image and credibility will suffer. Moreover, you will waste time explaining what your information means instead of addressing your more important goals.

3. Small, innocent mistakes (in both language and numbers) have a disproportionately negative impact on how your skills, professionalism, and intellect are perceived by others.

(continued)

4. The more important someone is, the more likely he or she is to reach these negative conclusions (about your presentation skills, professionalism, and/or intellect). And the more important someone is, the faster he or she will reach that conclusion.

5. All of the above points apply to presenting numbers as surely as they apply to any other communications; unfortunately, most of us haven't been formally taught the skills to do effective quantation. That's a shame, because quantation is a skill that can be taught and learned.

6. When a communication task involves quantation, doing it effectively is important both to the success of the task and to you personally:

   • When you are presenting numbers, the stakes are usually high.

   • If your job requires a lot of quantation (accounting, finance, or marketing analysis, for example) how you present numbers is a big part of your own professional image.

   • If your job doesn't require much quantation, when you do have to present numbers, the stakes are probably *very* high.

7. The quantation task is the least time-consuming task in a project involving collecting, summarizing, organizing, and presenting numbers. If it's done poorly, all of your other good work goes to waste. But if it's done well, it becomes the most important and valuable task in the project.

8. Quantation is not about numbers; it's about communicating to an audience (and you don't have to be the resident "numbers guy" to do it well). Generating clear, effective quantation is what this book is about.

I chose "The way you present says a lot about the way you think" as the epigraph for this Introduction because it relates to all of the reasons listed above. Perhaps Mr. Federman was specifically referring to standing up and giving an oral presentation, but I believe it is apt for *any* way you present information. When you present numbers, you expose every aspect of your thought process (or lack thereof) to your audience.

Please note: Nothing in this book is intended to be used as a cookbook. My goal is to give you the tools to enable *you* to design reports yourself that meet *your* quantation needs. Next is one example, of a printout I found taped to a table in the lobby of a county clerk's office. By the end of this book, you'll be able to identify everything that's wrong with this document, and you'll know how to improve it.

```
          MASS  CONVERSION  FOR  METERS  TO  FEET

   Divide  the  amount  of  meters  by  .3048  to  get
   the  proper  feet

           Meters                    Feet
           1,524                      5'
           1,5494                     5'1"
           1,5748                     5'2"
           1,6002                     5'3"
           1,6256                     5'4"
           1,651                      5'5"
           1,6764                     5'6"
           1,7018                     5'7"
           1,7272                     5'8"
           1,7526                     5'9"
           1,778                      5'10"
           1,8034                     5'11"
           1,8288                     6'
           1,8542                     6'1"
           1,8796                     6'2"
           1,905                      6'3"
           1,9304                     6'4"
```

The Ultimate Goal

As any good artist or teacher will tell you, you don't create a great painting because you went to the best art schools, used all the available colors, or knew the latest brushstroke techniques. The test of a great painting lies more in the answers to questions like: Does the painting tell a story? Is the viewer led to *care* about that story? Has the artist revealed the essential nature of the subject, regardless of how big or small the canvas is? My goal in *Painting with Numbers* is to give you all you need to know to communicate financials and other numbers so that you can tell your story in a way that is clear, comprehensible, concise, elegant, and, most of all, effective.

Some Notes about Reading This Book

Painting with Numbers covers what you need to know to do quantation effectively. It's divided into four sections: The Rules, The Tools, Real Mastery, and Wrap-Up.

Part I: The Rules discusses the rules and practices that can help you "be literate" when you're doing quantation—much the same way understanding grammar and using it effectively help you communicate and "be literate" when you write or speak. It's critically important for you to understand *why* these rules and practices work, so I'll discuss that as well. The topics covered in this section are:

- **Chapter 1**—numerals—describes how to use the Arabic numeral system, not just correctly, but to your advantage.
- **Chapter 2**—visual appearance—addresses how to convey information just by how you lay it out on the page, and how to use visual effects to enhance your reports.
- **Chapter 3**—words—examines the importance of getting the *words* right, and not just the numbers.
- **Chapter 4**—the audience—reveals how people in general, and your audience in particular, process information, what that means for the way you do quantation, and how the way you present information sends loud signals about your respect for your audience

Part II: The Tools offers a practical, tactical discussion about how to use the principal software tools to maximum advantage in your quantation.

- **Chapter 5—Instant Payoff Tips** for spreadsheets—focuses on skills to help you to be a *faster* user of Excel, so that being under time pressure will not be a barrier to effective quantation. The Instant Payoff Tips will make your work go faster *every* time you create and deliver a spreadsheet.
- **Chapter 6**—Long-Term Payoff Tips for spreadsheets—focuses on how to use Excel to make your life easier when you revisit spreadsheets long after you first delivered them, and how to improve the lives of people who are *users* of your spreadsheets (or inherit your work).
- **Chapter 7**—graphs—discusses how to make visual information comprehensible and meaningful to your audience.
- **Chapter 8**—presentations and PowerPoint—addresses the special factors to consider when you're presenting numbers to a live audience.

Part III: Real Mastery addresses the importance of subject-matter expertise when delivering quantation, examines practical applications of quantation, and provides examples of widely used reports, with particular emphasis on applying the rules and techniques from the chapters in Part I.

- **Chapter 9**—real professionalism—discusses the perspective you'll want to bring when you actually sit down to develop your own reports, and interact with your audience as a peer.

- **Chapter 10**—key indicators—discusses how to use ratios and other metrics together with the basic report information to add even more meaning to your quantation, and to make the information easier for your audience to understand.

- **Chapter 11**—the "natural P&L"—examines the challenge of management financial reporting, with a detailed review of the one report that is (or at least should be) the central management report for most organizations.

- **Chapter 12**—GAAP—provides a nontechnical examination of when and how management financial reporting differs from the reporting required by generally accepted accounting principles (GAAP). This chapter might be of particular interest and importance to readers with a professional accounting background, and those dealing with the reporting issues of publicly traded companies.

- **Chapter 13**—U.S. income taxes—reviews in detail how quantation can be used to clarify public policy issues, using the U.S. individual income taxation system as a case study.

- **Chapter 14**—quantation in ordinary life—offers quantation examples from other, more mundane walks of life, and illustrates how quantation shows up in the news and other unexpected places, in ways you might not think of.

Part IV: Wrap-Up is exactly that. Chapter 15 includes my thoughts on ethics, honesty, character, and other cosmic issues, and how all that relates to quantation. Chapter 16 provides a summary of all that we covered, and includes a discussion of how good quantation *begins*. In the Appendix, we revisit all of the Deadly Sins (defined momentarily) in one place, and from some unusual perspectives.

Important Elements to Aid Your Memory. Throughout *Painting with Numbers* you will find structural elements intended to drive home the main points of the book. These elements can be collected in quick lists for future reference. The principal elements are "The Deadly Sins of Presenting Numbers" and "Strong Advice," both of which appear sprinkled throughout these pages. There are also chapter-specific elements, including the "Instant Payoff Tips" and the "Long-Term Payoff Tips" for efficient and effective spreadsheet delivery, and the "Characteristics of a Well-Designed Natural P&L."

The Deadly Sins of Presenting Numbers is my metaphor to drive home the notion that seemingly small errors can say more than you ever want (or deserve) about your thought process. The Deadly Sins are quantation errors that you should avoid at all costs, because they are:

- Distracting, defocusing, or annoying to your audience (and not just something people recognize and disregard as a minor error)

- Relatively common
- Easily avoided
- Indications that you don't respect your audience, don't understand what they are looking for, or don't have any idea how to help them understand your information

As an antidote to the Deadly Sins, from time to time I introduce suggestions labeled as **Strong Advice**. I make numerous suggestions in these pages, and most of them are just that—suggestions—but the "Strong Advice" items are counsels that you should *always* follow. When you do, they will make your quantation powerful indeed.

The chapter-specific elements are groups of suggestions that you will find useful in highly tactical situations. The "Instant Payoff Tips" and the "Long-Term Payoff Tips" will be of use in making you a *faster* spreadsheet user. In fact, you might find them most useful if you're *not* a frequent or regular spreadsheet user and haven't had a chance to build up your habits and your memory of the tricks of the trade. The "Characteristics of a Well-Designed Natural P&L" in Chapter 11 is a list of characteristics that will be useful when you have to design a management P&L, but also when you have to manage your organization from reports provided to you.

The Exhibits: No Previous Accounting Experience or Graphics Arts Talent Needed. The majority of the exhibits and corresponding discussions relate to a variety of business situations, but I have designed them so that the discussion will be meaningful even if you have had only a passing exposure to financial statements and no technical accounting experience at all. Moreover, the purpose of the exhibits is to illustrate presentation techniques and not the underlying accounting. So if, when it comes to numbers, you think of yourself as a "poet," take heart—this book is for you, too. There may be a couple of chapters late in the book that you might choose not to focus on, but that would be because they lack relevance to you, not because they're over your head.

Just as I believe that financial and accounting experience are *not* prerequisites to reading and understanding *Painting with Numbers*, neither is any skill in graphics arts. Every single exhibit in this book was created by me, a real non-artist, using off-the-shelf Microsoft Excel 2010 with an ordinary font (Arial 10 points), and then *pasted* into the pages of this book. In other words, these exhibits look *exactly* like reports that you might generate yourself in Excel. I've tried to make sure that the print in all of the Excel exhibits was sized equally; because of the space limitations of a book page, that meant a somewhat smaller print size than you would see on a paper printout, but the exhibits are still easily readable. For the few exhibits that needed further size reduction, my apologies, but please understand that the main point for those exhibits was about layout, and the readability of the numbers themselves was of less concern. The spreadsheet design practices used here are nothing more than habits I've developed in the nearly 30 years since I was first exposed to spreadsheets. Producing good-looking, clear, and effective quantation doesn't require talent, but it does require attention to detail, a passion for delivering a high-quality product, and—something that gets more than a passing mention in this book—building habits and setting standards for yourself that enable you to produce beautiful information *every* time you sit down to design a report.

The Footnotes—Sometimes Informative, Sometimes Entertaining, Not Necessarily Essential. Throughout this book I have added technical and other details that you might find useful. They offer historical or theoretical context for points made in the text, or they are my own opinions or other relevant personal observations. While I hope you will find them interesting and valuable, I present them as footnotes because they are not essential to the narrative flow of the text, and you will not miss any of the fundamental essence of *Painting with Numbers* by ignoring them.

NOTES

1. **quantation** (kwŏn-tā'-shən) *n.* [English, c. 2008, from QUANTitative + communic-ATION]. The act of presenting numbers, such as financial results, electronically or in written form for the purpose of informing an audience. (Note: *Quantation* is the word I coined to describe the subject of this book, because no single word for it exists. It is not a word you will find in the dictionary, as of this writing.)

2. By "audience," we don't just mean a live audience at an oral presentation. Your audience could be reading hardcopy printouts, receiving e-mail messages, or sitting right next to you.

3. With these types of reaction in mind, if you don't know whether *its* or *it's* is appropriate in any given situation, do yourself a favor: *Find out. Right now.* It's a mistake that rarely makes a sentence hard to understand, but even so it might be the English grammar mistake most likely to cause you to be perceived as stupid and illiterate. For a similar perspective on this topic from the perspective of someone who cares deeply about the quality of written English, I highly recommend *Eats, Shoots & Leave: The Zero Tolerance Approach to Punctuation*, by Lynne Truss. A close second to the *its/it's* error are the *your/you're* exacta and the *there/their/they're* trifecta. Moreover, if you're relying on the built-in error-checking features in today's word processing software to protect you from boneheaded mistakes, guess again—all of the mistakes I've cited are *very* unlikely to be caught by built-in software.

PART I

THE RULES

CHAPTER 1

Numerals Matter

A facial expression of total astonishment.

—How a tribe in South America expresses numbers greater than 3, since their language has no word for those numbers (*1963 Guinness Book of World Records*)

You never know where a great idea will come from. That's why I'd like to start this chapter with a heartfelt thank-you to the Arabs. Let's consider what this summary of Vaporware and Software Technologies Corp.'s six-year financials might have looked like if history had been a little different (Report 1-1).

Report 1-1						
VASTCo -- MCMXCVIII-MMIII Financial Highlights						
(in $M)	**MCMXCVIII**	**MCMXCIX**	**MM**	**MMI**	**MMII**	**MMIII**
Revenues	DCXCIX	CML	MCDXCIII	MMCXXXVIII	MMCMX	MMMCMXCVIII
Expenses	DCLXII	DCCC	MCCVII	MDCXXXIX	MMCCCXLVIII	MMMCCCXLIII
Operating Profit	XXXVII	CL	CCLXXXVI	CDXCIX	DLXII	DCLV

REPORT 1-1: VASTCo MCMXCVIII–MMIII Financial Highlights

So, is VASTCo doing well? Would you buy their stock? Do you have any idea what this table is saying?

Let's try this again with a slightly different look at the same set of VASTCo financials (Report 1-2).

Report 1-2 VASTCo -- 1998-2003 Financial Highlights						
(in $000)	**1998**	**1999**	**2000**	**2001**	**2002**	**2003**
Revenues	699	950	1,493	2,138	2,910	3,998
Expenses	662	800	1,207	1,639	2,348	3,343
Operating Profit	37	150	286	499	562	655

REPORT 1-2:   VASTCo 1998–2003 Financial Highlights

Now *this* table is a lot easier to understand. As it turns out, VASTCo is one hot company, with revenues growing and profit growing even faster. And the reason this table is so much more comprehensible is *because of the Arabic numerals*. So what makes Arabic numerals so special?

- **You need to know only ten symbols.** In the Arabic numeral system, you need to know only the numerals 0 through 9 to recognize every single number, no matter how big or small. These ten symbols are also simple to learn, even for a child.

- **It's easy to spot the biggest (or the smallest) numbers.** More digits always means larger, and if two numbers have the same number of digits, you simply compare the leftmost digit.

- **A quick glance can tell you everything you need to know.** By taking advantage of these two features *together*, you can pick out key information in the blink of an eye.

The point here is that our number system is an immensely powerful communications tool when we take full advantage of it. Thank you, Arabs![1] To understand just how effectively you can communicate when you present numbers correctly—and how *ineffectively* you communicate if you don't—let's look at some more examples.

Lining Up the Numbers

Report 1-3 shows a company's sales by product. The three columns (Versions A, B, and C) contain identical numbers, but differ in presentation. Look at each version by itself, covering up the other two, and try to pick out at a glance which products have the highest and which have the lowest sales.

Almost everyone will say that getting the essence of the information in the table in Report 1-3 is much easier in Version A than Versions B or C. Why is that?

- **The largest numbers** (Charlie, Echo, Hotel) **stand out visually.** In the Arabic numeral system, numbers with more digits always have a larger absolute value than those with fewer digits, so Charlie, Echo, and Hotel have the

Report 1-3 Corporate Sales, by Product			
	Version A	**Version B**	**Version C**
Product	**Sales**	**Sales**	**Sales**
Alpha	1,163	1,163	1,163
Bravo	500	500	500
Charlie	15,695	15,695	15,695
Delta	7,863	7,863	7,863
Echo	37,638	37,638	37,638
Foxtrot	3,550	3,550	3,550
Golf	645	645	645
Hotel	22,500	22,500	22,500
India	10	10	10
Juliet	5,007	5,007	5,007

REPORT 1-3, VERSIONS A,B,C: Corporate Sales by Product

most digits. The same goes for the smallest number (India) but in reverse. The visual discrimination is harder in Version B, because half of the length difference in the numbers shows up on the left side and half on the right.

- **The numerals visually sticking out are the *important* numerals.** In Version A, it's easy to see that Echo has the biggest sales, followed by Hotel, and then Charlie, simply by looking at the leftmost digits: a *3*, a *2*, and a *1*, respectively. In Version C, the rightmost digits stick out, and these rightmost digits are the least significant.

- **The commas line up vertically only in Version A.** If the commas (or the decimal points, for that matter) line up, that also means the 1's digits all line up, and the 10's, and the 100's, and so on.[2] Also, when the commas don't line up, it simply looks strange to the eye.

- **The format mirrors the way we were taught.** Think back to how we've been taught to add a column of numbers, or multiply two numbers together. How were you taught? Do you line up the numbers at the left edge or at the right?

These observations bring us to the first Deadly Sin of Presenting Numbers:

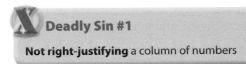

Deadly Sin #1

Not right-justifying a column of numbers

You might think this mistake is too obvious to mention, but alas, it isn't. I see this particular error in board meetings, financial reports, and sales presentations all the time. As you've just experienced, making a point *always* to right-justify is one of those small formatting choices that has a powerful impact on the readability of your information, and on your audience's ability to comprehend it quickly.

The Units of Measure

As long as we're talking about how the placement of your numbers on the page can affect audience understanding (and speed of comprehension), let's take a look at different ways to present the units your numbers are measuring, such as dollars, or square inches, or miles per hour. Here's Report 1-3 again, with three new versions. This time, all three have right-justified numbers, but they show different ways of presenting the units of measure. As with the previous presentation of this report, look at each version by itself, covering up the other two, and form an opinion about which is the easiest to read.

	Report 1-3 Corporate Sales, by Product		
	Version D	**Version E**	**Version F**
Product	**Sales**	**Sales**	**Sales ($)**
Alpha	$1,163	$ 1,163	1,163
Bravo	$500	500	500
Charlie	$15,695	15,695	15,695
Delta	$7,863	7,863	7,863
Echo	$37,638	37,638	37,638
Foxtrot	$3,550	3,550	3,550
Golf	$645	645	645
Hotel	$22,500	22,500	22,500
India	$10	10	10
Juliet	$5,007	5,007	5,007
TOTAL	$94,571	$ 94,571	94,571

REPORT 1-3, VERSIONS D,E,F: Corporate Sales by Product

Almost everyone will say that Version D is by far the hardest to read, because it takes extra effort to separate visually the numeric digits from the currency symbol. Moreover, the currency symbol is obscuring the leftmost digit, which is the single most important digit in the number. It would help a little if there were a space or two between the currency symbol and the digits, but not much, and furthermore you should ask yourself: Is the dollar sign really necessary for each number? [3]

Version E addresses these issues with the convention commonly used in formal accounting reports, which is to (1) put the currency symbol at the left edge of the column, far from the digits, and (2) include the currency symbol only next to the number at the top of the column and with the total at the bottom. This approach works fine visually, but it involves some extra effort by the presenter because it means formatting two cells—the one at the top of the column and the total at the bottom—differently from the other cells in the column.

Personally, I prefer the approach in Version F, which completely omits the currency symbol from the numbers in the body of the report, and includes it in the column heading instead. I like this approach because it's clean, minimizes extraneous characters, and requires a little less column width, which may come in handy in reports where space is a concern. (And frankly, you can usually assume that everyone in your audience knows the national currency of your financials!) But even when you use a minimalist approach, it's important to remember:

Strong Advice

Always make sure that your audience has a way to determine the **unit of measure** for *all* of the numbers in your reports. You can never be certain who will look at your reports, and what they do and don't know.

This discussion of how to identify the units of measure, especially currency notation, can sound like nitpicking, but it illustrates two larger points. First, small differences in formatting can have a large enough impact on the readability of your information to be worth considering carefully. Failing to get this right can alienate your audience, if only subconsciously. Second, *you have choices.* This will be a recurring theme in this chapter and throughout this book. Even with something as mundane as formatting spreadsheet cells, the choices you make will enable you to make information clearer and your presentations more effective.

Note

The choices you make will enable you to **put your own personal stamp** on the way you present numbers. You should never make presentation choices solely to make your reports unnaturally distinctive, but you still have an opportunity to create a "personal brand identity" by generating reports that are always well-organized and easy-to-read (an opportunity we discuss extensively in *Painting with Numbers*). Ideally, you could become one of those people who gets comments like "I always enjoy getting your reports; the news is not always good, but I can always understand what the numbers mean!"

Precision

But wait, there's more! You also have choices as to the level of detail you offer the audience, depending on the purpose of your presentation. Let's revisit the same VASTCo financial highlights we first saw in Reports 1-1 and 1-2. Take a look at five versions of the same report (Reports 1-4A through E), and form your own conclusions about how readable each one is, and how effectively it presents information. *(There is no one right answer here, since all the reports present exactly the same data.)*

Report 1-4, Version A
VASTCo -- 1998-2003 Financial Highlights

(in $MM)	1998	1999	2000	2001	2002	2003
Revenues	1	1	1	2	3	5
Expenses	1	1	1	2	2	3
Operating Profit	0	0	0	0	1	1

Report 1-4, Version B
VASTCo -- 1998-2003 Financial Highlights

(in $MM)	1998	1999	2000	2001	2002	2003
Revenues	0.7	0.9	1.5	2.1	2.9	4.7
Expenses	0.7	0.8	1.2	1.6	2.3	3.3
Operating Profit	0.0	0.1	0.3	0.5	0.6	1.4

Report 1-4, Version C
VASTCo -- 1998-2003 Financial Highlights

(in $000)	1998	1999	2000	2001	2002	2003
Revenues	699	950	1,493	2,138	2,910	4,733
Expenses	662	800	1,207	1,639	2,348	3,343
Operating Profit	37	150	286	499	562	1,390

Report 1-4, Version D
VASTCo -- 1998-2003 Financial Highlights

(in $)	1998	1999	2000	2001	2002	2003
Revenues	699,350	949,990	1,492,858	2,138,044	2,909,750	4,733,091
Expenses	662,423	800,018	1,207,132	1,638,979	2,348,148	3,342,593
Operating Profit	36,928	149,972	285,725	499,065	561,602	1,390,498

Report 1-4, Version E
VASTCo -- 1998-2003 Financial Highlights

(in $)	1998	1999	2000	2001	2002	2003
Revenues	699,350.30	949,990.10	1,492,857.66	2,138,044.05	2,909,750.42	4,733,091.00
Expenses	662,422.57	800,017.98	1,207,132.20	1,638,979.09	2,348,148.11	3,342,593.00
Operating Profit	36,927.73	149,972.12	285,725.46	499,064.96	561,602.31	1,390,498.00

REPORT 1-4, VERSIONS A,B,C,D,E: VASTCo 1998–2003 Financial Highlights

Which ones work for you? Personally, I find Version A (in millions, with no decimal places) completely useless, because it provides no sense of year-to-year variations that might be of great interest and importance to the reader. And Version E (numbers down to the penny) is almost as bad, because the additional digits just get in the way of visual comprehension without adding any useful information whatsoever.

My own preference is the middle one, Version C (in thousands, with no decimal places), which the astute observer will notice is identical to Report 1-2, because it's a well-balanced combination of readability and precision. But remember that I was a chief financial officer for many years, and while CFOs need to have more than just a passing acquaintance with the numbers, they don't pay us the big bucks to get mired down in details. In other words, I like this report because it's at the level of detail a typical CFO needs, which just proves the adage, "Where you stand depends on where you sit."

On the other hand, a member of the board of directors might be completely satisfied with Version B (in millions, with one decimal place), because it certainly provides enough precision to enable the reader to identify significant trends. And for the same reasons this is most likely the right level of detail for a presentation to investors. Moreover, investor presentations are often slideshows or PowerPoint documents, where you don't have room for lots of digits and characters, and where you don't *want* the conversation to go down the details rat hole.[4]

At the opposite extreme is someone reconciling different financial reports to each other, or using the report to determine compensation. I say this because when you are dealing with paychecks, people can be comforted to know that amounts are being calculated exactly. For these particular purposes, the level of detail shown in Version D (to the nearest dollar) might be essential.

There are two important lessons to learn from this discussion about the number of digits:

1. **"Precision" and "accuracy" are *not* the same concept.** To illustrate this point, suppose you are holding a jar containing 6,037 jellybeans, and you ask two friends to tell you how many jellybeans are in the jar. Friend A says, "8,488," and Friend B says, "About 6,000." Friend A's answer is the more precise one, but Friend B's is the more accurate one. The various versions of Report 1-4 above are all equally accurate, but differ greatly in precision.

2. **You have choices!** The differences between the five versions of Report 1-4 are a simple matter of Excel formatting,[5] and no additional time or effort is involved. There are valid reasons for choosing at least three of the five versions (and some highly compulsive person could probably justify Version E as well). Your choice depends on factors such as how the audience is using the information, the forum for presenting the information, and how much time is available for the presentation.[6]

Note

One suggestion: An experienced and highly practical finance manager I know addresses the decision about precision with a very simple rule: **no number in a report should have more than five digits.** While this may not be the right choice if consistency is one of your presentation objectives (more on that topic later), her instincts are spot-on for what is comprehensible to an audience.

Negative Numbers: What Do They Mean?

No discussion of numbers and numerals would be complete without at least a passing mention of **negative numbers**. And here, too, you have an opportunity to add meaning and clarity to your quantation[7] *by making intelligent choices.* When you see a column of a table where the numbers could be either positive or negative, what exactly does the distinction between positive and negative mean? Here are some examples (note that the first and the last are applicable to single numbers, but the other three require a comparison of one number to another):

What the number means if it is. . .

Positive	Negative	Examples
Greater than zero	Less than zero	Profit Cash flow
More than another number	Less than another number	Comparison to a "standard" (target, quota, etc.)
Increasing over time	Decreasing over time	Comparison to the prior period (year, quarter, month, etc.)
"Good"	"Bad"	Budget variance Opinion scoring
Debit	Credit	Accounting systems[8]

Sometimes the right choice is obvious. For example, if you're presenting net income or cash flow, virtually everyone understands that positive and negative numbers discriminate between turning a profit and losing money, or generating cash and burning cash. This is an example where the distinction between "more than zero" and "less than zero" is straightforward and well understood.

To appreciate some of the distinctions in the above table, and to illustrate the choices you have, let's take a look at a couple of examples, starting with Report 1-5.

```
┌─────────────────────────────────────────────────────────┐
│                       Report 1-5                          │
│             VASTCo -- Results for 2001 and 2002           │
│                                                           │
│                            2001    2002     Y/Y           │
│   (in $000)              Actual  Actual  Change           │
│                                                           │
│   Revenues                2,138   2,910     772           │
│   Expenses                                                │
│      Sales & Marketing      876   1,387     511           │
│      Research & Development 445     550     105           │
│      General & Administrative 318   411      93           │
│   Operating Profit          499     562      63           │
└─────────────────────────────────────────────────────────┘
```

REPORT 1-5:   VASTCo Results for 2001 and 2002

Looking at the "Y/Y Change" column, we see that VASTCo's change in Sales & Marketing expense between 2001 and 2002 was $411,000—a *positive* number. This aligns with the way we naturally think. We say to ourselves, "From 2001 to 2002, VASTCo Sales & Marketing expense increased by $411,000," and not, "2001 Sales & Marketing expense was less than the 2002 number by $411,000." In contrast, for General & Administrative expense, which *decreased* slightly from 2001 to 2002, the change shows up as a negative number.

Well, that was easy. We *always* think about year-over-year change as the later-year number minus the earlier-year number, and not the other way around. But sometimes you should stop and think about how to do the arithmetic, and the best example of that is the *budget variance*.

A budget variance is the difference between the actual result for a period and the amount that was budgeted. This is a corner of the quantation world where good and evil actually *do* exist, because the difference between actual and budget is sometimes *good* and sometimes *bad*. At the same time, consider that we have strong connotations with the words *positive* and *negative* when they are used in a nonmathematical sense. So you have a golden opportunity to merge your left brain with your right brain in a single seamless act of quantation! (See Report 1-6.)

(in $000)	Version A			Version B		
	← 2002 →			← 2002 →		
	Actual	Budget	Var.	Actual	Budget	Var. F(U)
Revenues	2,910	2,800	110	2,910	2,800	110
Expenses						
Sales & Marketing	1,387	1,125	262	1,387	1,125	(262)
Research & Development	550	580	(30)	550	580	30
General & Administrative	411	395	16	411	395	(16)
Operating Profit	562	700	(138)	562	700	(138)

Report 1-6
VASTCo -- 2002 Results, Actual vs. Budget

REPORT 1-6, VERSIONS A and B: VASTCo 2002 Results, Actual versus Budget

The two versions of Report 1-6 show two ways of calculating budget variances. In Version A, the variance is calculated the same way for every line, just like "Y/Y Change" in Report 1-5: the variance is the 2002 Actual number, minus the 2002 Budget number. Now, for Revenues, we would all say that the 2002 Actual of $2,910,000 is *better* than the Budget of $2,800,000. So far, so good. But when we come to Sales & Marketing expense, we see an Actual of $1,287,000, and a Budget of $1,125,000. When you spend more than you budgeted, is that a good thing? Probably not! And yet, the variance shows up as *positive* $162,000.

Version B fixes this error (and *error* is definitely the right word to use here) by calculating the variance as Actual minus Budget for the revenue and profit line items, *but Budget minus Actual* for the expense lines. Using this method, negative variances indicate problems (that is, Actuals that are *worse* than Budget), and positive numbers indicate results that are okay (that is, Actuals that are *better* than Budget). Please note the *Var F(U)* column caption. *F(U)* is commonly used notation to indicate that positive numbers are "Favorable" and negative numbers are "Unfavorable." The notation *B(W)* is sometimes used as well, to indicate whether the Actual result is "Better" or "Worse" than Budget. This captioning choice would have been inappropriate for Version A, since there is no subjective notion associated with whether the number is positive or negative, so the column caption is simply *Var.* instead.

I can tell you that the wrong budget variance presentation choice has provided me with many hours of cathartic irritation over the years. And I am not alone: almost every senior manager and corporate director I've talked to gets very annoyed when they see budget variances presented as in Version A of Report 1-5, because they can't pick out the "problem" variances at a glance just by looking for the negative numbers in the variance column.

What's important here is that it takes only a small amount of effort to get the spreadsheet formulas to present the variances correctly, and it's a nice thing to do for people who sometimes have to measure the time they can spend reviewing reports like this in seconds. And if you don't provide this courtesy, you risk having your audience conclude from a teensy oversight that you are *lazy*, not to mention totally unaware of how information gets used by an audience.

Let's recap the main points from this chapter:

- Our number system is based on the Arabic numeral system, which makes it incredibly easy to present numbers in a way that they can be understood visually and intuitively.

- If you want to take full advantage of the capabilities of the Arabic numeral system, *right-justify columns of numbers!*

- Be thoughtful about gunking up the numbers with units-of-measurement notations such as dollar signs. Ask yourself whether you're adding distinctions that justify making the numbers themselves harder to read.

- *Precision* and *accuracy* are not the same thing. How many digits you show your audience depends on how much space you have on the page, who your audience is, and what the report is going to be used for.

- The distinction between negative and positive numbers is important and informative. Remember that it matters, and present accordingly.

- In all aspects of quantation, *you have choices.* Making wise choices will dramatically improve the effectiveness of the information you present.

Understanding how to use numbers to do effective quantation is important. It's as important as good grammar and proper spelling are to effective writing. It's hard to be a truly effective communicator if you don't know have these skills, because grammar and spelling errors disturb the natural reading flow and may even make it harder for people to read and understand your writing. Similarly, you can't be an effective presenter if you don't know how to present numbers so that people can understand them quickly and get the maximum meaning from them.

But lest you think I am being unduly negative here, let me offer one more way to think about it: *Numbers are just words presented with a different set of characters.* And in the same way you choose your words carefully to have an impact, the choices you make in presenting numbers will make a big difference in how well your audience understands your message.

NOTES

1. To be completely fair, India deserves credit, too. Positional notation (that is, having the amount that a digit represents depend on its relative position within the number) was first developed by the Indians, and then spread throughout the western world by the Arabs. In fact, the Arabic term for this system actually translates as "Indian numerals." Originally, there were only nine numerals until the crucial addition of the zero in the ninth century, most likely by the Arabs. In any case, the invention of "Arabic numerals" is no different from any other great invention: we usually associate it with the person who sold it to us, not the one who invented it in the first place.

2. The convention in some European countries for commas and periods is the reverse of U.S. usage. They use a comma as the decimal point and a period as a separator between thousands, millions, and so forth. Don't get confused.

3. For single-character currency notations like $, €, or ¥, you have some real trade-offs. For other dimensions, such as *lbs.*, *sq. ft.*, or *units*, that's less true, because the dimension notation takes up too much space just to tell readers what they probably already know. Even if the notation is only next to a couple of the numbers in the column, the entire column has to be wider to accommodate it, which uses up space on the page you may not be able to spare.

4. If you just can't get enough of this fascinating topic, or you don't have anything better to do, I will observe that the difference between thousands and millions is subtle, but occasionally

important. Note that I use the notation *MM* to indicate millions, and *000* to indicate thousands. In the United States, *M* is also common notation for millions, and *K* for thousands. In many European countries, *M* means thousands (remember the Roman numeral *M*?) and *MM* means millions (i.e., thousand thousands). Avoiding the *M* notation for either amount eliminates any ambiguity.

5. All of the exhibits in this book are produced by the Microsoft Office® products Excel and PowerPoint. The raw numbers are identical in Reports 1-1, 1-2, and 1-4 (all five versions)—the only difference is how they are formatted (with the exception of the Roman numerals, which uses the ROMAN( ) function). You can even use Excel to truncate the last three or six or nine digits to present numbers in thousands, millions, or billions, respectively. Use the Format.Cells.Numbers command sequence. Check it out!

6. This is a book about *presenting* information, and so my focus is on the choices you can make about *precision*. But if this book were instead about *collecting* information, there might be a similar discussion about the choices around the *accuracy* of the information. Given additional time and resources, it is always possible to improve the accuracy of information. The question becomes whether the additional accuracy is worth the effort, or whether that amount of effort would have been better spent making the existing information more comprehensible. Forgive me for wearing my heart on my sleeve, but this question is central to the discussion of whether the Sarbanes-Oxley legislation actually made investors in U.S. public companies better off. I am one of many who question whether the stockholders of American public companies got good value from the roughly one-half trillion dollars (i.e., $500,000,000,000.00) of their money that has been spent on Sarbanes-Oxley compliance.

7. **quantation** (kwŏn-tā′-shən) *n.* [English, c. 2008, from QUANTitative + communicATION]. The act of presenting numbers, such as financial results, electronically or in written form for the purpose of informing an audience. (*Note: quantation* is the word I coined to describe the subject of this book, because no single word for it exists. It is not a word you will find in the dictionary, as of this writing.)

8. I include the *debit/credit* distinction for completeness, and not because it's likely to be relevant or interesting to you. In the world of double-entry bookkeeping, *debit* means "left" and *credit* means "right," and nothing more. (Or maybe it's the other way around—I can never remember.) In a computerized accounting system, all the debits are negative numbers and the credits are positive numbers and if the books are balanced, as they should be, the whole gigantic mess adds up to zero. There is no meaning to positive versus negative numbers other than that: there are actually accounting jokes (yes, such things exist!) about the fact that even highly experienced accountants sometimes get debits and credits confused—and this perspective tends to render professional accountants totally oblivious to the connotations that the distinction between the words "positive" and "negative" can have for normal humans.

CHAPTER 2

Looks Matter

Form ever follows function.

—Louis Sullivan (1856–1924), American architect considered the "father of the skyscraper"

Beauty is only skin-deep, but ugly goes clean to the bone.

—Dorothy Parker (1893–1967), American writer

Looks matter in quantation, just as they do in many avenues of life. First impressions are important, and when it comes to numbers, the first impressions you make as a presenter come from how you lay out your information on the page. How the page *looks* can tell your audience whether you're professional or unprofessional, well-prepared or sloppy, familiar with your audience or completely out-to-lunch.

Moreover, how you lay out the information on the page can be an important part of the *content* of your report. By using "white space" intelligently, you can tell your audience how they should group your information in their minds, what's important and what's not important, and where you want them to focus first. Also, visual clues (like font styles, point sizes, and color and shading) can help you highlight important data points, distinguish calculated values from user inputs, contrast raw information from key indicators, and highlight actual results from future or *pro forma* results.

If anything, all of this matters *more* with numbers than with words. People typically read written documents in a standard pattern—left to right, then top to bottom, one paragraph after another, and then on to the next page. Within the document, each paragraph starts with a sentence that lays out the main points, followed by the supporting detail, and then a concluding sentence.

Quantation doesn't work that way, because there is no standard way people read through quantation documents. Even though the principles of clear exposition and presentation flow are similar for *any* type of written communication, you've got much more flexibility about how to lay out the information on the page when you're dealing with numbers. This is a powerful capability, and if you use it wisely, it can work to your great advantage.

The *Tabula Rasa* Decision

Let's start with a clean, blank sheet of paper. In the United States, a sheet of paper is a rectangle 8½" by 11". It's slightly different in Europe and other places, but not by much. You need to have reasonable margins at the top, bottom, right, and left edges of the page. Not only are margins visually appealing, but they ensure that no information will be lost when your work is photocopied or three-hole punched.

The very first presentation decision you need to make is whether you want to orient the pages for your report using "portrait" (i.e., 8½" wide and 11" tall) or "landscape" (i.e., 11" wide and 8½" tall). Here is a rough idea of the size of the largest table you can fit in each orientation:

Page Orientation	Rows	Columns
Portrait	45	8
Landscape	30	13

With this information in hand, you can make an intelligent decision about how to lay out your reports. The question is: Which orientation is most likely to make your reports look good without forcing you to perform unnatural acts (like changing font sizes or playing with margins) to fit all your information on the page?

As a default orientation, I strongly recommend that you choose landscape. First, most well-designed reports don't require more than 30 rows, whereas having only 8 available columns for your report can be a significant restriction. Second, landscape is the most readable orientation for those who review reports on their computer monitors rather than in hardcopy. Finally, even if it's true that some of the reports in your package fit better in landscape and some fit better in portrait, it's irritating for readers to have to keep flipping the paper back and forth between the two orientations. Mark my words on this, because as we'll discuss in Chapter 4, consistency is essential to effective quantation.[1]

Another demonstration of consistency that your audience will appreciate is to have each of the typical report "dimensions" (i.e., time, organizational units, product lines, income statement line items, etc.) appear in every report in the same place on the page: that is, either *horizontally*, with the captions across the top of the page, or *vertically*, with the captions down the side. For the same reason that your audience doesn't enjoy *physically* flipping back and forth between landscape and portrait pages, they won't enjoy *mentally* flipping back and forth between the horizontal axis and the vertical axis. This means that if you choose landscape, you can be assured that your report will fit on one page if it requires 13 (or fewer) columns and 30 (or fewer) rows.

Note

For the sake of consistency, you should always try to present the time axis horizontally across the top of the page. Reports rarely present more than 12 months of data when the information is monthly, or more than two years if the information is quarterly. As a result, the limitation on the number of columns (especially if you're using landscape orientation) will rarely be a problem for the time dimension. Moreover, because this idea is so commonly held and widely understood, reports where the time axis runs vertically along the side of the page are rare and therefore jarring and confusing to many readers.

The "Where's Waldo?" Effect

A typical page has lots of characters (both Arabic numerals and Roman letters) that have the potential to be just a giant blob of toner marks to the reader's eye. Let's start the ball rolling by looking at VASTCo's summary income statement by month (Report 2-1).

Report 2-1, Version A VASTCo -- 2006 Income Statement, by Month													
(in $000)	Jan	Feb	Mar	Apr	May	Jun	Jul	Aug	Sep	Oct	Nov	Dec	Total
Licenses	987	1,263	1,698	1,029	1,317	1,770	1,071	1,371	1,842	1,113	1,430	1,894	16,785
Services	446	475	518	465	495	540	484	515	562	503	535	584	6,120
Total Revs.	1,433	1,738	2,215	1,494	1,812	2,310	1,555	1,886	2,404	1,616	1,965	2,478	22,905
Cost of Sales	205	229	266	214	239	277	223	249	289	232	259	300	2,982
Gross Profit	1,227	1,509	1,949	1,280	1,573	2,032	1,332	1,637	2,115	1,384	1,706	2,178	19,923
Sales & Mktg.	568	594	632	594	597	665	612	646	670	645	655	689	7,568
Resch. & Dev.	343	340	352	346	360	376	374	389	390	397	397	412	4,477
Gen. & Admin.	254	256	258	254	266	270	264	272	269	272	276	280	3,191
Total Op. Exps.	1,165	1,190	1,242	1,194	1,223	1,312	1,251	1,307	1,329	1,314	1,329	1,381	15,236
Operating Profit	62	319	707	86	350	720	81	330	786	70	378	797	4,687

REPORT 2-1, VERSION A: VASTCo 2006 Income Statement by Month

What do you think? Is this report easy to read? Could you find a result quickly if you had to make a snap decision? Most of us would say no, and let's explore why this true:

- There are 130 numbers in this report, and there's really no visual way to distinguish one number from another. You cannot quickly distinguish revenues from expenses, raw numbers from totals, or monthly results from the annual total. Putting underscores above the totaled numbers (i.e., Total Revs., Gross Profit, Total Oprg. Exps., and Operating Profit) will help a little, but not a lot.

- There are no visual cues to make it easier to locate and zero in on a number right in the middle of the table. For example, how quickly can you find R&D expenses for July?

Trying to read a report like this is a lot like playing "Where's Waldo?"[2] It's a fine way to pass the time if you're in the backseat of a car on a long, boring road trip, but not if you need the information to help you make some important decisions quickly.

Report 2-1 does have one saving grace, however: *the important stuff is around the edges.* In a report as densely crammed with stuff as this one is (and just imagine if it had many more than ten rows of numbers!), the only places where you can find anything quickly and easily are around the edges. Think about it: in numerical reports prepared in virtually all western languages, the *words* on the report are usually at the top and at the left edge, and the rest of the page is the numbers, just as they are in Report 2-1. Is this an accident? Of course not! The words are critical, because without them you have no idea what the numbers are measuring. So we use two of the edges of the report for the words.

But that still leaves you the right and bottom edges to use to your advantage. Think about it: you often hear businesspeople stress the importance of maximizing the "top line" (i.e., revenues) or the "bottom line" (i.e., profits). Are they important to maximize because they are the numbers at the top and the bottom of the page, or are they at the top and bottom of the page because they are important? (Have you ever heard a CEO or a CFO talk about the importance of maximizing the "middle line"?)

This point isn't quite as obvious for columns as it is for rows, as evidenced by the fact that you don't hear businesspeople talk about maximizing the "left column" or the "right column." But the vertical edges still do matter. In Version A of Report 2-1, we presented 12 monthly columns, but the single most important column—the Total for the twelve months—occupies the place of honor at the right edge.

So before we've even begun to discuss anything else about the visual appearance of effective quantation, we've learned one lesson:

 **Strong Advice**

Put the important numbers where they're easy for the audience to find, which is usually around the edges.

White Space Is Your Friend

One of your most effective tools for avoiding the "Where's Waldo?" effect is not the stuff that's printed on the page, but the stuff that isn't: the white space. To understand this better, let's look at a slightly reformatted version of the report we've just seen (see Report 2-1, Version B).

Report 2-1, Version B
VASTCo -- 2006 Income Statement, by Month

(in $000)	Jan	Feb	Mar	Apr	May	Jun	Jul	Aug	Sep	Oct	Nov	Dec	Total
Licenses	987	1,263	1,698	1,029	1,317	1,770	1,071	1,371	1,842	1,113	1,430	1,894	16,785
Services	446	475	518	465	495	540	484	515	562	503	535	584	6,120
Total Revs.	1,433	1,738	2,215	1,494	1,812	2,310	1,555	1,886	2,404	1,616	1,965	2,478	22,905
Cost of Sales	205	229	266	214	239	277	223	249	289	232	259	300	2,982
Gross Profit	1,227	1,509	1,949	1,280	1,573	2,032	1,332	1,637	2,115	1,384	1,706	2,178	19,923
Sales & Mktg.	568	594	632	594	597	665	612	646	670	645	655	689	7,568
Resch. & Dev.	343	340	352	346	360	376	374	389	390	397	397	412	4,477
Gen. & Admin.	254	256	258	254	266	270	264	272	269	272	276	280	3,191
Total Op. Exps.	1,165	1,190	1,242	1,194	1,223	1,312	1,251	1,307	1,329	1,314	1,329	1,381	15,236
Operating Profit	62	319	707	86	350	720	81	330	786	70	378	797	4,687

REPORT 2-1, VERSION B: VASTCo 2006 Income Statement by Month

This report is visually much easier to absorb. First of all, we reinstated the underscores, but equally important, this report also relies on intelligent spacing decisions. And in addition to making the report easier to read, there's actual logic underlying the spacing decisions, including:

- The most important elements stand apart (i.e., the Operating Profit row, and the Total column).

- The main row groups are distinguishable from each other (i.e., Revenues, Cost of Sales (and Gross Profit), and Total Operating Expenses).

- The captions for the rows that are *totals* are indented to further distinguish them[3] (i.e., Total Revenues, Gross Profit, Total Operating Expenses, and Operating Profit).

- The 12-month time scale is broken down into 3-month chunks (quarters). This not only works visually, but quarters are a time concept that most of us grasp intuitively, especially people in finance-related jobs or those working for public companies.

To illustrate a point about how this "better" version was constructed, let's take another look at it, but this time showing the cell gridlines (see Report 2-1, Version B (with Gridlines)).

Report 2-1, Version B (with Gridlines)													
VASTCo -- 2006 Income Statement, by Month													
(in $000)	Jan	Feb	Mar	Apr	May	Jun	Jul	Aug	Sep	Oct	Nov	Dec	Total
Licenses	987	1,263	1,698	1,029	1,317	1,770	1,071	1,371	1,842	1,113	1,430	1,894	16,785
Services	446	475	518	465	495	540	484	515	562	503	535	584	6,120
Total Revs.	1,433	1,738	2,215	1,494	1,812	2,310	1,555	1,886	2,404	1,616	1,965	2,478	22,905
Cost of Sales	205	229	266	214	239	277	223	249	289	232	259	300	2,982
Gross Profit	1,227	1,509	1,949	1,280	1,573	2,032	1,332	1,637	2,115	1,384	1,706	2,178	19,923
Sales & Mktg.	568	594	632	594	597	665	612	646	670	645	655	689	7,568
Resch. & Dev.	343	340	352	346	360	376	374	389	390	397	397	412	4,477
Gen. & Admin.	254	256	258	254	266	270	264	272	269	272	276	280	3,191
Total Op. Exps.	1,165	1,190	1,242	1,194	1,223	1,312	1,251	1,307	1,329	1,314	1,329	1,381	15,236
Operating Profit	62	319	707	86	350	720	81	330	786	70	378	797	4,687

REPORT 2-1, VERSION B (WITH GRIDLINES SHOWN):   VASTCo 2006 Income Statement by Month

With the gridlines in place, it's easy to see that the main change from Version A to Version B was simply the creative use of the Column Width and Row Height functions in Excel. The effort took me just a few minutes, but it makes all the difference in how easy to read (and therefore how effective) the report is.

...But White Space Is Not *Always* Your Friend

Using white space to group your numbers visually on the page makes your reports much easier to read, but be sure to identify a grouping approach that will make intuitive sense to your audience. Report 2-2, Version A, is an example that *doesn't* make intuitive sense; it's a report showing the same income statement rows as Report 2-1, but with columns showing actual, budget, and variance for both the current quarter and the year-to-date (and somewhat different row names, for the sake of illustration).

Report 2-2, Version A						
VASTCo -- 2006 Q3 Income Statement, Actual vs. Budget						
	Quarter Ended 9/06			Year-to-Date		
(in $000)	Actual	Budget	Variance F(U)	Actual	Budget	Variance F(U)
Licenses	4,284	4,064	220	12,348	11,792	556
Professional Services	1,561	1,530	31	4,498	4,321	177
Total Revenues	5,845	5,594	251	16,846	16,113	733
Cost of Sales	760	667	(94)	2,192	1,899	(293)
Gross Profit	5,084	4,927	157	14,654	14,214	440
Sales & Marketing	1,928	1,915	(13)	5,579	5,517	(61)
Research & Development	1,153	1,167	14	3,270	3,312	42
General & Administrative	805	798	(7)	2,363	2,313	(50)
Total Operating Expenses	3,887	3,880	(6)	11,212	11,142	(70)
Operating Profit excluding Impairment	1,198	1,046	151	3,442	3,072	370

REPORT 2-2, VERSION A: VASTCo 2006 Q3 Income Statement, Actual versus Budget

This looks a little strange, doesn't it? Here's why:

- The gaps between columns don't have a logical, intuitive meaning. Note that the two Variance columns are physically far away from the Actual and Budget columns from which they are derived, and in fact the Variance column for the Quarter is right up against the Year-to-Date Actual and Budget columns, from which it is *not* derived.

- There's a lot of white space immediately to the right of the row captions, which makes it harder to sight down the row and associate the numbers with their correct row captions. And what would happen to this report if it had even more columns, like three additional columns for the monthly results? If it did, you wouldn't be able to fit the report onto one page without committing some sort of "unnatural act."

This example shows that white space *can* be your friend, but it isn't *always* your friend. So let's fix this problem by using more reasonable column widths as shown in Report 2-2, Version B.

Report 2-2, Version B
VASTCo -- 2006 Q3 Income Statement, Actual vs. Budget

(in $000)	Quarter Ended 9/06			Year-to-Date		
			Variance			Variance
	Actual	Budget	F(U)	Actual	Budget	F(U)
Licenses	4,284	4,064	220	12,348	11,792	556
Professional Services	1,561	1,530	31	4,498	4,321	177
Total Revenues	5,845	5,594	251	16,846	16,113	733
Cost of Sales	760	667	(94)	2,192	1,899	(293)
Gross Profit	5,084	4,927	157	14,654	14,214	440
Sales & Marketing	1,928	1,915	(13)	5,579	5,517	(61)
Research & Development	1,153	1,167	14	3,270	3,312	42
General & Administrative	805	798	(7)	2,363	2,313	(50)
Total Operating Expenses	3,887	3,880	(6)	11,212	11,142	(70)
Operating Profit Excluding Impairment	1,198	1,046	151	3,442	3,072	370

REPORT 2-2, VERSION B: VASTCo 2006 Q3 Income Statement, Actual versus Budget

We've addressed the two problem issues described above, but the report *still* looks strange because when we reduced the column widths, several column captions and row captions ended up taking two rows to print.[4] Not only have we now lost the intuitive visual grouping of the *rows*, but the row heights themselves might be a problem, because those rows now take up space that you might not be able to spare if the report had more rows than it does in the above example.

So let's get this thing fixed once and for all (see Report 2-2, Version C).

Report 2-2, Version C VASTCo -- 2006 Q3 Income Statement, Actual vs. Budget						
	Quarter Ended 9/06			Year-to-Date		
(in $000)	Actual	Budget	F(U)	Actual	Budget	F(U)
Licenses	4,284	4,064	220	12,348	11,792	556
Prof. Svcs.	1,561	1,530	31	4,498	4,321	177
Total Revenues	5,845	5,594	251	16,846	16,113	733
Cost of Sales	760	667	(94)	2,192	1,899	(293)
Gross Profit	5,084	4,927	157	14,654	14,214	440
Sales & Marketing	1,928	1,915	(13)	5,579	5,517	(61)
Research & Dev.	1,153	1,167	14	3,270	3,312	42
General & Admin.	805	798	(7)	2,363	2,313	(50)
Total Oprg. Exps.	3,887	3,880	(6)	11,212	11,142	(70)
Operating Profit	1,198	1,046	151	3,442	3,072	370

REPORT 2-2, VERSION C: VASTCo 2006 Q3 Income Statement, Actual versus Budget

Now I think we're done with this one. With a *thoughtful* shortening of some of the row and column captions, and the row heights and column widths we discussed for Report 2-1, we now have a report that's easy to read and intuitive to understand.

Grouping your numbers on the page in a logical and intuitively appealing way is so vitally important to the readability of your reports that I now introduce another Deadly Sin:

Deadly Sin #2

Basing column width or row height on the **length of the caption**

A quick comparison of Version C to the earlier versions of Report 2-2 shows you why this is a Deadly Sin. It takes minimal effort to come up with intelligent-but-terse captions, and to space the rows and columns so your audience can organize the information visually. And the good news is that you need only do this once, when you first design the report. Now, you have a report where the reader can focus on the numbers themselves, and not waste time just figuring out how to read the report.

There may be times when you can't shorten the column captions in a meaningful way. In this situation, you may want to consider angled captions. Angled column captions can be an option when you need to maximize your caption space in a crowded spreadsheet without creating too much white space, much the way municipalities maximize parking spaces on busy downtown streets. Report 2-3 shows an example of angled captions.[5] (Don't worry about the numbers in this report; it's the column headings we're interested in.)

Report 2-3
VASTCo -- Customer Relationship Tracking Worksheet @ 12/31/06 (in $000)

Customer	Sr. Sales	E-Staff	Marketing	Engrg.	Year-to-Date Sales			Forecast Pipeline		
					License	Service	YtD Total	License	Service	Fcst. Total
American Flywheel	X		X	X	986	230	1,216	681	143	823
General Earthworm		X			479	139	619	551	184	735
Jones Mufflers		X		X	865	198	1,064	580	89	669
Okoboji University			X		963	228	1,191	886	193	1,079
State of California			X		1,269	295	1,565	1,574	454	2,028
Xanthous Solutions	X			X	623	183	806	423	85	508

REPORT 2-3:   VASTCo Customer Relationship Tracking Worksheet @ 12/31/06 (in $000)

Angled captions result in column widths that are no greater than they need to be, but allow easy-to-read captions that don't use up too much white space.

Time and Other Dimensions: Across or Down?

In most reports where time is one of the dimensions, the time scale runs horizontally along the top edge of the report. Why is that so? Take a look at these two versions of Report 2-4, each representing exactly the same content. This is a report you've already seen (Report 1-2, from Chapter 1).

Report 2-4, Version A
VASTCo -- 1998-2003 Financial Highlights

(in $000)	1998	1999	2000	2001	2002	2003
Revenues	699	950	1,493	2,138	2,910	4,733
Expenses	662	800	1,207	1,639	2,348	3,343
Operating Profit	37	150	286	499	562	1,390

REPORT 2-4, VERSION A: VASTCo 1998–2003 Financial Highlights

Report 2-4, Version B
VASTCo -- 1998-2003
Financial Highlights

(in $000)	Revs.	Exps.	Op. Prof.
1998	699	662	37
1999	950	800	150
2000	1,493	1,207	286
2001	2,138	1,639	499
2002	2,910	2,348	562
2003	4,733	3,343	1,390

REPORT 2-4, VERSION B: VASTCo 1998–2003 Financial Highlights

Which version do you prefer? Most of us are more comfortable with Version A, perhaps for reasons we can't articulate. But here are four reasons that choice is valid and appropriate:

1. **Reading flow.** In most of the western world, we read from left to right and *then* from top to bottom. I suggest that this is no different: if you are scanning for a trend in any of the three line items (Revenues, Expenses, or Profit), reading horizontally across the page is more comfortable.

2. **Mathematical logic.** Profit = Revenues – Expenses. That's how we think about it, of course, and we were schooled to write out the calculation as: (1) Revenues above (2) Expenses, then (3) an underscore below Expenses, and then (4) the difference (i.e., Profit) below that. The underscore is a visual clue to show the reader that Profit is the result of an operation involving Revenues and Expenses, and it's is a visual clue that is missing in Version B.

3. **Consistency.** Version A presents the time axis the way you will see it in almost every report you're likely to encounter. Any other way of presenting time, therefore, looks strange.

4. **Caption length.** It's virtually impossible to commit Deadly Sin #2 if the width of the caption is less than the width of the numbers that it is identifying. Every unit of time measurement (years, quarters, months, even days of the week) can be expressed in four characters or less. Here are some examples:

Years	2004	2005	2006									
	'04	'05	'06									

Quarters	04q1	04q2	04q3	04q4								
	Q1	Q2	Q3	Q4								

Months	Jan	Feb	Mar	Apr	May	Jun	Jul	Aug	Sep	Oct	Nov	Dec
	J	F	M	A	M	J	J	A	S	O	N	D

Days	Mon	Tue	Wed	Thu	Fri	Sat	Sun
	M	Tu	W	Th	F	Sa	Su

But what if time *isn't* one of your two report dimensions? You might, for example, want to present product line revenues by geographic sales region, or hours spent by each engineer on different projects, or how many points each of the girls on your daughter's basketball team scored in each game. Here, the same rules apply; each decision you make about which dimension is vertical and which is horizontal can have a modest, but noticeable, impact on the readability of your reports. If you need guidance, the four criteria above will lead you to good decisions.

Borders, Shading, and Other Visual Effects

Everything on the page can send some kind of message to your audience. So far, we've focused on visual groupings and where the white space is (and isn't). But white space is about the *absence* of something, and there are plenty of effects where their actual *presence* sends a message. These include:

- Cell borders
- Text effects such as boldface, italics, color, font style, and font size
- Cell shading

Cell Borders. There may be times when you have too many numbers to present for white space to be a luxury you can afford. Let's take a look at Version C of Report 2-1, the VASTCo monthly income statement, which you've already seen in the two versions of Report 2-1.

Report 2-1, Version C
VASTCo -- 2006 Income Statement, by Month

(in $000)	Jan	Feb	Mar	Apr	May	Jun	Jul	Aug	Sep	Oct	Nov	Dec	Total
Licenses	987	1,263	1,698	1,029	1,317	1,770	1,071	1,371	1,842	1,113	1,430	1,894	16,785
Services	446	475	518	465	495	540	484	515	562	503	535	584	6,120
Total Revenues	1,433	1,738	2,215	1,494	1,812	2,310	1,555	1,886	2,404	1,616	1,965	2,478	22,905
Cost of Sales	205	229	266	214	239	277	223	249	289	232	259	300	2,982
Gross Profit	1,227	1,509	1,949	1,280	1,573	2,032	1,332	1,637	2,115	1,384	1,706	2,178	19,923
Sales & Mktg.	568	594	632	594	597	665	612	646	670	645	655	689	7,568
Research & Dev.	343	340	352	346	360	376	374	389	390	397	397	412	4,477
General & Admin.	254	256	258	254	266	270	264	272	269	272	276	280	3,191
Total Op. Exps.	1,165	1,190	1,242	1,194	1,223	1,312	1,251	1,307	1,329	1,314	1,329	1,381	15,236
Operating Profit	62	319	707	86	350	720	81	330	786	70	378	797	4,687

REPORT 2-1, VERSION C: VASTCo 2006 Income Statement by Month

The borders we've added to this report serve the same purpose as the white space we used earlier in the chapter: to group the columns into three-month quarters and separate the quarters from the total for the year; to group the rows into Revenues, Cost of Sales and Gross Profit, and Operating Expenses; and to separate the Operating Profit line from the rest of the lines. Moreover, I used doubled lines (= and ‖) to place further emphasis on the all-important Total column and Operating Profit row.[6]

Note

A digression on lines: Underscores and bottom borders are *not* the same thing; do not use them interchangeably. An underscore has a very specific mathematical meaning: it means that the number just below the underscore is the result of an operation (e.g., addition, subtraction) on the numbers above the underscore.[7] Use cell borders only for visual separation; confusing cell borders with underscores is an example of yet another Deadly Sin that you will see shortly.

Text Effects. If your report is even moderately loaded with numbers, you will want to give your audience some help picking out the important numbers from the supporting ones. So far, we've used visual effects to help organize and lay out your information, but you can also use text effects to provide more information *about the numbers themselves.* You can use text effects to:

- **Identify the more "important" numbers.** These could be annual totals, as opposed to the month or quarter results, or fundamental objective results (like total revenues or gross margin or profit) in contrast to the "raw numbers."

- **Distinguish numbers by their "origin."** These could be actual numbers versus budget numbers, or actual results versus future forecasts.

- **Highlight particular numbers.** You might, for example, want to highlight numbers that are particularly surprising, either in a good or a bad way, or numbers that speak to issues that have been the subject of extensive discussions.

- **Denote cells that serve a particular purpose in the spreadsheet.** This is especially useful when you are presenting a business or mathematical model and you want to identify the cells containing key parameters or assumptions that drive the values in the rest of the spreadsheet. You may even want to highlight the cells that the users would want to modify when they play "what-if?" with the spreadsheet.

For the most part, your choices are found within the Font menu in Excel, and they include **boldface**, *italics*, color, and cell shading. Of course, you can select more than one of these effects for any given cell. Yes, you can really cut loose!

Report 2-5 is an example of a report that uses several of these effects. It presents the same income statement information you've seen presented in Reports 2-1 and 2-2, but it was generated after the third quarter. In this report, "Budget" refers to the one prepared before the year began, and a good portion of VASTCo management's incentive bonus is tied to performance against this Budget (specifically, the yearly variance). "Outlook" refers to what management expects will occur over the remainder of the year, based on the best current information. The purpose of this report is to indicate how VASTCo has performed over the first three quarters, and to provide a sense of how the entire year is likely to turn out.

Report 2-5										
VASTCo -- 2006 Income Statement, Actuals thru Q3 & Outlook for the Year										
(in $000)	Actual Results							Outlook for Full Year		
	Q1	Q2	Q3	YTD Tot.	Budget	F(U)	Q4	06 TOT.	Budget	F(U)
Licenses	3,948	4,116	4,284	**12,348**	11,792	556	4,500	**16,848**	16,000	848
Services	1,438	1,499	1,561	**4,498**	4,321	177	1,620	**6,118**	5,940	178
Total Revenues	**5,386**	**5,615**	**5,845**	**16,846**	16,113	733	6,120	**22,966**	21,940	1,026
Cost of Sales	701	731	760	**2,192**	1,899	(293)	765	**2,957**	2,600	(357)
Gross Profit	**4,685**	**4,885**	**5,084**	**14,654**	14,214	440	5,355	**20,009**	19,340	669
Sales & Marketing	1,794	1,856	1,928	**5,579**	5,517	(61)	2,019	**7,598**	7,510	(88)
Research & Dev.	1,035	1,082	1,153	**3,270**	3,312	42	1,191	**4,461**	4,542	81
General & Admin.	769	790	805	**2,363**	2,313	(50)	825	**3,188**	3,138	(50)
Total Oprg. Exps.	3,597	3,728	3,887	**11,212**	11,142	(70)	4,035	**15,247**	15,190	(57)
Operating Profit	**1,088**	**1,156**	**1,198**	**3,442**	3,072	370	1,320	**4,762**	4,150	612

REPORT 2-5:   VASTCo 2006 Income Statement, Actuals through Q3 and Outlook for the Year

In this report, we are using:

- **Boldface text**—to highlight the "important" rows (i.e., Total Revenues, Gross Profit, and Operating Profit) and columns (i.e., Actual YTD Total, and Full-Year Outlook, Budget, and Variance). And the Variance is especially important because it's the number that will determine the bonuses.
- Blue text—to identify all Budget numbers.
- *Italicized text*—to identify all numbers that depend on results that are not yet "real" (i.e., Q4 Outlook, full-year Outlook, and full-year Variance).
- Double-line borders —to highlight the most critical sections of the report (i.e., the Operating Profit row, and the columns for the full-year results).
- Single-line borders —to separate the main sections of the income statement (i.e., Revenues, Cost of Sales/Gross Profit, and Operating Expenses), and quarter results from YTD and full-year results.

Report 2-5 is admittedly a little more loaded with visual effects than most reports you'll see, and most readers will still need to review a report in this format at least a couple of times before they become completely comfortable with it. Even so, each different effect has a specific, identifiable, and valid purpose related to making the information easier to absorb and understand. Just imagine how confusing this report would be if it was also loaded with visual effects that *didn't* advance the comprehensibility of the report, were included just for looks, or were added to demonstrate the presenter's facility with the spreadsheet software. Using text effects carelessly or pointlessly brings us to another Deadly Sin:

Deadly Sin #3
Using visual effects for any reason **other than clarifying, distinguishing, or adding meaning** to information

Not only is an overdressed report hard to understand, but the impact of the visual effects that *do* have a valid purpose becomes diluted because the reader can't tell which effects are meaningful and which aren't. Moreover, using these features in Excel (and in Word and PowerPoint, for that matter) has become so easy that trying to impress people with your familiarity with the tools may backfire. Astute readers could easily conclude that you are using the tactic to mask a poor grasp of the subject matter, or to hide content that you would rather the audience didn't understand.

Cell Shading. Cell shading is one visual effect I haven't discussed yet, but deserves some mention here. As effects go, cell shading is a bit of an "atomic flyswatter," because when you shade in an entire cell (or group of cells), you create a powerful visual distinction that may be more than you really need. Moreover, if you use the effect too much, and you use multiple colors, you risk creating something that looks more like a work by Piet Mondrian than like a report for the board of directors.

Nevertheless, there are some types of presentations where cell shading is a good choice. One of them is spreadsheet *models*, where the entire model is driven by inputs to a handful of cells. Report 2-6 is an example of such a model—a pricing worksheet for a printing company. The Base Price/Copy is a function of the number of square inches (i.e., Width × Height), and the Volume Discount on that price depends on the number of Copies the customer is ordering.

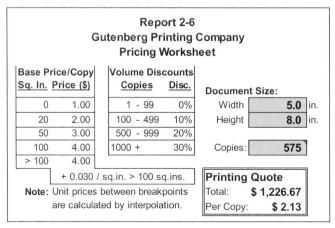

REPORT 2-6:   Gutenberg Printing Company Pricing Worksheet

In this example, the only numbers the user needs to specify are the Width and Height (in inches) of each unit, and the number of Copies. The rest of the spreadsheet is either values that are company policy and shouldn't be changed by the user,[8] calculated cells, or the resulting price quotation (both the Total and the Per Unit prices). Here, cell shading draws a clear distinction between the three cells permitted for user input and the rest of the spreadsheet.

Another use of cell shading is to *highlight blocks of information*. Report 2-7 presents the Gutenberg Printing Company's price list again, but without the areas for calculating a price quotation. This is a report that the company might be using as marketing collateral to hand out to customers and prospects, not for calculating specific quotations. Actually, there *four* price lists here, because customers can choose between color and black and white, and two kinds of paper. Still, each price list is organized in the same way.

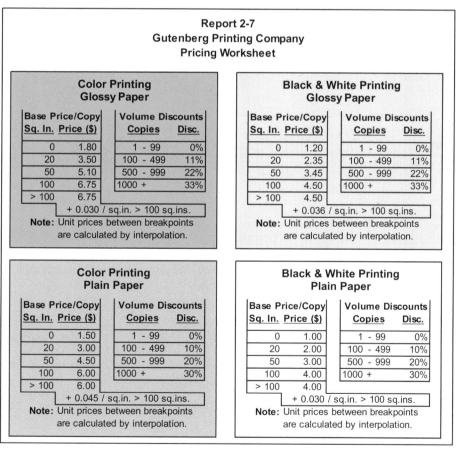

REPORT 2-7: Gutenberg Printing Company Pricing Worksheet

Since each of the four price lists is formatted identically, the shading of an entire block helps the reader pick out the price list of interest. And while it's a small touch, locating the right price list is helped by the fact that the two black-and-white lists are light gray and unshaded (i.e., white), while the two color price lists are shaded in primary colors.

Our discussion of text effects wouldn't be complete without a warning about using color in general, and cell shading in particular. Keep in mind that *things don't always look the same on paper, or projected on a screen, as they do on your own monitor.* You may find that information that looked just fine on your computer is indistinguishable from other information, or even unreadable, in other media. Or the shading that you so carefully selected is so dark when it's printed out that you can't read the words and numbers through the shading. And finally, remember that you don't always have control of how your reports are being reproduced: those colors that conveyed so much information disappear if they're printed on black-and-white printers and copiers. If you are worried that this will be a problem, some actions you can consider include:

- Sticking to visual effects that don't depend on the color being properly reproduced, or even being reproduced at all.
- Maintaining and distributing two versions of the document, one for color printing and one for black and white. Obviously, you'll need to consider whether any given document is worth your going to that much trouble, but sometimes it is.
- In the cover notes or transmittal document, or even in the document itself, making it clear that the document should be printed out in color. This may be sufficient if your document *will* be reproduced in color most of the time, and you're just trying to alert a few stragglers.

All that remains is a few short digressions on the subject of color:

Note

The term **red ink** to denote operating losses is so pervasive that Excel offers standard Number Format styles in which negative numbers are presented in red. My recommendation: *don't use these formats.* The problem is that red-versus-black is a very powerful visual clue, making very small negative numbers more noticeable than very large positive numbers. So don't use this style unless you are facing the unlikely situation where *any* negative number in your report is more significant than *any* positive number, regardless of size.

Note

Nearly 10% of all males, and over 5% of the whole population, have some form of colorblindness. In its most common form, people cannot distinguish reds from greens, so design accordingly. Also, if you happen to need a handy fact for your next trivia match, note that the frequency of colorblindness is ten times greater in males than in females.

Comments and Artwork

The number of features Excel offers for adding visual impact is just remarkable. In addition to borders, text effects, and cell shading, you can overlay additional visual "objects" onto the spreadsheet. Some of these features include:

- Text boxes and cartoon balloons
- Lines and arrows
- Geometric shapes
- Cell comments

The list of possibilities goes on and on, and you have plenty of flexibility for customizing each particular object. For example, enclosed shapes can be filled with shading or left blank, and you can vary the transparency to affect the appearance of the contents of the cells underneath each object.

Let's set the stage for our first example: A company sells three software products (Products A, B, and C). It generates primarily license revenues, but also some services revenues related to its license sales. It has a backlog of orders as of 12/31/08 that will generate both license and services revenues several years into the future. Company managers want to explain to the board of directors how they expect revenues from the existing backlog to be distributed over the next few years. Managers and board members are especially interested in license revenues and how they are distributed across their products, because the licenses are the biggest part of their business. Also, each services professional supports each of the three products, so services revenues by product is not a critical piece of information. Report 2-8 is a report management might deliver to its board.

Report 2-8
Backlog @ 12/31/08, by Product and Year of Realization

(in $000)	Backlog @ 12/31/08	Services	Licenses	Future Years 2009	2010	2011	2012+	
Product A	13,316	770	12,546	5,610	5,712	714	510	Licenses
Product B	2,818	728	2,090	660	550	440	440	
Product C	5,797	2,398	3,399	2,266	515	206	412	Services
	21,931	3,896	18,035	8,536	6,777	1,360	1,362	
				1,895	842	105	1,053	
				10,431	7,619	1,465	2,415	

REPORT 2-8: Backlog @ 12/31/08 by Product and Year of Realization

The total Backlog, in the leftmost column, is the sum of the Services and Licenses backlogs in the next two columns. The Future Years columns break out the Licenses revenues into the years in which the company expects to realize the revenue from the current backlog. Below the Future Years amounts for Licenses is a similar distribution for Services revenues, except that it's not broken out by product.

The Excel features we're discussing here help the readability of this report significantly. Future Years estimates for Licenses revenues for all three products are grouped in a gray rounded rectangle, as are the corresponding values for Services revenues. Cartoon balloons help to identify the contents of each rounded rectangle. Now, since we are slicing through this information in three different ways—by product, by Services versus Licenses, and by future year of revenue realization—we have situations where both row and column totals should agree with each other. This relationship is reinforced for the reader by the bent arrows that connect the Future Years numbers for Services to the total in the "Services" columns, and the grand total Future Years numbers to the total in the "Backlog" column.

Getting all these objects properly placed on this report was a little time consuming, but you can see that the effort makes an enormous difference in the comprehensibility of the report. Moreover, it's an effort you have to undertake only once, when you first design the report. If you have an audience that is senior enough, and pressed for time enough, the effort is definitely appreciated.[9]

Another useful Excel feature is comments on specific cells. Comments are text that you associate with specific cells, and they appear only when you float your cursor over the commented cell (a red triangle in the upper-right corner of the cell indicates that the cell has a comment attached to it). Comments do not appear when you print out the spreadsheet. For this reason, comments are ideal when your audience is looking at the spreadsheet itself, as opposed to looking at a paper printout. Report 2-9 is an example of how you might use this capability to add useful information to the "Copies" cell in the worksheet showing just the relevant portion of the pricing worksheet presented in Report 2-6.

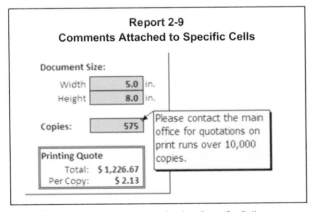

REPORT 2-9: Comments Attached to Specific Cells

As much fun as it is to use these effects, be afraid, be *very* afraid of . . .

The "Ransom Note" Effect

The careful reader might notice that I haven't discussed two easily available visual tools for distinguishing numbers from each other: font size and font style. This is because overusing these tools adds little to the visual impact of your reports, and you risk making your document look amateurishly produced.

Regarding *font size*, you've probably selected a standard font size for day-to-day use, and using a smaller font size risks making your information unreadable for your audience. *Increasing* the font size is even more pointless, since the only conceivable benefit of doing this is to use up more of the page's white space. If you want to increase the size of report titles and major headings by a couple of points just to improve readability, that's OK, but if you're looking for something to spice up your reports visually, look somewhere else.

Fooling around with the *font style* is an even worse idea, because that will make your reports look not merely strange, but bizarre. Take a look at Report 2-10. Is this the impression you really want to create?

Report 2-10 (1-2, revisited) VASTCo -- 1998-2003 Financial Highlights						
(in $000)	1998	1999	2000	2001	2002	2003
Revenues	699	950	1,493	2,138	2,910	4,733
Expenses	662	800	1,207	1,639	2,348	3,343
Operating Profit	37	150	286	499	562	1,390

REPORT 2-10 (REPORT 1-2, REVISITED):   VASTCo 1998–2003 Financial Highlights

Believe it or not, there is logic in this report. There were particularly noteworthy corporate events during each of the odd years, so the font size is larger for those years. The year 1998 got its own different font because that was the year VASTCo generated its first revenues. The company went public in 2001, so that year is italicized and in its very own font. Profit, being critical to success, is in larger type. Still, the whole report is a mess, with well-intentioned (but incomprehensible) visual effects.

The original ransom notes that gave rise to this expression looked the way they did because rather than typing or handwriting the message, the kidnappers created a collage of words and numbers cut out from various newspapers, magazines, and other printed material. Their purpose was to make the document devoid of any common themes, distinguishing patterns, or personal idiosyncrasies like handwriting. What I am suggesting you should try to achieve is the exact opposite, so please: Avoid **creating** the **RANSOM** note Effect with your **re**PORTS!

Two Truly Helpful Hints

My final suggestions may seem trivial, but they are useful all the same. The first one is a piece of Strong Advice:

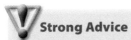

Strong Advice

As soon as you can, **turn off the gridlines** when you are designing your report.

The gridlines are a crutch that makes it easy to read large worksheets without getting confused, but it's not available to those in the audience looking at hard-copy or Print Preview.[10] So why not get used to the same image your audience is going to see, while you're in the process of working on it?

There's no need to make this a test of your concentration or your eyesight. Don't turn off the gridlines until you've put in enough of your visual elements (white space, borders, text effects) to make your report readable. You may find that doing this can actually make your spreadsheet design go *faster*, by making the layout design an integral part of the report creation process, and not just an afterthought.

Here is a second suggestion to help you visualize a report while you're developing it, and that is to do what your audience is going to do: actually *print it out*. Now, the Sierra Club may not thank you for all your test printing, but your goal here as a report designer is to make sure the report's overall look-and-feel is right so that your audience can understand its contents. The best way to ensure that is to look at your reports the same way your audience will.

A well-laid-out report, with visual cues to help your audience make useful distinctions, can be immensely effective. In this chapter, we discussed the following design tools:

- Choosing a page orientation that maximizes the likelihood that all your reports will fit properly onto a single page

- Locating key information where it is easiest to find, particularly around the edges of the report

- Using both white space and the absence of white space effectively

- Making intelligent decisions about whether specific report dimensions should run horizontally across or vertically down the page

- Using cell borders to group information and draw attention to important values

- Using text effects such as boldface, italics, and colors to distinguish different types of information

- Shading cells, or groups of cells, to highlight specific cells and distinguish entire sections of the page

- Using comments and artwork to add meaning in special situations

We also talked about not *overusing* the infinite number of choices offered by Excel and other software tools. Overuse of effects makes it hard for your audience to home in on the discriminators that are *really* important, and the "ransom note" effect can actually make your reports look unprofessional. Moreover, sometimes little, unnecessary things can stay with your audience and send them messages that you never meant to send. Beauty isn't always skin-deep, but ugly *always* goes clean to the bone!

The importance of looks to quantation is a lot like the importance of looks to written memos and articles. The visual impression of thoughtfully laid-out paragraphs, section headings, visual clues to identify key thoughts, and appropriate white space gives the reader comfort and makes the prospect of reading even the longest, densest documents less intimidating.

Remember that the *only* good reason to take advantage of the tools listed above is to help you present better information, not to make the report look fancy or demonstrate your mastery of the software. Knowing how to use the features of Excel won't make you effective at quantation, any more than knowing how to type fast makes you a good writer. Your goal is to create reports that look good to your audience, and the only reason they will look that way is if your audience finds them quick to decipher and easy to understand.

If you can sail clear of the treacherous cliffs of the "Where's Waldo?" effect and avoid the swirling whirlpool of the "ransom note" effect, you will find the placid waters of clear and truly effective quantation. You must seek those waters out, even if you have to order your colleagues or your staff to lash you to the mast and put wax in your ears so you are deaf to the misguided and insidious pleadings of the graphic arts Sirens in the marketing department. If you can achieve this, you will have smooth sailing to your longed-for Ithaca, or at least a corner office on the top floor.

NOTES

1. I want to stress that as strong as my expressed preference is, it is still a *personal* preference based on my own experience. If your quantation is being included in a package consisting mostly of plain text documents—for which most people, including me, would say the natural reading orientation is portrait—the choice is less clear-cut.

2. If you don't have children and weren't a child recently enough to have played it yourself, "Where's Waldo?" is a popular children's activity. "Where's Waldo?" picture books, or placemats, or wallpaper, have a picture of an incredibly busy scene like a city street or a popular sightseeing spot. Waldo, an affable young man with glasses, wearing blue jeans and a red-and-white-striped shirt and cap, is somewhere in the picture, and the object is to locate him. It's harder than it sounds.

3. Excel allows you to achieve this effect through the Increase Indent function (in Excel for Office 07, in the Alignment group). Alternatively, you can type a few spaces before the indented captions, or insert additional narrow columns within the row captions area. The choice is yours.

4. Excel automatically increases the row height to accommodate text on multiple rows if you turn on the Wrap Text cell formatting option. If you turn Wrap Text off, text that is too long for the cell will spill over into adjacent cells to the left and/or right (depending on whether your Justify choice is Left, Center, or Right, and only if those adjacent cells are blank). Similarly, if you use the Merge Cells option, text entered into a single cell will be distributed over the range of cells you've selected. The Merge Cells option is how I centered the "Quarter Ended 9/06" and "Year-to-Date" captions over the three columns they refer to, not to mention the titles at the top of virtually all of the exhibits in this book.

5. To do this in Excel 07, follow the Font/Alignment/Orientation command sequence. You can choose any orientation between +90º (caption running straight up) and –90º (straight down). I will also observe that this report is a somewhat less conventional use of quantation than most of the examples in this book, but a report design like this can be a very useful sales account management tool. You could, for example, sort the rows using the relationship columns as the "sort order" to identify at a glance which account relationships each functional area needs to pay attention to. Also, through a "recap" report at the bottom (or the top) of the report, you could identify the total amount of business on which each of the functional areas has a significant impact. See Chapter 5 for more detail about this type of presentation. Specifically, see the discussions on using Excel's Lookup and Reference functions and using Excel as a database.

6. Here's another useful Excel feature: you can align content not only *horizontally* within the cell (i.e., left, center, and right, with the default depending on whether the cell has numbers/formulas or text) but *vertically* (i.e., top, middle, and bottom, with the default always bottom). If you're using horizontal borders above or below cells, it's useful to take advantage of this capability to create a visual separation between the number in a cell and its border. For example, I used "middle" vertical alignment to make the Operating Profit numbers equidistant from the top and bottom borders. For reasons we'll discuss in Chapter 5, doing this by inserting blank rows or columns is usually a bad idea.

7. Note that a *double* underscore (e.g., 3,498) also has a highly specific meaning, but only in the world of accounting. A double underscore means Net Income or Earnings per Share (which is also, of course, a Net Income measure)—the true "bottom lines." Intermediate profit results, like Operating Profit and Pretax Income, are often more meaningful numbers to those responsible for day-to-day operations, but they should not be double-underscored.

8. If you are really concerned about the security issue, Excel offers extensive capabilities for managing which cells can and cannot be modified by various users. This is a two-edged sword, though, since these capabilities take real work to implement and manage, and sometimes have unintended consequences. If your primary concern is inadvertent errors by users, rather than security, you'll find that using the kind of visual cues discussed here, and doing some thoughtful user training, can go a long way toward easing that concern.

9. Report 2-8 is a variant of a real report that caused two members of the board of directors to smile when they first saw it. Yes, venture capitalists smiling at a financial statement! I am not making this up—I witnessed it myself. At subsequent board meetings, this was the report that the directors were most anxious to see first.

10. Unless, of course, your document has been set up to print *with* the gridlines. As far as I'm concerned, however, that particular look is cheesy and unprofessional.

CHAPTER 3

Words Matter

And now the basketball scores: 110–102, 125–113, 131–127, and in an overtime duel, 95–94. Boy, that was a squeaker! Oh, and here's a partial score: Pittsburgh, 37.

—George Carlin, as sportscaster Biff Burns (c. 1967)

When you are focusing on *numbers*, it's easy to forget that words matter, too. Imagine receiving a report that contains four pages of numbers, but no words. What kinds of conclusions could you draw from this report? How would you know what the numbers were measuring? What would the report actually *mean* to you? In the same way that books need titles and chapter headings, so do your reports. Your titles, row headings, column headings, and comments tell your audience what your numbers are measuring and help your audience reach conclusions about the contents of your reports.

Still, words by themselves won't guarantee that your audience will find your reports clear and easy to understand. You have to choose the *right* words to include in your presentations. And when it comes to quantation, the right words must be as precise and accurate as possible. The level of precision you employ with your words is completely your choice. You can choose the level of precision you want to employ with your words, just as you can choose the number of digits you want to present. However, just like the choices you have with numbers, you often face trade-offs between adding accuracy to your words and making your reports clean enough that your audience can quickly grasp what's important.

In addition, how you organize the words on the page can have a big impact on the readability of your reports. This is especially true for the *rows* in your report, because the way you order your rows affects the reading flow and communicates essential information about your content.

Mean What You Say and Say What You Mean

Words add either clarity or confusion to your quantation. Whether your audience is clear or confused depends on whether they share your view about what specific words and phrases mean, and whether you have used common terms properly. Some words and phrases have highly specific meanings in most business contexts. Some words and phrases have specific meanings, *but only* within specific organizations or professions or industries.

Here are examples of terms you'll see frequently in numerical reports. Please note that I use **boldface** for the terms that have a clear, specific, and universal meaning, [plain text] for terms that are widely understood to have a common meaning, and *italics* for terms whose meaning is highly dependent on local interpretation:

The Top Line

Term	What It Means
Revenue	**Business volume reported in accordance with generally accepted accounting principles (GAAP) for that period**
Collections	**Cash received from customers**
Bookings	*Amount of contractual commitments recorded*
Sales	*Some notion of business volume*

Resources Consumed

Term	What It Means
Expense	**Consumption of a resource in the current period as determined according to GAAP**
Expenditure	Cash outlay
Cost	*Some notion of the total amount that will be spent, eventually*

The Bottom Line

Term	What It Means
Gross Profit	**Revenues minus Cost of Sales (i.e., expenses directly associated with producing a unit of the good being sold)**
Operating Profit	**Revenues minus Operating Expenses (i.e., the total resources the company consumes in its effort to generate revenues)**
Pretax Profit	**Operating Profit plus/minus below-the-line items (i.e., items with a financial impact but not directly related to the company's main line of business, such as interest income, interest expense, gain/loss on asset disposition, and the ever-popular "extraordinary items")**
Net Income	**Pretax Profit minus income tax expense**
Earnings	**The same meaning as Net Income, but usually used only in the term "Earnings per Share"**
Contribution	*Some notion of revenues minus selected expenses*

Financial Statements

Term	What It Means
Income Statement	A report reflecting *all* revenues and expenses of an organization, with the bottom line equal to Net Income (or Operating Profit or Pretax Profit, if below-the-line items are omitted). This report is typically prepared in accordance with GAAP requirements, and even when the formatting of the Income Statement is different from what is usually seen in corporate annual reports, the top-line and bottom-line numbers are no different.
Profit & Loss (or P&L)	*A statement showing selected revenues and/or expenses, with Contribution as the bottom-line result. One use of P&L reports is to give an organization's managers a sense of how much they are contributing to corporate profitability when considering only the expenses those managers can control. For example, a sales organization's P&L might include all of the revenues credited to that organization, but the only expenses included would be the cost of revenues associated with the products sold and the expenses incurred by the sales staff.*

Commitments or Predictions

Term	What It Means
Plan	The company's overall top-level intentions, typically for one or more years into the future
Budget	**The Plan, translated into line-by-line, item-by-item expectations for the entire organization and for the individual functional areas within that, typically for one year at a time**
Quota	The top-line expectations for individuals or groups of individuals. The meaning is similar to "Budget," except that it frequently applies to individuals, and "Quotas" are the term of art in communicating compensation plans
Outlook	*What the presenter thinks the future results will be*

Nuances

Term	What It Means
%	One number (the numerator) expressed relative to another (the denominator)
% Change (or Growth, or Difference)	The magnitude of the difference between two values of the same measure (e.g., revenues this year versus last year, or our productivity versus a competitor's)
Percentage Points	Typically, a *difference* between two percentage numbers[1]
Profit[2]	*Some notion of profitability, measured in total dollars*
Margin	*Some notion of profitability, measured as a percentage of revenues*

The differences among these terms are sometimes subtle, but sometimes not. For example, here are three groups of related terms that you must use properly to avoid unnecessary confusion:

- *Revenue* versus *Collections*, *Bookings*, or *Sales*. *Revenue* is a number that is calculated strictly in accordance with the rules of generally accepted accounting principles (GAAP). Publicly traded companies must report GAAP revenue to their stockholders. *Collections*, *bookings*, and *sales* are important to a company's operating outlook (and often form the basis for sales or executive compensation because of the complexity and sometimes seemingly arbitrary nature of GAAP-based revenue recognition), but these terms should never be used interchangeably.

- *Expense* versus *Expenditure*. An *expense* occurs when an asset is used for its economic purpose, and *expenditure* occurs when the payment occurs. For example: Employee X's target bonus for the year 2008 is $30,000, to be earned by achieving on-target performance throughout the year; the actual bonus amount is calculated and paid as a lump sum within 60 days after the end of the year. If performance was right on target throughout the year, the company's *expense* for this bonus was $2,500/month for January 2008 through December 2008,[3] but there was no *expenditure* until February 2009, when the company paid the $30,000 bonus.

- *Budget* versus *Outlook*. A *budget* is both a commitment by management to achieve a revenue level, and an expense pool available to management as long as they are achieving that revenue objective. It is frequently the basis for management's incentive compensation. An *outlook* is simply a prediction of what future results will be. While we can only hope that the agreed-upon budget was based on an outlook that was realistic at the time, reality may change, but budgets don't, except by formal agreement.

These are examples of "slight" wording differences that I have seen pointlessly consume endless amounts of time. The conversations that ensue from wording mix-ups like these remind me of a fight between two blindfolded boxers—each fighter swings away with great skill and precision, but neither has a clue as to where the other person is.

Before we wrap up this section, I'd like to introduce another set of terms that often cause a great deal of confusion:

Economic Metaphysics

Term	What It Means
Price	*The amount of money asked for or given in exchange for a good or service*
List Price	*The amount that a provider publishes or announces as the price for the good or service it is offering*
Cost[4]	*The amount a purchaser spends to obtain a good or a service*
Value	*The amount that the speaker believes would be a fair price for the good or service in question*

Although each of these definitions comes from a dictionary, they are all in italics, because their definitions remain immensely subjective. Their meanings depend entirely on who is using the word, and understanding this fact can save you lots of confusion and grief in your quantation. If you need any confirmation that this is a real issue, note that one of the dictionary definitions of *price* is "cost," and one of the definitions of *cost* is "price." (And if the dictionary can be confusing, anyone can!)

Confusion surrounding the above terms is frankly much more likely to come up in the public policy arena than in business. For example, I recently overheard a person who had just returned from a vacation in France, where he had gone to the hospital: "I broke my leg, took an ambulance to the hospital, spent two hours in the emergency room, had a pin put in my leg, and got a cast. And you know what? The whole thing cost only $250. Why is it so expensive here in the United States?" Now, I don't know what orthopedic surgeons make in France, but I would guess that it "cost" more than $250 for the ambulance, emergency room stay, surgery, pin, and cast. Now, he might have spoken more accurately if he had said, "cost *me* only $250," but regardless, his last question suggests that he is unclear on the distinction between what it costs to provide services and who pays for them. Remember: One man's price is another man's cost.

If it seems like I'm being overly dramatic about the importance of word choice, let me suggest a simple exercise. Ask yourself the following questions:

- What is a minute of your time worth?
- How many minutes of your time will it take to get the words clear, and just right?
- What is a minute of time worth to each member of your audience?
- How many minutes is the average person in your audience hoping to spend reviewing your report in the first place?
- How many extra minutes will it take each audience member to resolve a wording ambiguity in your report?
- For those in your audience who can't resolve the ambiguity by themselves, how many extra minutes will it take you to have a conversation about it?
- How many such conversations are you willing to have?

With the answers to these questions in hand, it's easy to determine: (1) the value of your time to get the words right, (2) the value of your time spent unnecessarily if you *don't* get the words right, and (3) the value of your audience's time spent unnecessarily if you don't get the words right. If you are sensing that we are in Deadly Sin territory, you are correct. Your time and your audience's time are simply too valuable to commit:

Deadly Sin #4

Unclear, imprecise, or (worst of all) **incorrect** row and column headings

Getting the words wrong is just as harmful as getting the *numbers* wrong, and this sin is an easy one to avoid committing.

Choosing between Precision and Presentability

With respect to words, you want the reader to be able to glance *quickly* at the captions to understand the report's organization, and then move on to the numbers. Precision is important, but if you need to increase your caption length to achieve a certain level of precision, you may force your readers to stop and absorb the words, ultimately doing yourself and your readers a disservice. This is especially true if you have increased the column width or row height to accommodate the longer captions and thereby committed Deadly Sin #2, rendering the report more difficult to understand.

The easiest way to preserve the clarity of your words without committing Deadly Sin #2 is simply to *make the words shorter*, through the intelligent use of shortcuts like acronyms and abbreviations. However, like any shortcuts, acronyms and abbreviations can be used for both good and evil. At their most effective, these shortcuts enable you to achieve complete verbal precision without having to compromise on the visual characteristics that make it easy for readers to find and understand the numbers. But poorly chosen acronyms and abbreviations add nothing to the audience's ability to understand your quantation; sometimes, the mere fact that you are using shorthand can be annoying or offensive to your audience.

Here are a few examples of acronyms widely used in business quantation:

Acronym	Meaning	Explanation
GAAP	Generally accepted accounting principles	The accounting principles U.S. publicly traded companies must comply with when reporting their financial results to their stockholders.
COGS	Cost of goods sold	Fully burdened cost of manufacturing, producing, or delivering the products or services included in reported revenues.
EPS	Earnings per share	Net income divided by weighted average shares outstanding (both calculated in accordance with GAAP).
EBITDA	Earnings before interest, taxes, depreciation, and amortization	Just what it says. This fairly widely used metric is intended to provide some sense of a company's ability to generate cash flow from its operations.[5]
MBO	Management by objective	Correctly used, this describes an approach to management in which employees all have specific, detailed achievement objectives. But it has also become widely used to refer to employee incentive compensation based on the MBO approach.

Here are some examples of abbreviations you will often see in quantation:

Income Statement (Rows)	
Abbr.	**Meaning**
Revs.	Revenues
Svcs.	Services
Mfrg.	Manufacturing
Mktg.	Marketing
Engrg.	Engineering
Admin.	Administration
Oprg. or Op.	Operating
Inc.	Income

Columns & Other	
Abbr.	**Meaning**
Yr.	Year
FY	Fiscal year
Mo.	Month
Qtr.	Quarter
Tot.	Total
Avg.	Average
Bud.	Budget
Var.	Variance
Chg. or Δ	Change
HC or H/C	Headcount

As you can see, most of these abbreviations are intuitively clear and, given the right context, can be just as easy to understand as the full words they are abbreviating. I have the following suggestions if you are planning to take this approach:

- Use abbreviations *consistently* to avoid confusion.
- Use a period (.) after the abbreviation to tell the readers that they are looking at an abbreviation. It's a small thing, but it helps.

When deciding whether to use acronyms or abbreviations for your row and column captions, consider the following questions:

- Is the term used widely and often enough that it will be familiar to your audience?
- Would the term be likely to be confused with another term? And if so, is there a more obvious term you could use?
- Is your audience confined to insiders familiar with the term, or do you have a broader audience?

If these questions give you pause, but you still want to use abbreviations for visual reasons, consider adding a "key" to your terms similar to the "Notes" in Report 3-1.

The last consideration with respect to acronyms and abbreviations is a little more subjective. Shorthand terms can certainly establish you as a knowledgeable insider, but they can also alienate some people in your audience if you're not careful. This experience is like being at a cocktail party where you happen to be the only one who is not a neurosurgeon. You may want to contribute heartily to the banter, but you find yourself feeling completely left out when one of the guests relates an apparently hilarious anecdote involving the medulla oblongata and several cavernous angiomas.[6] Be sure to use great care when employing acronyms and abbreviations with an audience who is senior to you, such as a board of directors. These people may not spend enough time with your organization to be fully familiar with all the shorthand terms, and you will get no benefit from making them feel like outsiders. (In other words, if you're going to be condescending, save it for your peers.)

Sometimes you have to choose between the lesser of two evils when using shortcuts. But if you can't stand the thought of committing either Deadly Sin #2 (basing column width or row height on caption length) or Deadly Sin #4 (unclear, imprecise, or incorrect captions), you can use notes as an alternative. Report 3-1 is an example presenting the same report we looked at in Report 2-2, and taking a page from the "Comments and Artwork" discussion in Chapter 2.

Report 3-1
VASTCo -- 2006 Q3 Income Statement, Actual vs. Budget

	Qtr. Ended 9/06			Year-to-Date			
(in $000)	**Actual**	**Budget**	**F(U)**	**Actual**	**Budget**	**F(U)**	
Licenses	4,284	4,064	220	12,348	11,792	556	**Notes: Budget** is revised budget
Prof. Svcs.	1,561	1,530	31	4,498	4,321	177	approved at Jul board mtg.
Total Revenues	**5,845**	**5,594**	**251**	**16,846**	**16,113**	**733**	**Cost of Sales** includes
Cost of Sales	760	667	(94)	2,192	1,899	(293)	only 3rd party royalties
Gross Profit	**5,084**	**4,927**	**157**	**14,654**	**14,214**	**440**	**Oprg.Exps.** excludes exps.
Sales & Marketing	1,928	1,915	(13)	5,579	5,517	(61)	of division divested in 4/06
Research & Dev.	1,153	1,167	14	3,270	3,312	42	
General & Admin.	805	798	(7)	2,363	2,313	(50)	
Total Oprg. Exps.	3,887	3,880	(6)	11,212	11,142	(70)	
Oprg. Profit	**1,198**	**1,046**	**151**	**3,442**	**3,072**	**370**	

REPORT 3-1:   VASTCo 2006 Q3 Income Statement, Actual versus Budget

This approach is particularly useful if extensive clarification would be helpful to your readers, or if a few more characters (or another whole word) aren't enough to provide the clarity you need.

Obviously, where you place your notes is dependent on where you happen to have the extra space. The notes in Report 3-1 are on the right simply for space efficiency in this book, but in general, I recommend putting notes at the *bottom* of the report for the following reasons:

- Notes at the bottom interfere less with readers' ability to scan through the numbers. (Remember that we normally read first from left to right, and then from top to bottom.)

- In most report designs, you're more likely to have space available at the bottom than at the right for notes, even with landscape orientation.

- When notes are at the right, the row heights you've chosen for your report rows will affect the text spacing, possibly making the comments harder to read. And, if you delete any of the report rows, you need to be careful not to inadvertently delete your notes as well.

Treating Words Like Numbers

In quantation, the way you order your rows must seem natural to your readers, so you want to choose an ordering of words or phrases that makes your reports easy to read. People naturally sort and order numbers, but they *also* naturally sort and order words and concepts. Here are some examples:

- When asked to name their children, parents of three or more children will almost always list them *in descending order of age.*
- When asked to list their significant assets, people will typically list them *in descending order of value*, even if they weren't asked to state the values.
- When asked to list all 50 U.S. states, most people *visualize a map of the United States*, and start in one corner and work their way across the map to the opposite corner. Very few people can name all 50 states alphabetically.[7]

To understand why it's important to order your captions properly, let's look at three versions of the same report, listing major donors to a charity (Report 3-2). The question is: Which of these three versions is the correct one to present?

Report 3-2, Version A Targeted Major Donors		Report 3-2, Version B Targeted Major Donors		Report 3-2, Version C Targeted Major Donors	
Donor	**Donation**	**Donor**	**Donation**	**Donor**	**Donation**
Jones, Jonn	100,000	Ace Car Wash	35,000	Zinker, Aaron	60,000
Smith, Marie	90,000	Brando, Marlon	40,000	Ace Car Wash	35,000
Roberts, Robert	75,000	Brown, Georgia	20,000	Lincoln, Abraham	33,333
Louie's Pizza	75,000	Davis, Mavis	25,000	Lawyers-R-Us	50,000
Zinker, Aaron	60,000	Harmonicas Forever	15,000	Jones, Jonn	100,000
Lawyers-R-Us	50,000	Jones, Jonn	100,000	Peterson, Fiona	18,000
Brando, Marlon	40,000	Lawyers-R-Us	50,000	Roberts, Robert	75,000
Ace Car Wash	35,000	Lincoln, Abraham	33,333	Smith, Marie	90,000
Lincoln, Abraham	33,333	Louie's Pizza	75,000	Ott, Fred & Ginger	15,000
O'Riley, Zbigniew	25,000	O'Riley, Zbigniew	25,000	Brown, Georgia	20,000
Davis, Mavis	25,000	Ott, Fred & Ginger	15,000	Brando, Marlon	40,000
Brown, Georgia	20,000	Peterson, Fiona	18,000	Louie's Pizza	75,000
Peterson, Fiona	18,000	Roberts, Robert	75,000	Davis, Mavis	25,000
Harmonicas Forever	15,000	Smith, Marie	90,000	O'Riley, Zbigniew	25,000
Ott, Fred & Ginger	15,000	Zinker, Aaron	60,000	Harmonicas Forever	15,000

REPORT 3-2, VERSION A:
Targeted Major Donors

REPORT 3-2, VERSION B:
Targeted Major Donors

REPORT 3-2, VERSION C:
Targeted Major Donors

In Version A, the donors are sorted by size of donation, and in Version B the donors are listed alphabetically. If you can figure out the logic behind the ordering in Version C, you have a rare gift indeed, since I used a random number generator to arrange the rows. But it *could* have been an actual ordering of the rows in the spreadsheet, if the administrator had simply added a new row at the bottom every time another donation was received and no one had bothered to rearrange the rows before presenting the report. In other words, let's assume that in Version C the rows are arranged in the order the donations came in.

As far as which version of Report 3-2 is "correct," the answer depends on what this report is going to be used for:

- Version A would be the best choice if the purpose was to *recognize the largest donors*, or to *identify the best prospects* to target in an upcoming fundraising round.

- Version B would be the best choice if the purpose was to *provide a complete list* of all significant donors, or to provide a basis for deciding who in the organization should contact each significant donor in an upcoming fundraising round.

- Even Version C might be a good choice if the main purpose was to *report on how the fundraising had progressed* (although the reader would need more information, like the donation dates and the cumulative amount raised at each date).

The point is that *each* of these versions might have reflected an understandable (but not necessarily intelligent or logical) basis for presenting this information, but the *right* choice requires further thought by the presenter.

So far, we've identified two possible choices for ordering your row captions: size (that is, sorting the rows based on the values in one of the numerical columns) and alphabetical order. There is also a third approach, which I call *intuitive* ordering, where the rows are ordered by some sort of logical relationship between the rows that makes sense to you and your audience. Here are some examples of intuitive row ordering (we won't bother with reports with numbers this time):

Expenses	Departments	Sales Regions	Works of Music
Salaries	Sales	Northeast	Baroque
Bonuses	Technical Support	Southeast	Classical
Benefits	Professional Services	Midwest	Romantic
Travel & Lodging	Marketing	Mountain States	Modern
Office Costs	Engineering	Far West	
Accounting & Legal	Finance		
Trade Shows	Administration		
Other			

There is an underlying logic to the ordering of each of these sets. The Expenses captions at the top of the list are those expense categories most directly related to headcount, and the captions at the bottom are those least directly related to headcount. (See Chapter 11 for a deeper discussion about choosing and ordering the line-item categories for the management P&L.) The Departments are listed roughly in descending order of proximity to and interaction with customers. The Sales Regions are ordered roughly geographically, scanning east-to-west across a map of the United States, and the lines under Works of Music list the principal eras in chronological order.

The above intuitive orderings are admittedly arbitrary, but even so, once readers understand the logic it's much easier for them to find the row they're looking for without having to scan the entire list. What you want to avoid is forcing readers to break their natural reading flow to find what they're looking for, especially when your reports have more than just a small number of rows. Once again, *you have choices*, and some of the pros and cons of your ordering choices are as follows:

Sort Order	Pros	Cons
Size	• Rows with largest numbers are easy to find.	• Row ordering changes from one report to the next. • A specific row is hard to find if you don't have a prior knowledge of how big its number is. • Choice of which column for sorting sometimes seems arbitrary.
Alphabetical	• Same ordering every time report is produced (if the row captions don't change). • Easy to find a specific name, even in a long list.	• Important numbers are hard to find if you don't know the row caption beforehand. • No logical relationship between adjacent rows.[8]
Intuitive	• Same ordering every time report is produced. • Adjacent rows have a logical relationship to each other, making rows easy to find and the whole report structure appear "natural."	• Ordering logic may make sense to you, but it must also make sense to the audience. • Extra time and effort are needed to design the appropriate ordering.

If you are presenting your rows by size or alphabetical order, you can make the initial choice and let the spreadsheet software do the rest of the work. Using an intuitive approach may require you to use more judgment and discretion when you design the report, but it's very useful in reports where (1) there is no particular mathematical relationship between the rows and (2) you want the report to have the same layout every time you produce it.

Remember the Title. Please.

Titles also matter, often much more than we recognize. Readers look first at the top of the page so they can (1) determine whether this is something they need to read and (2) prepare their brains for what they are about to read. Titling is not a perfunctory task, but a responsibility you should take as seriously as naming a child.

Every parent I know has agonized over this choice, with questions like: Is this name too strange? Is it too generic? Does it honor a family member we want to honor? Does it fit the kind of person we want our child to turn out to be?[9] Even if all your title does is blandly and correctly describe the contents of your report, a dull title is better than no title at all. After all, would you select a book from the bookcase to read if it didn't have a title on its spine? This leads us to the next Deadly Sin:

Deadly Sin #5

No title or timestamp (date *and* time) on printed spreadsheets

How you format your report titles is up to you. Although I don't follow this practice in this book for space reasons, here is an example of my own title layout preference:

Vaporware and Software Technologies, Inc.
2006 CORPORATE INCOME STATEMENT

The title is in **boldface** and slightly larger font size for readability, and I use ALL CAPS to make the description of the report content more noticeable. (All caps is not necessary for the company name, since it will be the same for most of the reports.) I do strongly suggest that once you settle on a format you like, *you be consistent about it.*

Painting with Numbers is, of course, a book about presenting numbers, not words. Even so, the clear, precise, thoughtful use of words is essential to effective quantation. The key topics we discussed in this chapter include:

- Using precise words and using them properly, so your audience can quickly understand what the report is about and move on to the important business of focusing on the numbers

- Balancing the trade-offs between precision and too much verbiage

- Choosing a logical order for your captions in your report (especially the rows) so that the conceptual flow is natural for your audience

- Remembering to put a title at the top of your report.

Getting the words right in your quantation reports is not a particularly time-consuming task, but it's immensely valuable. Being too creative (or careless) about the words you use in quantation is an overt presentation flaw, and it is a mistake similar to taking words willy-nilly from a thesaurus and assuming that will enable you to create a good piece of writing. Unless you use all those potential synonyms properly and in their appropriate context, you're more likely to confuse your audience than to inform or entertain them.

The interplay between words and numbers in quantation is like the interplay of people at a formal dance. The women go to great lengths to be beautiful, selecting gowns that show them to best advantage and command attention. The men are expected to look just as formal and put-together, but not in a way that calls attention to them specifically, other than a few small accessories. (The men are often compared to penguins!)

While both people in each couple appear equally sleek at the ball, we all speculate humorously on how much more time the women spent dressing than the men did. And finally, while the strongest visual impression at the dance itself is of the couples dancing *together*, what we remember afterwards is how the *women* looked. We rarely comment later, "Boy, Fred sure looked slick in that tuxedo!"

Quantation is also like that. The *numbers* are the centerpiece of your reports, and it is the differences among the various numbers in the report that readers are most interested in. The *words* are merely the "helpers," but it's essential that they be crisp, precise, and free of unnecessary flourishes. You spend much more time collecting, organizing, and laying out the numbers than you spend fine-tuning the words around the edges of the page, but the precision and presentation of both the words and the numbers are equally essential to effective quantation. While it's true that the words and the numbers must work together to help the audience understand the fundamental messages, what your audience should remember afterwards is the *numbers*.

NOTES

1. For example, if Operating Margin grew from 8% to 12%, you could say that Operating Margin had increased by 4 percentage points, whereas an increase from 8% to 12% represents a 50% increase in the percentage. Newspaper articles are notorious for failing to be clear about the distinction.

2. Note that "Profit" and "Margin" measure the same bottom-line result, but "Profit" measures the result in total dollars and "Margin" measures the result as a percentage, typically of Revenues. For example, if a business had total Revenues of $200 and total Operating Expenses of $146, then Operating Profit would be $54 ($200 − $146), and Operating Margin would be 27% (Operating Profit of $54 ÷ Revenues of $200). This is not a hard-and-fast rule, but

sticking to it anyway avoids confusion. See Chapter 10 for a more detailed discussion of using ratios as key indicators.

3. In fact, only in the accounting world is *to expense* used as a verb, meaning that an amount of money is treated as an expense. In the above example, it would be accurate to say, "We *expensed* $2,500 per month for Employee X's bonus."

4. Yes, I know "Cost" appeared in another table as well. Alas, some words have many meanings.

5. I will refrain from devoting too much space to editorializing about the EBITDA metric, but I can't resist a brief mention. The mechanics of accounting for depreciation, amortization, interest expense, and taxes are complex and often require true professional skill, but these expenses are every bit as real as those paid for with cash when incurred. Put another way, the English-language translation of *EBITDA* is "our company's earnings, if you don't count a bunch of expenses we'd really rather not talk about." EBITDA is the kind of arcane, semi-meaningful metric that causes some people to be suspicious of financial statements, and suspicious of the people who present them.

6. If you actually *are* a neurosurgeon, imagine instead that you are in an analogous situation involving a cocktail party where everyone else is a former world champion big-wave surfer who has had a near-death experience. If you are *both* a neurosurgeon *and* a former world champion big-wave surfer who has had a near-death experience, I am not interested in your problems.

7. But those who *can* name all 50 states alphabetically, win a lot of free drinks!

8. Avoid presenting report rows in alphabetical order unless that choice clearly makes sense. While it's easy to alphabetize with today's spreadsheet software, it makes information hard for the reader to find because the rows have no logical relationship to each other, and the most significant numbers aren't in any particular place on the page. If you keep the books for small businesses and startups, take note: I've talked with many senior managers and investors who find this particular approach to financial reporting extremely annoying, and attribute their irritation to presenter laziness.

9. For an intelligent and entertaining analysis of the economic consequences of child-naming choices, I highly recommend *Freakonomics*, by Steven D. Levitt and Stephen J. Dubner.

CHAPTER 4

Your Audience Matters

Boy, the food at this place is really terrible.
Yeah, I know; and such small portions.

—Alvy Singer (Woody Allen), recollecting a tough audience's conversation
at a Catskills resort restaurant (the opening lines of *Annie Hall*, 1977)

When you present numbers, your information is always *for* someone, *for* a specific purpose. Your audience is a key component of your presentation, and understanding how your audience thinks and uses information is another aspect of effective quantation.

Your audience can be the people you work for, the people who work for you, individuals in another functional area who depend on you for support, your board of directors, your investors, or any other group of people who need your information. Specific audiences may want specific things, but *every* quantation audience whose approval or decision you need wants:

1. The **right amount** of data—not too much and not too little

2. **Appropriate emphasis** on critical information

3. **Consistency in form and approach**—not only within your report package, but every time a report is delivered, and across all report packages

4. **Meaningful and relevant** numbers in a self-contained reporting package

5. Your demonstrated **respect** for their time

If you pay attention to these five universal audience wishes as you design your reports, you will have consistently appreciative audiences.

The Right Amount of Data

The *amount* of data you produce has profound implications for your relationship with your audience, and the impact that your information has on them. Your audience is made up of human beings, and humans beings tend to respond in predictable ways when numbers are involved. The best way to describe this dynamic is to introduce you to Bolten's Law[1] and its corollaries:

 The Laws of Quantation

Bolten's Law of Discretionary Disclosure: If you present a number, your audience will ask about it.

If you want to keep your audience focused and the conversation on track, *don't* put irrelevant information in your reporting package. It's a good idea to think carefully about how much data you are presenting and limit the contents of your presentation to what is absolutely necessary. However, lest you think that minimizing the amount of information in your report will keep you out of trouble, Bolten's Law has a corollary:

 The Laws of Quantation

Corollary #1 to Bolten's Law: If you don't present a number that the audience was expecting, they will ask you why it's not there.

A conversation about why a particular number is not in your report is not a conversation you want to have. Even if there's a perfectly innocent explanation, the discussion will be time-consuming and defocusing. One way to avoid this is to include the extra numbers the first few times you deliver the information, and then take out what seems to be unimportant or irrelevant later. Unfortunately, this may put you face-to-face with the second corollary:

 The Laws of Quantation

Corollary #2 to Bolten's Law: If you don't present a number that the audience was expecting because it had been included in previous reports, not only will they ask you why it's not there, they will question the motives behind the omission.

Ask any CFO of a public company about this topic, and you are sure to hear painful stories about investor reactions to suddenly missing information. So, when making the decision of what to include and exclude, ask yourself whether you will even have the opportunity to explain what your motives were for omitting data.

If you get this opportunity, you can count yourself lucky, because of the third corollary to Bolten's Law:

The Laws of Quantation

Corollary #3 to Bolten's Law: The likelihood that your audience will express their concern about your motives for not presenting information is inversely proportional to the harshness of the conclusion they are in the process of forming.

In other words, if the audience thinks you left out something simply because you *forgot,* someone will raise his hand and ask you about the apparent oversight. If, on the other hand, the audience believes that you are trying to pull a fast one, you may encounter silence (especially if your audience is composed of people who dislike confrontation).

So are you damned-if-you-do-and-damned-if-you-don't? Not at all; Bolten's Law and its corollaries are simply a pithy reflection of some of the maddening characteristics of audiences and how they typically behave around numbers. When you are deciding which data to include (or omit) in your reports, you have many tactics available to fend off and manage the symptoms of Bolten's Law and its corollaries. Here are some of them (with a nod to *Who Wants to Be a Millionaire?*):

- **Ask the Audience.** Pardon this penetrating glimpse into the obvious, but before you distribute a reporting package, and even before you finish the design and layout, I strongly suggest that you seek out key members of your audience for their feedback. Not only does this help you deliver a better package, but it can give you political cover if any of the corollaries kick in, since you can honestly assert that what was included and omitted in your package was based (at least partly) on audience feedback.

- **Phone-a-Friend.** It is always good to have friends who are generally insightful and loaded with common sense. Running your reports past a knowledgeable friend can be really helpful, *especially* if the audience for your report(s) is large or cuts across multiple functional areas or management levels of your organization. Phone-a-Friend can give you another perspective when your audience is varied (that is, when Ask the Audience may not provide a consistent, coherent answer).

- **Ask the Expert.** It is a near-certainty that you are not the first person in history charged with delivering this particular type of reporting package. Go find someone who has done this before and find out what they know. You can consult people in your organization, textbooks or articles in your professional area, or other professionals in your area. (This is one of the reasons why networking and membership in professional associations can be so valuable.)

Consulting your audience, phoning a friend, or asking the experts are great tactics *anytime* when you're trying to do something well, but they are especially helpful if you're concerned about running afoul of Bolten's Law and its corollaries. Remember, you're not looking for the kind of help that requires others to get deeply immersed in your quantation problems; you're just looking for feedback on *how much* data to present and what information is critical. Beyond these "lifelines," here are a few more tactics at your disposal:

- **Confront omissions head-on.** If you are going to remove data from a reporting package, you will be a more credible presenter if *you* tell your audience what you've done before *they* figure it out on their own. The phrase, "I'm not presenting that data (or that report) anymore because . . ." can be followed by many plausible reasons, including:
  - "The information no longer serves any useful business purpose."
  - "It created more confusion than clarity."
  - "The package was getting too large and unwieldy (but I'll put it back in if you really want it)."
  - "Not one of you fine people has ever made a single comment or asked a single question about it, so I presumed no one was interested." (See Chapter 9 for a longer discussion about managing audience feedback.)
- **Establish your credibility.** Your reputation as a straightforward and ethical presenter of information is the most valuable thing you can have when facing the wrath of Corollaries #2 and #3. If you are perceived as clear and above-board, you are more likely to hear the questions your audience may have about your choice of data.

Being able to demonstrate that you are aware of Bolten's Law and its corollaries will help you deliver effective quantation and generate consistent audience respect.[2]

Appropriate Emphasis on Critical Information

In Chapter 2, we discussed specific visual effects you can use to emphasize certain numbers in your report. The chapter had examples, but we didn't really discuss *why* you might want to emphasize some numbers, because that's an audience-dependent discussion that belongs in this chapter. Basically, there are two reasons for emphasizing numbers:

1. The number is **generically important** because of what it's measuring (e.g., results rows like Total Revenues and Net Income, columns like annual totals when months or quarters are also presented).

2. The number is **specifically important** because of its magnitude, or because it's been the subject of particular attention from this audience (e.g., budget variances that are large on either a raw dollar or a percentage basis, other numbers that are pleasant or unpleasant surprises).

Most of the time, numbers highlighted in reports are of the generically important variety, and this makes life easy for you. Once you design and format your spreadsheet, you don't have to mess with it because each iteration of the report has the same numbers emphasized (typically in specific rows and columns).

Emphasizing specifically important numbers has its place as well. You can do this using the visual effects we've discussed in Chapter 2, but you can also use Excel's "conditional formatting" capability so that numbers that meet certain criteria are formatted differently (e.g., variances greater than 20%, or the three highest numbers in a column). Conditional formatting is a very powerful feature and fun to use. But before you dot the landscape with colorful, energized numbers, be sure to consider:

- **The "ransom note" effect.** Especially if you are also emphasizing generically important numbers, does your report have too much going on?

- **What you are not emphasizing.** Are the *un*emphasized numbers *un*important? When you emphasize specifically important numbers, you are injecting your opinion about what is (and is not) worth emphasizing. This is fine to do, of course, as long as you're doing it intentionally.

- **Whether the audience will appreciate your effort.** This is a subtle point, and very audience-dependent. Some audiences may feel your most important contribution is to deliver information in clear, readable reports (and extracting meaning from the information is *their* job). To that kind of audience, reports that also tell them which information is and is not important may seem irritating and inappropriate.

- **Your time and your sanity.** Although conditional formatting can bring a little order to the process, you should be reviewing the report every time you publish it, just to make sure there's nothing unintended in the report. This takes extra time and extra care. Is conditional formatting worth your effort?

- **Whether it's necessary.** In my experience, the need to emphasize specifically important numbers often arises out of reports that are so poorly designed and overloaded with data that additional measures are necessary to help the audience glean any information at all from the reports. Clear, effective quantation of the kind I'm describing and advocating in *Painting with Numbers* can make those additional measures unnecessary.

I'm not trying to talk you out of emphasizing specifically important numbers, but be sure to review the points above so you can consider the pluses and minuses carefully.

If you choose to emphasize *both* generically and specifically important numbers, it's an exceedingly good idea to use different visual effects for the different types of emphases. Report 4-1 is an example, using Report 2-5 from Chapter 2.

Report 4-1 (2-5, Revisited)
VASTCo -- 2006 Income Statement, Actuals thru Q3 & Outlook for the Year

(in $000)	Actual Results						Outlook for Full Year			
	Q1	Q2	Q3	YTD Tot.	Budget	F(U)	Q4	06 TOT.	Budget	F(U)
Licenses	3,948	4,158	4,326	12,432	11,792	640	4,500	16,932	16,000	932
Services	1,438	1,518	1,580	4,536	4,321	215	1,620	6,156	5,940	216
Total Revenues	5,386	5,676	5,906	16,968	16,113	855	6,120	23,088	21,940	1,148
Cost of Sales	701	739	769	2,209	1,899	(310)	765	2,974	2,600	(374)
Gross Profit	4,685	4,937	5,136	14,759	14,214	545	5,355	20,114	19,340	774
Sales & Marketing	1,794	1,874	1,961	5,629	5,517	(112)	2,019	7,648	7,510	(138)
Research & Dev.	1,035	1,111	1,176	3,321	3,312	(9)	1,191	4,512	4,542	30
General & Admin.	769	800	813	2,381	2,313	(68)	825	3,206	3,138	(68)
Total Oprg. Exps.	3,597	3,786	3,950	11,332	11,142	(190)	4,035	15,367	15,190	(177)
Operating Profit	1,088	1,152	1,187	3,427	3,072	355	1,320	4,747	4,150	597

REPORT 4-1 (REPORT 2-5 REVISITED):   VASTCo 2006 Income Statement, Actuals through Q3 and Outlook for the Year

The generically important numbers are emphasized just as they were in Report 2-6, using **boldface**, blue text, and *italics*, and the specifically important numbers are circled. The circled numbers that are notably positive results are circled in purple, and the "problem" numbers are circled in red. Finally, the Operating Profit variance for the full year—the single number on which the bulk of the management bonus will be based—has four purple arrows pointing in toward it, just in case anyone in management needs a reminder! In this example, I use a different visual effect for each different reason for emphasizing a number. And the effects I use for the specifically important numbers are noticeably different from the ones I use to emphasize the generically important numbers.

Another way to emphasize specifically important numbers is to use that other powerful communications tool: *words*. Words give you a way to emphasize specifically important numbers, but through explanation rather than through visual effects. Report 4-2 is a re-presentation of an exhibit you've seen before

(Report 2-2 from Chapter 2), with comments at the right (and the other columns squeezed together a little to make room on the page).

Report 4-2 (2-2, Revisited)
VASTCo -- 2006 Q3 Income Statement, Actual vs. Budget

(in $000)	Quarter Ended 9/06			Year-to-Date			Comments
	Actual	Budget	F(U)	Actual	Budget	F(U)	
Licenses	4,284	4,064	220	12,348	11,792	556	GM deal didn't close -- bailout
Prof. Svcs.	1,561	1,530	31	4,498	4,321	177	Expanded scope, fewer deals
Total Revenues	5,845	5,594	251	16,846	16,113	733	
Cost of Sales	760	667	(94)	2,192	1,899	(293)	
Gross Profit	5,084	4,927	157	14,654	14,214	440	
Sales & Marketing	1,928	1,915	(13)	5,579	5,517	(61)	Hired new Sales VP in October
Research & Dev.	1,153	1,167	14	3,270	3,312	42	Version 3.1.6.a re-engineered
General & Admin.	805	798	(7)	2,363	2,313	(50)	
Total Oprg. Exps.	3,887	3,880	(6)	11,212	11,142	(70)	
Oprg. Profit	1,198	1,046	151	3,442	3,072	370	

REPORT 4-2 (REPORT 2-2 REVISITED):   VASTCo 2006 Q3 Income Statement, Actual versus Budget

Using words not only clarifies the meaning of significant numbers, but it is also one way to address questions of *why* certain numbers were or weren't emphasized.

Consistency

Consistency is a recurring theme in *Painting with Numbers* because it's a critically important idea. To make your audience more comfortable with your quantation, I suggest that you develop a consistent and recognizable look-and-feel for your quantation, because it will enhance your audience's ability to grasp the essence of your information quickly. Moreover, consistency isn't merely an approach you should apply to a single report or reporting package. *It should be applied across all of the different quantation products you deliver.* Some of the benefits to this approach are:

- The audience can absorb the content much more quickly, because they know where to look for the information they're most interested in.
- The audience becomes comfortable with your reports and has confidence in their quality and accuracy, because they've seen the same reports many times before.
- Audience confidence applies even when you are delivering a completely new report on a completely new subject.
- The audience comes to expect a certain level of quality from you, which can go a long way toward enhancing the reputation of your department as well as your own personal brand image.

At the beginning of Chapter 2, we discussed a simple example of consistency: the choice between landscape and portrait orientation. It doesn't matter which orientation you choose (personally, I recommend landscape as your default); what matters is doing it the same way as often as possible, so your audience gets comfortable with it.

Reporting packages that make the reader flip back and forth between portrait and landscape can risk looking sloppy and unprofessional, giving the impression of a bunch of disparate reports stapled together and not an integrated package. In addition to page orientation, some of the other elements to consider in the name of consistency include:

- Typeface and font size
- Location and format of the "housekeeping" elements on the report, like title, timestamp, pagination, confidentiality legend, filename, and author
- Wording and format for the captions of commonly used report dimensions, like time (year, quarter, month, day), income statement line items, balance sheet line items, and divisions/departments
- Standard approaches for highlighting important information, or distinguishing one type of information from another (e.g., actual results, budgets, and forecasts)
- Standard approaches for visually separating various portions of the report, like white space and cell borders
- Number formats (especially when truncating digits) and number of decimal places

To cap off this discussion of consistency, I'd like you to consider a very specific consistency problem, one that has earned the coveted Deadly Sin award. Look at each of the two versions of Report 4-3, covering up one version while reading the other.

Report 4-3, Version A (1-2, revisited) VASTCo -- 1998-2003 Financial Highlights						
(in $000)	**1998**	**1999**	**2000**	**2001**	**2002**	**2003**
Revenues	699	950	1,493	2,138	2,910	4,733
Expenses	662	800	1,207	1,639	2,348	3,093
Operating Profit	**37**	**150**	**286**	**499**	**562**	**1,640**

REPORT 4-3, VERSION A (REPORT 1-2, REVISITED): VASTCo 1998–2003 Financial Highlights

Report 4-3, Version B VASTCo -- 1998-2003 Financial Highlights						
(in $000)	2003	2002	2001	2000	1999	1998
Revenues	4,733	2,910	2,138	1,493	950	699
Expenses	3,093	2,348	1,639	1,207	800	662
Oprg. Profit	1,640	562	499	286	150	37

REPORT 4-3, VERSION B: VASTCo 1998–2003 Financial Highlights

Obviously, they are the same report, with Version A presenting the columns in forward chronological order and Version B in reverse order. *Which version do you prefer?*

As with many of my other shooting-fish-in-a-barrel examples, people have a strongly one-sided preference, which in this case is Version A. As I've said before, in most of the western world, we read from left to right. And when we think about multiple time periods, we usually think of them in chronological order. When we consider these two cognitive approaches together, it's easy to see why Version B looks odd to most of us.

In the world of quantation, confusion on this issue can have serious consequences: people taking a quick glance at a row of numbers will perceive an upward trend as a downward one, and *vice versa*, if they've gotten the time progression confused. For this reason, I strongly believe that *time-period information should always be presented in forward chronological order*, that is, from left (earliest date) to right (latest date) if it runs horizontally across the page, or from top to bottom if it runs vertically down the page.

Now, there are some people who prefer reverse chronological order. I have no idea why. However, whichever method you choose, please do not commit:

Deadly Sin #6

In a package with more than one multiple-time-period report, presenting **some reports in forward and some in reverse chronological order**

Never do this! You will dramatically increase the probability that someone in your audience will come to a conclusion that is exactly the opposite of the one he or she should, and all because you didn't grasp the importance of *consistency*.

Meaningful and Relevant Numbers

Report 4-4 was just presented to the board of directors. What kind of grade would you give it?

Report 4-4 VASTCo -- 2006 Income Statement	
(in $000)	2006 Total
Licenses	16,785
Services	6,120
Total Revenues	**22,905**
Cost of Sales	2,982
Gross Profit	**19,923**
Sales & Marketing	7,568
Research & Dev.	4,477
General & Admin.	3,191
Total Oprg. Exps.	15,236
Operating Profit	**4,687**

REPORT 4-4:   VASTCo 2006 Income Statement

Well, it seems to be about the right level of detail for a corporate director, it follows the "looks" guidelines we discussed in Chapter 2, and we have every reason to assume that the information is accurate. Does that make this a good report? NO! This report gets an *F*! Why? Because of the following:

The Laws of Quantation

de Urioste's Law: There is no such thing as a stand-alone number.[3]

It's virtually impossible for normal humans to look at a single number (e.g., $22,905,000 in Revenue), and form a conclusion about it. You can't tell from a number sitting all by itself whether it's high or low, or better or worse than expected, or whether you should be pleased or displeased. People need some way to make useful comparisons (against prior periods, or against the budget, or against investor expectations), and the only practical way to do that is to include those comparison numbers in the same report. After all, most people do not have photographic memories. This is especially true of corporate directors (if for no other reason than it's often been three months or more since they last looked at information about your company).

It's critical that you *include all of the numbers your audience is likely to want for comparison in one single report.* Don't make people have to dig out last quarter's report and put both reports side by side. Each report, or each page in the report package, should be able to stand on its own as a meaningful document. With that in mind, let's take another whack at that report that got an *F*, so it can get a passing grade (see Report 4-5).

Report 4-5
VASTCo -- 2006 Income Statement

(in $000)	2006 Total	vs. Budget 2006 Total	vs. Budget Var. F(U)	vs. Prior Year 2005 Total	vs. Prior Year Y/Y Change
Licenses	16,785	16,000	785	12,365	4,420
Services	6,120	5,940	180	4,436	1,684
Total Revenues	**22,905**	**21,940**	**965**	**16,801**	**6,104**
Cost of Sales	2,982	2,600	(382)	2,372	610
Gross Profit	**19,923**	**19,340**	**583**	**14,429**	**5,494**
Sales & Marketing	7,568	7,510	(58)	5,775	1,793
Research & Dev.	4,477	4,542	65	2,840	1,637
General & Admin.	3,191	3,138	(53)	2,815	376
Total Oprg. Exps.	15,236	15,190	(46)	11,430	3,806
Operating Profit	**4,687**	**4,150**	**537**	**2,999**	**1,688**

REPORT 4-5: VASTCo 2006 Income Statement

Now the numbers in this report have meaning! With minimal effort, your audience can tell how VASTCo did against budget expectations for the year and against its prior year. Presenting numbers without proper context is a grievous error—in fact it warrants its own Deadly Sin:

 Deadly Sin #7

Presenting numbers with **no context** whatsoever—no comparison to prior periods, to plan/budget, to competitors, or to anything else

This is a serious sin that is committed most often by people who view reporting as an act of compliance, not an act of communication. Presenting numbers without context wastes your audience's time and damages your relationship with them, because it renders your report practically useless.

While we're on the subject of what you choose to include (or exclude) in your reports, remember that *everything* about your quantation guides your audience toward what is important. For example, look at Report 4-6, showing revenues from just two product lines.

Report 4-6
Corporate Sales, for Products A & B (in $000)

Product	2002	2003	2004	2005	2006	Total
Product A	586	950	1,045	963	1,201	4,745
Product B	400	525	650	887	843	3,305
Total	986	1,475	1,695	1,850	2,044	8,050

REPORT 4-6: Corporate Sales for Products A and B (in $000)

Here's the question: *Do the Totals (either the row or the column) belong in this report? Are they relevant?* The answer is a resounding and unequivocal *maybe*. It depends completely on the context of the report.

Let's start with the Total *column* at the right, and ask ourselves: Is there any particular meaning to the years 2002–2006? If not, why are we bothering to present the total of those five years? If the company was *founded* in 2002, then this report is showing the company's entire five-year revenue history, in which case the Total through 2006 might be of some interest. The audience for the report might be interested, for example, in the total cumulative installed bases of the two products. But beyond an explanation like that, it's hard to understand why a reader would be interested in the total revenues of each product over an arbitrarily chosen five-year period.[4]

Let's turn now to the Total *row* at the bottom. *Does it belong there? Is it relevant?* If Products A and B were the company's *only* products, the answer is a straightforward *yes*, since the Total row therefore represents the company's total revenues, and total revenues are almost certainly of interest. But if Products A and B were only two of, say, seven different products the company offers, why would the sum of those two products have any meaning whatsoever? And if instead you were presenting these two products just to show the *comparison* between A and B, then the Total row is not only meaningless, but it actually gets in the reader's way, because it's extraneous information.

The larger point here is that every number in your report has meaning, or at least *should* have meaning. With respect to totals, this naturally brings us to:

Deadly Sin #8

Omitting totals where they would be appropriate, **or presenting totals** where they aren't appropriate

I recognize that this is one of the subtler of the Deadly Sins, but I'm including it because it goes right to the heart of one of the most important principles of quantation:

The Laws of Quantation

Your audience is entitled to presume that every number in a report is meaningful, and if data are omitted, it's because they are less meaningful.

Presenting (or not presenting) totals appropriately demonstrates that you have a sound understanding of what the numbers mean and how your report should be used.

Respect for your Audience's Time

Finally, let's talk about time—specifically, *your audience's* time, and even more specifically, *not wasting* your audience's time. Not wasting your audience's time is a gesture of courtesy and respect, and it can be essential to you and to your organization, because your audience may choose not to take the time needed to understand your quantation fully, or even worse, just ignore your reports altogether. Let's review some obvious ways to demonstrate respect for your audience's time, starting with the pages of your reports:

- **Use a title to tell them what the report is about.** Omitting the title is a Deadly Sin.

- **Keep reports to *one* page.** If you can't get your information onto a single page, perhaps you didn't spend enough time thinking about the best way to lay out the information. Yes, that elegant report you just designed doesn't quite fit on one page, but beware of thinking impure thoughts, and thereby committing:

 Deadly Sin #9

Shrinking font size in order to fit a report onto a single page, or creating a "single page" **with the help of Scotch tape**

You are creating a report, not an eye chart, so don't mess with the font size. And no matter how you slice it, if you have to Scotch-tape your document, it has too much data on it for most readers to find it useful. If you cannot fit your report onto a single page without committing Deadly Sin #9, *the problem is with your report design, pure and simple, so fix it!*

- **Timestamp your reports.** Many, if not most, reports are "living documents"; they provide information based on the best data you have now, which everyone expects will change over time. If you give your audience up-to-the-minute information, you must give them a way to figure out which reports are now out-of-date, so those can be thrown away. This prompts us to revisit:

 Deadly Sin #5

No title or timestamp (date *and* time) on printed spreadsheets[5]

- **Insert document information.** You would do well to make sure every page of your quantation also includes the following items (and preferably *in the same place on every page* so people know where to find them):

- The **filename**, so your audience can find the source document if necessary
- **Page numbering**, if the reporting package has multiple pages
- The **"Confidential"** legend, if appropriate[6]

Using a title, keeping the report to one page, including the appropriate time-stamp, and inserting basic document information are all simple things that you can do for your audience to demonstrate your respect for their time. There are also some larger actions you can take to ensure that your audience can access the information they need easily and quickly:

Think about the Best Ways to Distribute Your Reports. My views here might be a little controversial in a world of "empowering" employees to get their own information (and concern for our natural resources), but there is just no substitute for *putting the information in people's hands yourself*. Distributing hardcopy (i.e., paper) is most effective, closely followed by an e-mail with an attachment. I cannot begin to tell you how many people have told me they see red when they hear the words, "Let me tell you how you can get the information off the server." The intensity of the red they see is directly proportional to their seniority. After all, how many CEOs actually *know* how to get information off the server?

Make the Information Easy to View. Once the reports have been distributed, your audience has to be able to read them. As much red as people see when they are told to go retrieve documents from the server, they see *even more* red when they go to print out a spreadsheet, and what should be one page turns into four pages: the bulk of the report on page 1, the rightmost column on page 2, the bottom row on page 3, and the lower right-hand cell, all by itself on page 4. To the thunderous applause of these red-seers, I now present:

 Deadly Sin #12

To print the finished report, requiring the audience to **do more than just click the "Print" icon**[7]

It's a simple matter to set the Print_Area in Excel before you distribute the document, and look at it yourself with Print Preview, if for no other reason than to make sure your audience is going to see what you want them to see.

Note

More and more people prefer to look at reports on their computer screens rather than in hardcopy. This reduces, *but does not eliminate*, your need to make sure that it's easy for your audience to view your reports. Many people view the reports using Print Preview in Excel, so the same issues apply that apply to paper printouts. Also, readers who use notebook computers may get annoyed having to scroll up and down and left and right because of screen-size limitations. So, before you distribute your reports, make sure that your audience will have a comfortable experience reading them, regardless of the way they choose to do it.

Help Readers Find What They Need. In addition to creating well-designed reports that make it easy for your audience to find important information, there are several other actions you can take that will help your audience understand what they are receiving and frame your entire package:

- Attach a **cover memo** briefly describing the package and introducing new reports and other major changes in the package format and organization. You might want to summarize the key conclusions that the reader should review.

- If your package has more than two or three reports, provide a **table of contents**.

- If your package is being distributed in hardcopy and some of the reports have several pages, attach **divider tabs** so people can get to a specific page quickly.

The entire package should be structured to enable readers to get the most important nuggets of information out in the least amount of time. This should be evident in the way the individual reports are designed and laid out, and in the organization of the overall package. Don't find yourself committing a common Deadly Sin, by uttering:

 Deadly Sin #13

"Well, I can see why you reached that conclusion, but that's because you didn't review the whole package."

If you find yourself saying this, the first thing you should do is look in the mirror and have a conversation with yourself. Then go back and examine how you have organized and laid out your information.

In this chapter, we discussed the characteristics of effective quantation that all audiences need:

- The **right amount** of data. Bolten's Law and its corollaries describe the risks of providing too much data (or too little) to your audience.

- **Appropriate emphasis** on critical information. The way you use visual cues to highlight *generically* important information, as well as *specifically* important information, will help your audience home in on the critical information.

- **Consistency.** An underrated but critically important element of effective quantation is presenting information in the same way, and in the same places on the page, every time you deliver reports. This applies to *all* the reports you deliver, not just too recurring presentations of the same information package.

- **Meaningful, relevant** numbers (de Urioste's Law). Numbers are meaningless to an audience without *something* to compare them to. It is important to include any essential context that your audience may need to understand your reports. Your audience is also entitled to assume that all the numbers they're seeing are important, and what's *not* there is *not* important.

- **Respect** for their time. When the audience looks at one of your reports, they should *immediately* understand its subject, how it's organized, and whether it's current. You can also make accessing and printing out your quantation faster and more painless for your audience. If you don't take the time to think through these steps, you risk annoying your audience even before they start looking at the numbers.

It's no accident that almost half of the Deadly Sins in *Painting with Numbers* are introduced in this chapter. Your audience is a critical component of your quantation; the most important thing you can do is keep their needs in mind when you design your reports. If you want to inform, enlighten, advise, guide, warn, or even entertain, the most important thing you must do is *reach your audience*. No matter what your objectives are, if you can't reach your audience, you won't be able to communicate with them.

That said, all audiences are tough audiences, one way or another. Sometimes they're short of time, patience, interest, grasp of the subject, or plain-old native intelligence. Sometimes they have *too much* of one or more of these traits, and that's not always pleasant, either. The quote from Alvy Singer at the beginning of this chapter applies to quantation audiences as readily as it applies to life in general. Regardless of the toughness of your audience, when you communicate numbers, your job is no different from when you speak or write.

When you write a memo or an article, you choose words and language appropriate for your audience's grasp of the subject matter, and an amount of detail appropriate for their time and interest level. When you speak to a group, you dress appropriately for that audience, you balance formal and colloquial speech to fit them and the setting, and you allocate the necessary time for questions. Effective quantation involves exactly the same kind of attention to detail. You need to have a sound understanding of how your audience processes information, you need to know how to interact successfully with them, and you need to show respect for their time and their intelligence. Effective quantation also requires you to understand how your *particular* audience is unique. If you can demonstrate a deep understanding of these principles, your audiences will appreciate you over and over again.

NOTES

1. I have always felt that it would be just lovely if a Law, or a Theorem, or a Principle, were named after me. I might add that I would not have been satisfied with a mere "lemma," "question," or "paradox."

2. This chapter's text description of Bolten's Law and its corollaries is the lay interpretation of a highly technical principle. The mathematically correct formulation is:

   $$L_{n,p} = v\, I_n^{-1}\, T_p^{-2}$$

   where: $L_{n,p}$ = the length of the conversation about data point n in reporting package p (in minutes)

   v = Verbosity Constant (generally assumed to be an arbitrarily large number)

   I_n = the importance of data point n ($0 < I_n \le 1$)

   T_p = total time available for discussion and analysis of reporting package p (in hours)

   My ultimate objective is nothing less than a trip to Stockholm. The white tie and tails are packed!

3. George de Urioste is a friend and fellow CFO. This particular pronouncement, delivered over lunch in a fine local restaurant, deserves to have the force of law. I was so impressed when I heard it that not only did I offer to pick up the tab, I agreed to supersize.

4. Note also that if instead of the years 2002–2006, the columns showed revenues for the months January–December, or quarters 1–4, we would all agree that a total for the year is probably meaningful, since in the business world a full year is not an arbitrary period of time.

5. Please note that the timestamp you can put into an Excel Header or Footer tells you when the report was *printed*, not when the spreadsheet was last saved or last worked on. But it's better than nothing, and it happens automatically. If you want some way to memorialize when the report was *prepared*, put an "as-of date" in a cell somewhere in the worksheet, or even have some indicator of that embedded in the filename. More on this in Chapter 6.

6. A word of advice from a non-lawyer about marking items as "Confidential": Don't put this legend on documents that clearly are *not* confidential. If things ever "get legal," one of the defenses an accused confidentiality violator can argue is that the "Confidential" legend was used so indiscriminately that no reasonable person could rely on it to tell whether a document was in fact truly confidential. If you're concerned about this, consult with your legal counsel.

7. The astute reader will notice that the number for this Deadly Sin is out of sequence, since it was immediately preceded by Deadly Sin #9. Stay calm. The elegant symmetry of my Jesuitical logic will be revealed in the Appendix ("Jazz Meets Theology").

Wrap-Up for Part I: The Rules

Chapter 4 concludes the first part of *Painting with Numbers*. In these chapters we codified the essential premises of this book:

- Quantation is a *communication* skill and not a numbers skill.

- Effective quantation requires you to follow a set of basic rules and best practices (not unlike the rules for grammar, diction, paragraph structure, etc.).

- Your quantation is constantly sending all kinds of messages to your audience.

- Small errors in your quantation can have a disproportionately negative impact on your audience's understanding (as well as their opinion of you).

- When quantation is involved, the stakes are likely to be high.

With these considerations in mind, we focused on a number of specific quantation skill areas. The following table draws parallels between these quantation skills and various analogous writing and speaking skills:

Chapter	Quantation Skill	Analogous Skills	Consequences When Poorly Done
1	Using the Arabic numeral system effectively	• Correct spelling • Good grammar • Proper pronunciation	• Disturbing the audience's reading (or listening) flow • Occasional confusion or misunderstanding
2	Using the layout and visual appearance of quantation to enhance readability	• Paragraph organization • Using white space to organize your content • Using text effects (margins, font size, boldface, italics, etc.)	• Audience misses key points • Intimidating the audience • Presenter perceived as unprofessional
3	Using words properly and effectively in quantation	• Vocabulary sense (choosing words well) • Awareness of audience familiarity with jargon and abbreviations	• Audience confusion from poor choice of words • Audience feels left out or patronized
4	Respecting your audience and understanding how they process quantation	• Tailoring vocabulary and sentence structure to audience • Tailoring length of document or talk to audience's interest level • Making meaningful analogies	• Too much or too little information for audience needs • Audience misses key points • Audience gives up and stops reading (or listening)

You may have noticed a shift in emphasis as we progressed through these chapters. The early chapters focused on how to lay out your numbers clearly and precisely on the page to make it easy for your audience to understand the information. These skills are the foundation of quantation, just as correct spelling, good grammar, and strong vocabulary are the foundation of effective writing. The later chapters (especially Chapter 4) focused on how to present your information with an eye toward the needs, abilities, and interests of the particular audience you are trying to reach. By using these skills effectively, you show your audience not only that you *understand* them, but that you *respect* them as well. Showing respect for your audience is an important aspect of any form of communication. To put this another way (using terminology that should be especially meaningful if you have an accounting background):

Strong Advice

There is a difference between *compliance* and *communication*. When you have delivered information according to the rules for its presentation, you have complied. When your audience *understands* both the information and its meaning, you have communicated. Quantation that simply complies without communicating is at best ineffective and at worst destructive.

Doing quantation effectively can be hard work. It requires you to master a variety of skills and tactics. Moreover, you need to keep in mind at all times:

- You have choices.

- There are tradeoffs.

Please note that this book is *not* titled *The Idiot's Guide to Effective Quantation*. (Then again, I'm not aware of any books titled *The Idiot's Guide to Clear and Elegant Writing*, or *The Idiot's Guide to Eloquent Speaking*, either.) Effective quantation is both an art and a skill, but there are great rewards for being able to do it well, both for your audience and for you personally.

PART II

II

THE TOOLS

CHAPTER 5

You Can Pay Me Now . . .

You think in spreadsheets, don't you?

—A CFO, overheard remarking to one of his more imaginative financial analysts, c. 1987 (i.e., about the time that spreadsheets began to see widespread use)

If you're like most people tasked with presenting lots of information, your biggest challenge is time. Moreover, the time you spend organizing and presenting your information (i.e., doing quantation) is typically at the *end* of a long project, after you've done the hard work of collecting and analyzing the data, and when the pressure on you is most acute. This chapter and Chapter 6 will help you make the most of this time by showing you how to use Excel faster and more efficiently in two different ways. The tips in this chapter will help you save time by developing habits that make the work go faster each and every time you use Excel. The tips in Chapter 6 will help you save time by enabling you (or others who use your documents) to quickly resume working when you (or they) return to your spreadsheets sometime later. You'll be amazed at how using these tips and making them a habit will naturally translate into clear and effective quantation.

Developing effective spreadsheet habits is no different from learning how to play the saxophone proficiently or mastering a tennis serve. The secret is practice, practice, practice. As sports coaches like to say, you must develop "muscle memory" so that you can do a task well, every time, and under every circumstance. Having muscle memory means your body will take over and do the right thing when your mind is distracted by other pressures—like a national TV audience, or the state championship trophy, or the board meeting happening in just a few hours (or days). If you use the tips in this chapter on a regular basis, you will be building essential skills that will serve you well under pressure.

With this important idea in mind, my very first suggestion is to adopt the "board of directors meeting mindset." The board of directors meeting mindset is a way of thinking that says:

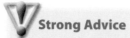

Strong Advice

Every time you design and deliver a spreadsheet or a reporting package, tell yourself that your audience is the board of directors.

Here are some of the reasons why this is a good idea:

1. If you treat every report as a report for your board of directors even when it isn't, the skills you need to get the task done efficiently will be right at your fingertips when you actually *are* preparing that report.
2. You will develop a reputation as someone who consistently delivers clear, high-quality information, regardless of the audience.
3. Sometimes, contrary to everyone's expectations, that report you thought was a throwaway actually *will* end up in front of the board of directors.

Aside from the obvious benefits of getting solid practice, and building a good reputation, the harsh truth about reports is that you don't control their final destination. The most trivial, innocently intended, casually requested report can take on a life of its own and start making its way around the world without any additional propulsion from you. Moreover, once it's out there, that report is *yours*, warts and all. If there are mistakes in it, or it is unprofessional looking because it was hastily prepared, it will still be thought of as *your* work. So, in recognition of the fact that the road to hell is paved with good intentions, let me introduce:

Deadly Sin #16

"I never intended for anyone else to use this spreadsheet."

Of all the Deadly Sins presented in *Painting with Numbers*, this one is unique because it doesn't necessarily describe a presentation error. It's simply an acknowledgment that you have allowed work that is not up to your professional standards to escape from its cage. Your report will have gone places you didn't intend, and your apparent lack of preparation will now be public knowledge. In this chapter and the next, I offer a whole set of tips on how to use Excel to support your quantation, and to protect you from ever having to hang your head in shame and utter those awful words. If you develop a regular habit of using these tips, you will save time, and avoid the pitfalls of hasty work during crunch time.

The Instant Payoff Tips

In this chapter, we focus on the Instant Payoff Tips. These are skills and habits that will give you an immediate time savings *every* time you build a spreadsheet. They include:

1. Set up templates and styles.
2. Customize your toolbar.
3. Learn some shortcut keys.
4. Use consistent formats.
5. Learn to use Excel as a database.
6. Learn to use the Lookup & Reference functions.
7. Organize data for easy computation.
8. Learn to use automated help.
9. Don't learn too many ways to do the same thing.

Some of the sections in this chapter and the next go into considerable detail about the nuts-and-bolts of Excel.[1] Even so, you will *not* find step-by-step instructions on how to execute spreadsheet functions, since there are many excellent books on that topic. Instead, you'll find explanations of why each tip is valuable and how to use it effectively. If you are a moderately experienced user of spreadsheets, some of the sections will suggest techniques and habits that you are already familiar with, so feel free to skim this chapter and read carefully only the sections that will help you the most. Now, you won't find any profound philosophical truths about quantation in this chapter. But I am confident that if you study and implement these tips, someday (as your parents have said) you will thank me for this.

Instant Payoff Tip #1: Set Up Templates and Styles

When you specify your page orientation, font sizes, number formats, report titles, footers, captions, and column alignments *each and every time you create a report*, you are wasting precious time. Even if you're spending only 10 or 15 minutes making each of your reports look professional, you could be doing something else with that time.

What's the alternative? Set up a template so that every time you create a new workbook or worksheet all of this will be taken care of. Using a template will cut your spreadsheet setup time from 10 or 15 minutes (or more) down to 1 or 2 minutes.[2] You'll still need to create a title for any new worksheet, but this will be your reminder to include a title (and thereby avoid committing a Deadly Sin).

Report 5-1 shows many of the elements you might want to define in an Excel template. Pay special attention to your Page Setup (page layout, margins, headers/footers) and Styles (standard formats for certain types of numbers or cells). Report 5-1 includes some standard number formats[3] you might want to specify. The template approach will help you get work done faster and will enable you to create a standard, consistent look-and-feel for your quantation.

Report 5-1
SPREADSHEET TEMPLATE EXAMPLE

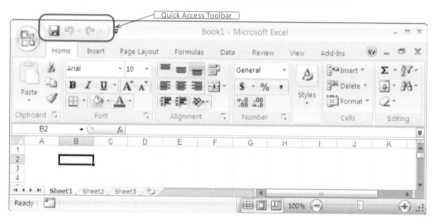

Vaporware & Software Technologies Corporation
TITLE OF THIS PARTICULAR REPORT

Company Name   Report Title   Top Margin

Left Margin   Right Margin

Standard Formats
1234567.89 General
1,234,567.89 Comma
1,234,568 Comma(0)
1,235 Thousands(0)
1,234.6 Thousands(1)   Bottom Margin
1 Millions(0)
1.2 Millions(1)

Author   Filename   Confidentiality   Date/Timestamp   Pagination
                                  Legend
rcb -- filename.xlsx   **VASTCo Confidential**   printed 11/15/10 1:35 PM p. 1/5

REPORT 5-1:   Spreadsheet Template Example

Instant Payoff Tip #2: Customize Your Toolbar

Having frequently used functions at your fingertips can help you become a much faster spreadsheet user. In Office 07, Microsoft allows you to customize your function interface with the Quick Access Toolbar. Shown here is the default Excel window with the Home ribbon visible (the Quick Access Toolbar is visible regardless of which ribbon you select). At the top is the default Quick Access Toolbar (circled in red). As you can see, Excel's out-of-the-box Quick Access Toolbar has only three function icons: Save, Undo, and Redo.

If you customize your Quick Access Toolbar, you can put a variety of Excel functions icons within easy reach. Here is an example of a customized toolbar:

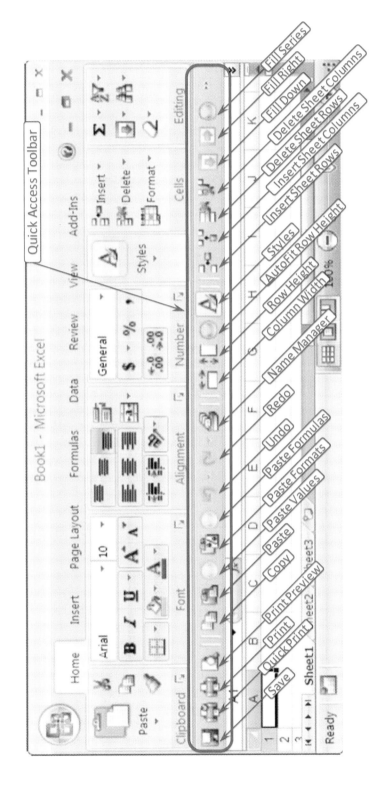

Quick Access Toolbar

Fill Series
Fill Right
Fill Down
Delete Sheet Columns
Delete Sheet Rows
Insert Sheet Columns
Insert Sheet Rows
Styles
AutoFit Row Height
Row Height
Column Width
Name Manager
Redo
Undo
Paste Formulas
Paste Formats
Paste Values
Paste
Copy
Print Preview
Print
Quick Print
Save

First, note that you can position the toolbar below the ribbon, rather than above it, which is a much more convenient place to put the most commonly used functions because it's closer to the cells themselves. Also, you can choose from virtually all of the Excel functions, and you can arrange them in any order, including putting space separators between different groups of icons. Finally, note that most of the functions included in this example relate to format and layout. I prefer having the format and layout functions on my toolbar because I use them over and over when I'm initially designing the spreadsheet as well as when I'm fine-tuning its appearance at the end of the process. But you have complete flexibility.[4] Customizing your Quick Access Toolbar (and then actually using it) shortens cursor travel and eliminates keystrokes and mouse clicks. It's nothing fancy, but will save you a *lot* of time.

Instant Payoff Tip #3: Learn Some Shortcut Keys

Like many software products, Excel offers you lots of way to do the same thing. Some of them are intended to be intuitively clear even if you're not familiar with the product (like clicking the function icons along the top of the window). Others aren't as obvious, but once you know them they can make your work go much faster. The shortcut keys fall into this category. There are lots of shortcuts in Excel, including the standard copy, cut, and paste, but here are a few that are the most important to know:

Operation	Keystroke Sequence
Highlight a single rectangular range of cells	(1) Left-click a cell that is one of the four corners of the range. (2) Do one of the following: • Without releasing the left-click, drag the cursor to the cell in the diagonally opposite corner of the rectangle. Then release the left-click, and the entire range will be highlighted. • Release the left-click. Then, move the cursor to the diagonally opposite cell, hold down the Shift key, and left-click that cell.
Highlight several noncontiguous cells or several rectangular ranges	(1) Highlight the first cell or rectangular range (as described above). (2) Hold down the Control key, and highlight the next cell or rectangular range. (3) Repeat until you've highlighted all the cells and rectangular ranges.
Clear contents (but not formats) of a range of cells	(1) Highlight the applicable range. (2) Hit the Delete key. (*Note:* Clearing only the content, but not the format, is especially important if you've spent a lot of time designing the report for maximum readability.)
Repeat what you just did	Ctrl-y (For example, if you've just entered a formula into or formatted a cell, you can select another cell or range of cells and repeat that operation.)

Undo what you just did	Ctrl-z (*Note:* Since everyone makes mistakes, this is a *really* useful shortcut! And Excel remembers the last several operations you did, so if you realize you goofed several steps ago, just keep hitting Ctrl-z until you've undone the operation in question.)
Enter the same formula into *all* the cells in a range	(1) Highlight the entire range. (2) In the formula bar, enter the formula. (3) Hold down the Control key and hit the Enter ↵ key (or click the √ button just to the left of the formula bar).
Fill right	(1) Highlight a range of cells. (2) Type Ctrl-r. Excel will copy the formula or value in the left-hand cell (or left-hand column) into all the cells (or columns) to the right.
Fill down	(1) Highlight a range of cells. (2) Type Ctrl-d. Excel will copy the formula or value in the topmost cell (or topmost row) into all the cells (or rows) below it.
Fill a series (i.e., create a sequence of numbers or dates)	(1) Enter values in the first two cells of the target row (or column). (2) Highlight these two cells. (3) Left-click the little square in the lower right-hand corner of the selection. (4) Without releasing the left-click, drag the cursor to the last cell in the row (or column) where you want the series. (5) Release the left-click. (*Note:* This operation is sometimes called "drag-and-drop.")

The last item in this table—filling a series—deserves a little more explanation because it can be a nice timesaver. Report 5-2 illustrates three such uses of this shortcut.

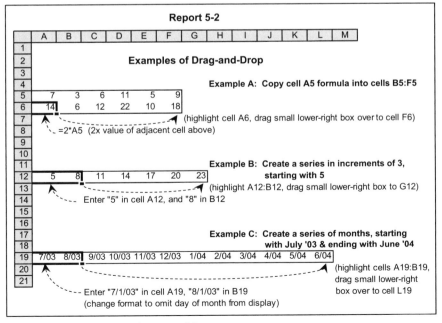

REPORT 5-2:   Examples of Drag-and-Drop

There are, of course, plenty of other shortcuts. Learn the ones for the actions that you find yourself performing most frequently.[5]

Instant Payoff Tip #4: Use Consistent Formats

Every time you build a spreadsheet, you make dozens of tiny little design decisions. The future of the world doesn't depend on any one of them, but each decision adds minutes or even hours every time you produce a new document. Some decisions, like the header, footer, style choices, and margins, can be taken care of with a template (see Instant Payoff Tip #1). But there are other design choices that don't lend themselves to templates, such as:

- **Columns.** Use standard captions for commonly used columns, including:
  - Time periods (years, quarters, months, weeks, days)
  - Types of information (actual, budget/plan, forecast/outlook, historical versus future)
  - Key indicators (growth rates, variances, etc.)
- **Rows.** Format your choices to distinguish different row captions (indents, boldface, italics, font size, font color).
- **Report numbers.** Format your choices to distinguish different types of numbers (actual, budget/plan, forecast/actual, totals versus individual numbers, key indicators, user inputs versus other cells).
- **Types of cells.** Format your choices and locations on your worksheet for different types of cell values, such as raw data, user inputs, key parameters, and summary information. See Long-Term Payoff Tip #7 for a more extensive discussion.
- **Overall.** Format your choices for grouping and distinguishing rows and columns (white space, row heights and column widths, borders, cell shading, text effects).

Your goal is to make these choices so that your reports are clear and intelligible, without making these choices your life's work. Any of the following approaches can save you a lot of time:

- **Create a style sheet.** This is a document you write for yourself that you can refer to every time you build a spreadsheet.
- **Cannibalize existing spreadsheets.** Copy elements you like from spreadsheets you've already built.
- **Create multiple templates.** A variant on Instant Payoff Tip #1 is to create more than one template, so that every time you create a new spreadsheet you can choose the appropriate template for the report you happen to be designing at the moment. Excel's user instructions will guide you through creating, storing, and organizing multiple templates.[6]

Another reason to take this approach is unrelated to the time you save: *Creating a consistent look-and-feel for your reports can help you develop your personal brand image.* If you do consistently excellent work, it's to your advantage to have your reports recognized as your own; having a consistent approach and style will help you earn that recognition.

Instant Payoff Tip #5: Learn to Use Excel as a Database

You may find yourself faced with an unwieldy heap of data from your organization's standard reporting systems. Your organization's financial statements from the accounting records, its sales forecasts from the customer relationship management (CRM) system, or its survey summaries from the HR database may provide excellent raw data, but you will need to present this data in a meaningful and comprehensible way for your audience.

This is when having database skills can be worth its weight in gold. You can address a variety of reporting issues by simply downloading the data from the back-office system into a file usable by spreadsheet software and then letting the spreadsheet's built-in database capabilities do the heavy lifting.

Report 5-3 is a simple example of an Excel spreadsheet tracking what a person ate at each meal over several days, with one row for each portion of food eaten at each meal, as well as the food group and calories of each item. This spreadsheet contains the raw data. (The squiggles indicate the omission of many rows of data.)

Report 5-3
Diet Record for 7/15-7/19

Seq	Date	Meal	Food	Group	Cal.
1	7/15	Bkfst	eggs	protein	160
2	7/15	Bkfst	toast, buttered	starch	225
3	7/15	Bkfst	orange juice	fruit	100
4	7/15	Lunch	yogurt	dairy	125
5	7/15	Lunch	apple	fruit	120

37	7/19	Lunch	tuna salad	protein	110
38	7/19	Lunch	hard-boiled egg	protein	80
39	7/19	Lunch	salad	vegetable	190
40	7/19	Dinner	spaghetti	starch	300

REPORT 5-3:   Diet Record for 7/15–7/19

To the untrained eye, Report 5-3 is just a plain, ordinary table, but it's really an honest-to-God *database*, with powers and abilities far beyond those of mere tables. Using standard Excel capabilities on this database, we can produce useful summary reports like Reports 5-4 and 5-5.

Report 5-4 — Calories Consumed at Each Meal 7/15-7/19						
	7/15	7/16	7/17	7/18	7/19	Total
Bkfst	485	455	460	585	125	2,110
Lunch	245	650	840	900	380	3,015
Dinner	1,100	560	540	1,425	830	4,455
Total	1,830	1,665	1,840	2,910	1,335	9,580

Report 5-5 — Food Group Calorie Distribution 7/15 - 7/19			
	Bkfst	Lunch	Dinner	Total
Protein	620	1,720	2,140	4,480
Starch	1,145	110	1,290	2,545
Vegetable	60	570	680	1,310
Fruit	100	490	0	590
Dairy	185	125	345	655
Total	2,110	3,015	4,455	9,580

REPORT 5-4: Calories Consumed at Each Meal 7/15–7/19

REPORT 5-5: Food Group Calorie Distribution

Or we can use the Data Filter capability in Excel to look at meaningful subsets of the data. For example, Report 5-6 shows all the portions in the database from the "protein" group that had at least 350 calories.

Report 5-6
Items Filtered from 7/15-7/19 Diet

Filter for "protein" group

Filter for "≥350" calories

S	Day	Meal	Food	Group	C
6	7/15	Dinner	steak	protein	750
13	7/16	Lunch	cheeseburger	protein	650
19	7/17	Lunch	burrito	protein	400
27	7/18	Lunch	club sandwich	protein	480
31	7/18	Dinner	ribs	protein	600

Icons indicate Data Filtering is on, and which columns are being filtered

REPORT 5-6: Items Filtered from 7/15–7/19 Diet

Note

A Presentation Tip: Presenting filtered data in real time can be very powerful. For example, in a companywide sales meeting, you could present the sales pipeline of each sales rep, one at a time on-screen (so that your audience can see the spreadsheet you're working on). Then you could view the entire company's big deals (say, $1 million or more) at a glance. Then you could look at all the deals needing some help from a senior executive in order to close that quarter (if your CRM system is set up to track that), and so on. Trust me: being able to do this on the spot can make you very popular with sales management.

Some of the "database" functions available in Excel are listed here. Each of them can be powerful and effective in its own way, but you should consider your own quantation needs and skill level when deciding which ones are appropriate for your own particular reporting situation.

Method	Brief Description	Pros	Cons
Pivot tables	From a database file, enables you to generate a table with totals in two dimensions (e.g., Sales Rep versus Product Line)	• Easy to learn and use • Actually produces the report table itself • Ability to drill down for more detail • Drag-and-drop capability to move rows and columns around	• Only does cross-totals, no capability for more complex queries • Formatting somewhat inflexible • May need to remember to "refresh" after updating underlying raw data
Array formulas	Formulas that calculate totals or other information from a database using a wide range of criteria[7]	• Immensely flexible and powerful, especially if you are constructing complex queries • Can meet virtually every reporting need, since you simply create formulas in a spreadsheet layout of your own design	• Requires skill to learn, even more skill to explain to others • Array formula syntax is "temperamental" and hard to debug
Database formulas	Formulas that calculate standard functions (like SUM, AVERAGE, MAX, MIN, COUNT, etc.) on columns in a database, subject to specified criteria[8]	• Can be used to structure many (but not all) of the complex queries possible using array formulas • Has the same report layout flexibility as array formulas	• Requires moderate skill to learn • Each query's criteria must be stored in a separate row of cells rather than entered into formulas; requires additional spreadsheet cells and limits query flexibility
Accessing SQL databases	Use commands written in Structured Query Language (SQL) embedded in Excel formulas to access data in large custom database systems like the accounting, sales, or H/R systems. (SQL is the standard format for queries to relational databases.)	• Take full advantage of SQL's "real database" capabilities • No need to recreate existing databases in your spreadsheet	• Generally requires understanding of how to structure SQL queries; very likely to require the support of IT professionals • Requires access to external files
Filtering	Used on a database file in a spreadsheet, enables user to sort data, or view only database rows meeting certain criteria	• Easy to learn and use • Very flexible for structuring all kinds of queries • Looks extremely cool in a real-time presentation	• More appropriate for real-time and interactive analysis rather than for producing printed reports

Excel's database features can be very powerful, and the dramatic increase in the data storage capabilities of personal computers and workstations has certainly made these features practical. (There was a time, not so long ago, when these functions were impossible without armies of nerds and buckets of money.)

Instant Payoff Tip #6: Learn to Use the Lookup & Reference Functions

You may not need to use Excel as a heavy-duty database. But even if all you want to do is extract information from your tables, you'll be amazed at how effectively you can do that if you're familiar with Excel's Lookup & Reference functions. These functions enable you to locate cells in an array that meet specific criteria, get information about those cells, and perform calculations involving those cells. Excel offers about 20 functions in its Lookup & Reference function library, but among them all, I find these the most useful:

- **INDEX**—returns the cell at the intersection of a particular row and column.
- **MATCH**—returns the position in an array of a cell that matches a specified value.
- **OFFSET**—returns the cell or range of cells that is a given number of rows and columns away from another cell.
- **VLOOKUP**—looks for a specified value in the leftmost column of a table and then returns the cell in that same row of another column in that table.
- **HLOOKUP**—VLOOKUP's recumbent twin, this does the same operation starting with the topmost row of a table.

A word of warning: these functions can have complex syntax and specific requirements for how your table must be organized for the formulas to work properly. For example, under some circumstances, cells must be sorted in either ascending or descending order. But once you get the hang of it, you'll find that these are very powerful functions that are well worth the trouble to learn.

These functions are especially useful if you want to present only specific pieces of information calculated from your database as opposed to an entire table of results (like Reports 5-4 and 5-5). For example, Report 5-7 shows the monthly sales production of five sales reps over a two-year period. The raw data is in cells A5:F30, and the columns for the sales reps are presented in the order of their rank within the sales organization. To the right of the raw data are examples of useful information extracted by using the Lookup & Reference functions described earlier. Remember as you examine this report:

- The input parameters are the shaded cells in column J.
- The calculated results are in boxed boldface , also in column J.

- To help make sense of the report, the red artwork provides information on how the formulas are calculated, and the functions used in the formula for each calculated result are identified in *gray italics*.

Report 5-7

	A	B	C	D	E	F	G H	I	J	K
1	**VASTCo -- 2008 & 2009 Sales Rep Production,**									
2	**by Sales Rep, by Month (in $000)**									
4	**Rank:**	**1**	**2**	**3**	**4**	**5**				
5		**Abel**	**Baker**	**Charlie**	**David**	**Eddie**				
6	Jan-08	236.3	149.6	110.2	166.2	60.0				
7	Feb-08	184.5	225.4	160.7	168.1	97.6				
8	Mar-08	255.0	174.6	142.0	171.9	64.1				
9	Apr-08	261.8	273.3	148.4	151.3	72.1				
10	May-08	204.9	237.5	178.2	76.1	91.6				
11	Jun-08	279.2	260.4	165.8	118.8	92.8				
12	Jul-08	153.0	207.9	112.7	123.5	108.6				
13	Aug-08	221.4	232.5	79.1	139.4	97.4				
14	Sep-08	189.6	199.2	126.2	158.2	69.5				
15	Oct-08	241.8	201.7	111.9	134.9	114.9				
16	Nov-08	213.4	152.5	140.3	75.9	63.9				
17	Dec-08	269.0	200.8	152.5	151.8	108.0				
18	Jan-09	323.0	178.8	89.0	156.8	109.8				
19	Feb-09	178.0	126.3	193.0	175.5	118.4				
20	Mar-09	274.0	213.3	159.0	99.2	129.2				
21	Apr-09	227.5	146.3	142.2	116.5	82.6				
22	May-09	191.0	290.8	164.9	81.1	89.2				
23	Jun-09	158.0	276.3	176.0	86.7	109.0				
24	Jul-09	288.5	165.4	161.2	105.9	105.6				
25	Aug-09	222.0	162.1	103.7	101.6	108.8				
26	Sep-09	342.0	128.8	133.2	144.0	109.4				
27	Oct-09	244.0	201.3	172.6	170.1	102.2				
28	Nov-09	350.0	228.3	147.6	111.7	68.4				
29	Dec-09	265.0	205.0	86.4	96.3	71.4				
31		Month	1							
32		Qtr	3							
33		Year	12							

Height of summed range depends on type of period specified (Month, Qtr, Year) in cell J13.

Rep's performance in a specified month:
Sales Rep: David
Month: Apr-08
Sales: 151.3   *Functions used: INDEX()*
                                    MATCH()

Rep's performance in a specified, variable time period:
Sales Rep: Baker
Period: Qtr
Ending: Jun-08
Sales: 771.3   *Functions used: OFFSET()*
                                    VLOOKUP()

Total sales for a specified month:
Month: Oct-08
Sales: 805.3   *Functions used: OFFSET()*
were   **8.5%**   *MATCH()*
of that year's sales

Performance of top X reps in a specified year:
The top   **2**   reps
            in   **2009**
Sold   55.2%   *Functions used: OFFSET()*
of that year's sales

Number of columns in summed range depends on number of sales reps specified in cell J24.

BONUS HELPFUL TIP: create drop-down lists with Data Validation tool to minimize user typing and avoid typos, when inputting rep's name, month, and type of time period.

Reference table , specifying the number of months that are in different time periods

REPORT 5-7:   VASTCo 2008 and 2009 Sales Rep Production by Sales Rep, by Month (in $000)

These functions *do* take some skill to use effectively. But they're very powerful and can enable you to provide rifle-shot information for your audience—you can provide the specific pieces of information that certain people will want without overwhelming them all with reams of reports.

Instant Payoff Tip #7: Organize Data for Easy Computation

It's simply amazing how much time you can save yourself just by organizing the data in your spreadsheet so that you can use it. Here are two valuable tips in this subject area: (1) avoid blank rows and columns, and (2) store time series data intelligently. There are many other tips like these that space does not permit, but a brief discussion of these two will give you a sense of what I'm talking about.

Avoid Blank Rows and Columns.   When entering formulas, it's always easier to work with a single rectangular array of cells (which may have only one row or one column). In Report 5-8, we revisit Report 2-1, Version B (with Gridlines), exactly as it appeared in Chapter 2. As with the original report, you can see the gridlines, and I've also included the row and column labels (1–14 and A–N, respectively). Note that the cells circled in red are the ones that require some sort of computation formula (as opposed to raw numbers extracted from the accounting system).

Report 5-8, Version A (2-1, Version B (with Gridlines), Revisited)

	A	B	C	D	E	F	G	H	I	J	K	L	M	N
1														
2					VASTCo -- 2006 Income Statement, by Month									
3														
4	(in $000)	Jan	Feb	Mar	Apr	May	Jun	Jul	Aug	Sep	Oct	Nov	Dec	Total
5	Licenses	987	1,263	1,698	1,029	1,317	1,770	1,071	1,371	1,842	1,113	1,430	1,894	16,785
6	Services	446	475	518	465	495	540	484	515	562	503	535	584	6,120
7	Total Revs.	1,433	1,738	2,215	1,494	1,812	2,310	1,555	1,886	2,404	1,616	1,965	2,478	22,905
8	Cost of Sales	205	229	266	214	239	277	223	249	289	232	259	300	2,982
9	Gross Profit	1,227	1,509	1,949	1,280	1,573	2,032	1,332	1,637	2,115	1,384	1,706	2,178	19,923
10	Sales & Mktg.	568	594	632	594	597	665	612	646	670	645	655	689	7,568
11	Resch. & Dev.	343	340	352	346	360	376	374	389	390	397	397	412	4,477
12	Gen. & Admin.	254	256	258	254	266	270	264	272	269	272	276	280	3,191
13	Total Op. Exps.	1,165	1,190	1,242	1,194	1,223	1,312	1,251	1,307	1,329	1,314	1,329	1,381	15,236
14	Operating Profit	62	319	707	86	350	720	81	330	786	70	378	797	4,687

REPORT 5-8, VERSION A (REPORT 2-1, VERSION B WITH GRIDLINES SHOWN, REVISITED):   VASTCo 2006 Income Statement by Month

It looks pretty simple, doesn't it? If you use the shortcut keys to enter the same formula into multiple cells (see Instant Payoff Tip #3), you have to enter formulas only into the five rectangular arrays that are circled: Total Revs., Gross Profit, Total Oprg. Exps., Operating Profit, and finally, the Total for the 12 months. As the cell gridlines indicate, the white space that's so helpful for visually grouping rows and columns (and avoiding the "Where's Waldo?" effect) is achieved by varying row heights and column widths.

Now let's look at Version B of the same Report 5-8, which will look visually identical to Version A when both are printed out without the gridlines and the

Report 5-8, Version B (2-1, Version B (with Gridlines), Revisited)

	A	B	C	D	E	F	G	H	I	J	K	L	M	N
1														
2					VASTCo -- 2006 Income Statement, by Month									
3														
4	(in $000)	Jan	Feb	Mar	Apr	May	Jun	Jul	Aug	Sep	Oct	Nov	Dec	Total
6	Licenses	987	1,263	1,698	1,029	1,317	1,770	1,071	1,371	1,842	1,113	1,430	1,894	16,785
7	Services	446	475	518	465	495	540	484	515	562	503	535	584	6,120
9	Total Revs.	1,433	1,738	2,215	1,494	1,812	2,310	1,555	1,886	2,404	1,616	1,965	2,478	22,905
11	Cost of Sales	205	229	266	214	239	277	223	249	289	232	259	300	2,982
13	Gross Profit	1,227	1,509	1,949	1,280	1,573	2,032	1,332	1,637	2,115	1,384	1,706	2,178	19,923
15	Sales & Mktg.	568	594	632	594	597	665	612	646	670	645	655	689	7,568
16	Resch. & Dev.	343	340	352	346	360	376	374	389	390	397	397	412	4,477
17	Gen. & Admin.	254	256	258	254	266	270	264	272	269	272	276	280	3,191
19	Total Op. Exps.	1,165	1,190	1,242	1,194	1,223	1,312	1,251	1,307	1,329	1,314	1,329	1,381	15,236
21	Operating Profit	62	319	707	86	350	720	81	330	786	70	378	797	4,687

REPORT 5-8, VERSION B (REPORT 2-1, VERSION B WITH GRIDLINES SHOWN, REVISITED):   VASTCo 2006 Income Statement by Month row and column headings. This time, a careful, well-meaning analyst has chosen to insert blank rows and columns to create the needed white space. From the standpoint of someone trying to get work done quickly, this was *not* an innocent, harmless design choice! Instead of having to enter a formula into five different rectangular arrays, you now have to enter formulas into 23 separate arrays to avoid putting formulas into cells that should be empty. Each of the four income statement totals or subtotals is now separated into four three-month groups of cells, and the blank rows have separated the Total column into seven groups of one or more cells. The effort required to input the formulas into this spreadsheet has increased by more than fourfold! Not only that, but having to work with all these different ranges makes this careful, well-meaning analyst much more likely to make simple clerical errors (or forget to enter formulas into some of the cells) when creating and modifying the spreadsheet.

Store Time Series Data Intelligently. Well-thought-out cell organization can make your life dramatically easier. If you don't believe me, take a look at the next two reports. Version A of report 5-9 shows a time series in row 6, with monthly data for the three years from January 2002 through December 2004 (not all of it is shown below). The purpose of the spreadsheet is to calculate the monthly average for the six months ending in the month entered into cell A8 and show that result in cell B8. The formula I created for this calculation is shown in *gray italics*. There's no need to understand the formula[9]—trust me that it works properly. (As with Report 5.3, the squiggles denote columns omitted for space reasons.)

REPORT 5-9, VERSION A: Monthly Results for 2002–2004, with Six-Month Moving Average

Let's look at another spreadsheet, Version B of Report 5-9, with the same data and the same computation objective. This time, our careful, well-meaning friend has organized the monthly data into three rows with one row for each year. His reasoning was that he wanted to create a nice, clean, compact visual presentation of the monthly data that fits easily onto a single page. Aside from that, the layout is the same as in Version A, with the target month entered into cell A9 and the result shown in cell B9. The answer is the same as in Version A, but feast your eyes on the formula now needed for this calculation (in *gray italics*).

Report 5-9, Version B

	A	B	C	D	E	F	G	H	I	J	K	L	M	N	O
1															
2	Monthly Results for 2002-2004, with 6-Month Moving Average														
3															
4		Jan	Feb	Mar	Apr	May	Jun	Jul	Aug	Sep	Oct	Nov	Dec		
5	2002	5.0	4.6	5.3	3.2	5.5	4.6	5.9	5.5	5.8	3.6	6.3	4.4		
6	2003	4.4	5.0	4.8	6.2	4.9	4.9	5.3	6.0	7.4	7.3	5.3	7.8		
7	2004	6.2	5.4	9.2	8.6	8.3	7.4	8.9	6.6	8.0	8.1	9.9	9.9		
9	Apr-03	**5.2** (6-month moving average)													

=(SUM(OFFSET($B$5,MATCH(YEAR($A$9),$A$5:$A$7,0)-1,MAX(0,MONTH($A$9)-6).,
MIN(6,MONTH($A$9))))+IF(MONTH($A$9)<6,
SUM(OFFSET($M$5,MATCH(YEAR($A$9),$A$5:$A$7,0)-2,
-(5-MONTH($A$9)).,6-MONTH($A$9))),0))/6

REPORT 5-9, VERSION B: Monthly Results for 2002–2004, with Six-Month Moving Average

If you thought the formula in Version A was hairy, the one in Version B is *four times* as long! The reason this immense formula is necessary is that (1) the formula needs to select one of three annual rows of the spreadsheet, and (2) if the date input is May or earlier, then the average must be computed from some cells in the chosen row and from some in the previous row. This formula was extremely difficult to write in the first place, and even harder to debug—and I'm a trained professional!

One suggestion: if it's truly important to lay out the raw data for the user (and you could argue that the layout in Version B is visually easier for that purpose), then store the monthly data in a single row (or column) of the spreadsheet—as is done in Version A—somewhere where it won't get printed out, and use that row (or column) for calculating the moving average formula. The values in the three-row table shown in Version B can also be derived from that single row of raw data, or vice versa, so you'll have to input the raw numbers into only one place in the worksheet.[10]

The moral of these examples is that how you organize the cells in your spreadsheet can have a significant impact on how much work you have to do when it comes time to create your formulas. If the formulas you're creating are causing you to crave alcoholic beverages, the problem may lie simply in the way you've laid out your spreadsheet.

Instant Payoff Tip #8: Learn to Use Automated Help

To some (you know who you are) this will come as a complete surprise: no one knows *everything*. This applies to spreadsheet knowledge just as it applies to less important subjects. Fortunately, one of the areas where Microsoft has made enormous improvements over the past several years is helping users understand their products. In fact, at some point in the previous century, Microsoft and many other software providers stopped including printed user instructions in the product packaging. Instead, all user documentation is accessible from inside the software itself, by clicking the "Help" or "?" icon.

In Excel 2007, help is also available in the following ways (most are available in recent earlier releases as well):

- Float your cursor over the command icons at the top of the Excel window to get a pop-up with a brief description of the function.

- Enter a valid function name into the formula bar to get a pop-up listing the arguments of the function.[11]

- Click the "f_x" icon next to the formula bar to get either (a) a pop-up list box, enabling you to select an Excel function, or (b) a dialog box describing in more detail the use of the function you just typed in.

- The "Help" function will often point you to additional documents, presentations, videos, articles, or other useful content available on the Internet.

Don't be diffident. Don't be proud. Don't be stubborn. Be confident in the fact that knowing how to use help features is like having an expert sitting next to you all the time.

Instant Payoff Tip #9: Don't Learn Too Many Ways to Do the Same Thing

Trying to remember how to use an astounding number of features can actually get in the way of simply remembering how to operate the software. A wise friend once described this mental dilemma as the "full bucket syndrome": once a bucket is full of water, you can't pour more into it without having some of the water slosh out.

Bear in mind that one of the reasons Excel offers so many ways to use a feature is that people are different, and there are lots of cognitive approaches and typing/keyboard styles. Once you know what's available, find the methods that work best for *you* and stick with them. You'll be surprised at how fast you'll become.

The past few decades have seen incredible advances in the tools available to do our jobs: the computer, word processing, spreadsheets, mobile communications—the list goes on and on. But as remarkable as all these innovations have been, most of them haven't fundamentally changed the way we do things. It's just that we're now able to do them faster, or more accurately, or from any location.

Spreadsheets are different. Together with the relational database model (which came into common usage about the same time), spreadsheets enable us to *think* about our businesses and many other major life activities in ways that simply weren't possible before. In other words, spreadsheets are among a very small number of killer apps introduced over the past 30 years.

(continued)

This is why being able to think in spreadsheets is so important. With the availability and usability of spreadsheets, it is possible for you to think about how you will *communicate* with your audience at the same time you are thinking about and understanding the underlying data. It's like a photographer strolling down a street and thinking instantly about the best place to take a picture while imagining how it will look, or a writer who can't watch an event unfold without thinking about how she would write about it. Both these professionals engage in their craft while keeping in mind how the final product will be experienced by others.

Perhaps more than most other communication skills, quantation is usually the final step in a long process of collecting and analyzing information, and therefore is often done under great time pressure. For this reason, you also need to be fast and efficient in the use of your tools. In this chapter, we reviewed the Instant Payoff Tips, which are ways to get your work done faster and more efficiently. In the next chapter, we show you ways to return to the same task much later without missing a beat or worrying about amnesia setting in.

NOTES

1. As in the rest of *Painting with Numbers*, we go into detail about Excel because it is the spreadsheet and presentation software that most people use. For the most part, though, the ideas in this chapter and the next will apply regardless of the software and other presentation tools you use. Moreover, my references are to Excel for Office 07, but the same capabilities apply equally to earlier versions of Excel and will almost certainly apply to later ones as well.

2. Note that you can create templates for either **worksheets** or **workbooks**. The workbook template applies when you launch Excel, and the worksheet template applies when you create a new worksheet within an existing workbook. The Help function will tell you all you need to know about how to set up and store templates.

3. Excel comes preloaded with a number of Styles you'll want to use, like Comma (commas every three digits), Currency, and Percent. You may want to create your own styles as well as modify the preloaded ones.

4. If you are using Office 03 or earlier versions of Excel, you don't have a customizable Quick Access Toolbar. However, the function toolbars across the top of the Excel window are customizable in much the same way, so similar capabilities exist for earlier versions of Excel.

5. Note that for many Excel shortcuts, as you float your cursor over the command icon at the top of the Excel window, the function description and shortcut key (if one exists) will pop up on your display.

6. This approach can be extremely useful if you are a consultant or a contractor with a number of clients. You can store templates for each client, making it much easier to deliver reports consistent with each client's design preferences.

7. You typically create array formulas by formulas with a nesting of IF() clauses, and then enter the formula while holding down the Shift and Ctrl keys simultaneously. {Brackets} shown around the formula in the formula bar indicate an array formula—those brackets were not created by typing those keys. The tables in Reports 5-4 and 5-5 were calculated using array formulas.

8. Database formulas are distinguished from their standard counterparts with a *D* at the beginning of the formula name. For example, DSUM() is the database formula equivalent of SUM(), DAVERAGE() of AVERAGE(), and so forth. Consult user documentation for a complete discussion of formula syntax.

9. But note that this is another formula that takes advantage of the Lookup & Reference functions discussed in Instant Payoff Tip #6.

   Also note that a correctly constructed formula would need to handle the computation differently if the date input was between January 2002 and May 2002, because then the average would have to be constructed from less than six months of data, or from data not in the spreadsheet you see. For simplicity, I've chosen not to throw that particular monkey wrench into the works.

10. The U.S. federal government has an enormous treasure trove of fiscal, employment, demographic, and all kinds of other time-series data, generated by agencies like the Congressional Budget Office, the Internal Revenue Service, the Department of Labor, and the Office of Management and Budget. All of this data can be downloaded into spreadsheets, but unfortunately much of it has the structural problems I've just described, with monthly data in tables that are twelve columns across and one row for each year for which there is data, and annual data in tables that are ten columns across, with a new row starting each decade. If you want to perform analysis or computations easily on this information, I would advise you to reorganize the data into rows or columns.

11. The "arguments" of a function are the values the function needs to know to calculate the value of the function. For example, for a function to calculate the total net price of a quantity purchase, the arguments would be the price for quantity 1 of the item, the number of items purchased, the discount from list price, and the sales tax rate.

CHAPTER 6

...Or Pay Me Later

Excellence is not a singular act, but a habit.

—Basketball star Shaquille "The Big Aristotle" O'Neal in 2001, quoting his favorite philosopher, upon receiving his first NBA Most Valuable Player award

We now move to the Long-Term Payoff Tips. Unlike the Instant Payoff Tips we discussed in Chapter 5, the Long-Term Payoff Tips don't necessarily save you time *every* time you sit down to build a spreadsheet. In fact, some may take you a bit *more* time. Still, the Long-Term Payoff Tips will make your quantation easier, faster, and more error-free in the following circumstances:

- You are responsible for generating similar reports regularly and frequently (e.g., weekly sales forecasts, quarterly board meetings, or new reports with significant opportunities to borrow layouts).

- Your work has complex computations or other design characteristics that you are unlikely to remember in detail for more than a few hours.

- Other people have to work with your spreadsheets (e.g., weekly sales forecasts to be prepared by staff in the regional sales organizations, budget models to be used by all departments companywide, or expense reports used by anyone requesting expense reimbursement).

- You are an independent consultant doing similar work for a number of different clients, with no desire to create your quantation from scratch each time.

■ There is a reasonable chance that your work will be handed off to or inherited by others when, for example, you step into that new position (which, of course, you qualified for because of the outstanding reports you delivered).

The Long-Term Payoff Tips

As I've said, the Long-Term Payoff Tips won't necessarily save you time when you first sit down to build a spreadsheet, but they will make your quantation much easier in the future. The tips include:

1. Use sensible, intelligent filenames and folder organization.
2. Use consistent formats.
3. Design intelligent, intelligible formulas.
4. Use named ranges.
5. Use named formulas or macros.
6. Links: A force that can be used for good or evil.
7. Make different types of cells visually distinguishable and physically separate.
8. Document your work!
9. Check your work!
10. Avoid cool new features.

Again, these tips do *not* constitute step-by-step instructions on how to build spreadsheets, since there are many better places to learn spreadsheet-building. Instead, you'll find a detailed explanation of why each tip is valuable and how to use it effectively. And if you are already a moderately experienced user of spreadsheets, you may prefer to skim this chapter to find the sections most useful to you.

Long-Term Payoff Tip #1: Use Sensible, Intelligent Filenames and Folder Organization

When you're returning to work you did weeks or even months ago, the first thing you'll need to do is *find it on your computer*. If you're like most people, you've got an awful lot of stuff on that thing. How are you going to find that one spreadsheet that you're looking for? The simplest tool to look at is your computer's file-listing utility.

Therefore, the first and most obvious step is a sensible approach to storing files in folders and subfolders. Don't just throw it all on your desktop. Put the sales forecasts in a folder called "Sales Forecasts," and the financial statements in a folder called "Financial Statements." Can you recognize a pattern here? Inside the "Financial Statements" folder you might have subfolders labeled "Balance Sheets" and "Income Statements."

You might also want to create folders for each year so that all the 2009 stuff goes in the "2009" folder, and so on. Whether the folders for each year are subfolders within the "Sales Reports" and "Financial Statements" folders, or vice versa, is up to you. What's important is to develop an approach that seems sensible and works for *you*, and then stick to it.

Even more important, and a little less obvious, is *intelligent filenames. Please* don't give files names like "Financial Analysis" or "Stuff for 9-30-08." The only way you'll ever figure out what's in those documents is to open them up and look at them. This can be tedious and time consuming. If it's a sales forecast, have "Forecast" or "Sales Forecast" in the filename.

Equally important to intelligent filenames, especially for documents you're generating monthly or weekly or even daily, is the *date* of the document. In the United States, our shorthand date convention is month/day/year, like 8/26/09 for August 26, 2009. For assigning names to your files, *this is a really bad idea.* Why? Because the computer's file-listing utility will sort your filenames for you. If you give your sales forecast of August 26, 2009, a filename of "Forecast 82609," it will appear *after* a file called "Forecast 11510" (for January 15, 2010), and *before* a file called "Forecast 82808," even though that file was generated in August 2008.

The only way to avoid this confusion is to use the year/month/day convention when naming your files, and insert a "0" in front of single-digit months and days. If you do this, the report for August 26, 2009 ("Forecast 090826") will always appear *after* the report for August 28, 2008 ("Forecast 080828") and *before* the report for January 15, 2010 ("Forecast 100115"), as it should.

The table presented here shows how Windows and other file management systems will sort the filenames for 24 monthly documents generated over a two-year period. Each of the date formats presented is in fairly common use, and the dates are sorted the way a computer would sort them:

The 24 Months, as Spelled Out, in Chron. Order	How a Computer Would Sort the 24 Dates, Depending on the Format Used				
	A yyyy-mm	**B** yyyy-m	**C** mm-yyyy	**D** mmm-yyyy	**E** yyyy-mmm
January 2008	2008-01	2008-1	01-2008	Apr-2008	2008-Apr
February 2008	2008-02	2008-10	01-2009	Apr-2009	2008-Aug
March 2008	2008-03	2008-11	02-2008	Aug-2008	2008-Dec
April 2008	2008-04	2008-12	02-2009	Aug-2009	2008-Feb
May 2008	2008-05	2008-2	03-2008	Dec-2008	2008-Jan
June 2008	2008-06	2008-3	03-2009	Dec-2009	2008-Jul
July 2008	2008-07	2008-4	04-2008	Feb-2008	2008-Jun
August 2008	2008-08	2008-5	04-2009	Feb-2009	2008-Mar
September 2008	2008-09	2008-6	05-2008	Jan-2008	2008-May
October 2008	2008-10	2008-7	05-2009	Jan-2009	2008-Nov
November 2008	2008-11	2008-8	06-2008	Jul-2008	2008-Oct
December 2008	2008-12	2008-9	06-2009	Jul-2009	2008-Sep
January 2009	2009-01	2009-1	07-2008	Jun-2008	2009-Apr
February 2009	2009-02	2009-10	07-2009	Jun-2009	2009-Aug
March 2009	2009-03	2009-11	08-2008	Mar-2008	2009-Dec
April 2009	2009-04	2009-12	08-2009	Mar-2009	2009-Feb
May 2009	2009-05	2009-2	09-2008	May-2008	2009-Jan
June 2009	2009-06	2009-3	09-2009	May-2009	2009-Jul
July 2009	2009-07	2009-4	10-2008	Nov-2008	2009-Jun
August 2009	2009-08	2009-5	10-2009	Nov-2009	2009-Mar
September 2009	2009-09	2009-6	11-2008	Oct-2008	2009-May
October 2009	2009-10	2009-7	11-2009	Oct-2009	2009-Nov
November 2009	2009-11	2009-8	12-2008	Sep-2008	2009-Oct
December 2009	2009-12	2009-9	12-2009	Sep-2009	2009-Sep

NOTE: Format for Column B is same as for Column A, except that one-digit months (i.e., Jan - Sep) don't have a leading zero.

Of the five formats shown for presenting dates, only the one shown in column A will get the dates sorted in the same order in which the months actually occur. Need I say more?

Long-Term Payoff Tip #2: Use Consistent Formats

We've already talked about this as Instant Payoff Tip #4. But also remember that the most important person you want to avoid confusing with your quantation is *you*. If you're picking up a spreadsheet for the first time in several months, format consistency—as well as a consistent approach to formulas, spreadsheet layout, and overall look-and-feel—can make a big difference in helping you remember what you did in the distant past, and why you did it that way.

Long-Term Payoff Tip #3: Design Intelligent, Intelligible Formulas

There is nothing more frustrating than opening a spreadsheet you haven't looked at in a few months to update it with a tiny little tweak, and realizing that you have no idea how you calculated some values, nor what you were thinking when you created the formulas in the first place. Wait—there *is* something more frustrating: it's when someone else who is now responsible for your spreadsheet asks you for help on how to decipher it and you can't remember how you constructed it! So, any time you are designing the formulas for your spreadsheet, always ask yourself, "Will I understand this formula when I come back to this spreadsheet later? Will other people?" Here are some ways to ensure that your answer is always *yes*.

Use Intermediate Values. Many people (myself included, I admit) take some perverse intellectual pride in how much logic they can pack into a single formula. This can get you into real trouble, and it's often a much better idea to break your formulas into bite-sized chunks. Report 6-1 is an example, which is just a re-presentation of the price list in Report 2-6. The only difference is the addition of the italicized boxes at the right, below the "Intermediate Values" heading.

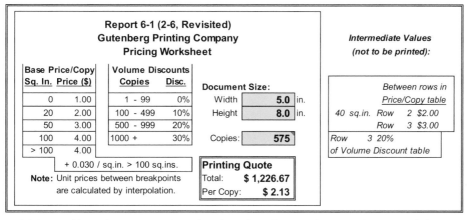

REPOR T 6-1 (REPORT 2-6, REVISITED):   Gutenberg Printing Company Pricing Worksheet

The pricing methodology at the Gutenberg Printing Company is to base the unit price per copy on the number of square inches, which is the width of the document times its height. The incremental unit price per square inch declines as the number of square inches per copy increases, from $1.00 for the first square inch down to $0.03 for each square inch above 100. Finally, the *total* price is that unit price times the number of copies, but adjusted for volume discounts that kick in at 100, 500, and 1,000 copies. When described in plain English, it's a sensible and comprehensible approach to pricing. But to cram all that logic into a single formula would be immensely difficult and even harder to debug or modify (let alone understand!) several months later. A simple, sanity-preserving approach is to create cells with intermediate values, like square inches and volume discount, in an unused portion of the worksheet, and then create the final price quotation formulas by using those intermediate values. (Note that there's no need to print all that extra stuff out when you're publishing the report.)

Avoid Constants. It's not unusual for a single piece of raw data to appear in more than one place in the same report, for reasons of narrative flow or audience comprehensibility. And if you're working with a workbook that has multiple related worksheets, it's a virtual certainty that the same piece of raw data will appear in multiple worksheets. For these situations, I offer this very simple suggestion for protecting you from yourself:

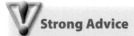 **Strong Advice**

Any given piece of raw data should appear in only one cell in your spreadsheet. Every other cell that uses that datum should be a formula referencing that particular cell. This applies to your entire workbook and not just within individual worksheets within that workbook.

The first reason to do this is that as you create formulas that utilize said piece of raw data, you will give yourself a consistent, coherent view of where that information came from, and you will have less trouble understanding your own formulas. A further helpful tip in this situation is to assign a name to the item, and use that name, rather than the cell reference, every time that value appears in a formula. See Long-Term Payoff Tip #4 for more on this topic.

An even more important reason this suggestion is useful occurs when the raw data is a constant value input by the user (rather than a formula referencing another document or system). If your spreadsheet calls for the input value to be entered in more than one cell of the spreadsheet, you risk the user forgetting to update *every* instance of the value if that value is updated. If some of the formulas in your spreadsheet refer to the cell that *wasn't* updated, you will introduce errors in your spreadsheet that are almost impossible to discover, let alone debug[1]—that is, until it's too late.

Avoid Hidden Cells. I have often seen spreadsheets with hidden rows or columns; you can tell that there are hidden rows or columns because there's a gap between adjacent numbers in the row headings at the left of the window, or between adjacent letters in the column headings at the top. Presumably, the cells that are visible have values that are derived from these hidden cells, but our good-ol'-well-meaning presenter no doubt wants to protect the audience from having to read extraneous information, or in some cases may even be trying to hide confidential information. *This is a bad habit.* First, it's bad spreadsheet design: any time you look at a formula for the purpose of modifying it or just plain understanding it, you should be able to see all of the other cells in the worksheet on which that formula depends at the same time.

Moreover, hiding rows and columns has the potential for offending some in your audience. The message you *might* be sending to your audience is that they are not competent to use the hidden information properly, or that that they're not smart enough to understand it, or that they can't be trusted with it. You certainly don't want to appear to be embedding your sense of moral or professional superiority in your communications, especially if that's not what you *meant* to do.

Finally, hiding cells *doesn't always achieve its intended purpose.* The very existence of hidden information tempts at least some in the audience to want to look at it. After all, how many of us see a "wet paint" sign, and find ourselves impulsively reaching out to touch the object to see if that paint is *really* wet?

If you really feel that you don't want to (or shouldn't) allow your audience to focus on all of the information in your spreadsheet, here are some alternative tactics you might consider:

- Rather than interspersing the undesired information with the information you do want your audience to read, put that information in a separate part of the worksheet. The information will be there, but not in your audience's main reading flow.
- Put the undesired information in a separate worksheet within the workbook, or even in a separate workbook (but see Long-Range Payoff Tip #6).
- If you absolutely don't want your audience to see the underlying information, send them an image of the desired report in a file in PDF format. That way, your audience can see the report as you want them to see it without exposing them to the information you want hidden.

Within Reason, Avoid References to Cells Outside the Current Worksheet. It's always harder to understand and debug a formula that references cells in another worksheet in the same workbook, or in another workbook entirely. First, you have no opportunity to look at the cells referred to in that formula while you are looking at the formula itself. Moreover, the additional characters needed to describe the access path fully just make the formula *longer*, and that alone makes it harder to understand and manage. Obviously, sometimes you just don't have a choice about referencing cells in other worksheets or workbooks, but one way to minimize those references is to have that external value stored in one cell in the current worksheet, so that other formulas in that worksheet can then point to a cell in the same worksheet. Another way is to use named ranges, as we discuss in Long-Term Payoff Tip #4.

Document Your Work. Often, the easiest way to make sure that future generations understand your work is to document it. See Long-Term Payoff Tip #8 for specific suggestions on how to do this.

Long-Term Payoff Tip #4: Use Named Ranges

Excel formulas can look really opaque, especially if you haven't touched that particular spreadsheet in weeks or months. Understanding the humongous formulas you've written is much easier if you can pick out a few recognizable English words in them. That's where named ranges come in. They come in handy in two principal ways: (1) in formulas, and (2) to identify sections of the spreadsheet you might want to highlight later. There is plenty of excellent documentation on using named ranges, so we'll just look at some examples here.

In Formulas. Rather than using cell references (e.g., $B$9, F63), give cells (or ranges of cells) a name and use that name in the formula. As an example, let's return to the pricing spreadsheet we used for Report 6-1 (first seen as Report 2-6).

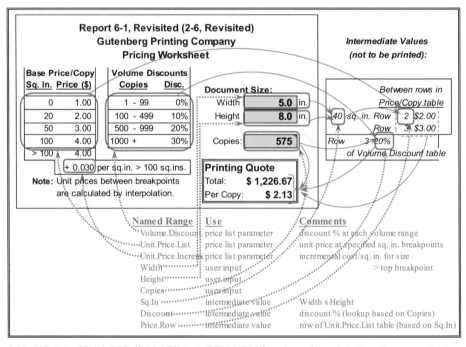

REPORT 6-1, REVISITED (REPORT 2-6, REVISITED):   Gutenberg Printing Company Pricing Worksheet

The spreadsheet itself hasn't changed, although I've added explanatory comments and artwork in red type. First of all, this spreadsheet has nine named ranges, as listed at the bottom of the exhibit. Each range name has a dotted line pointing to the cell or range of cells with that name. Rather than using cell references (e.g., "B6", "J15") in the formulas, the formulas instead use the above-named ranges. The solid lines emanating from each range point to the cells whose formula includes that range name. So, for example, the square inches formula would be "=*Width*Height*", and its value is 40 in the current example. There's no question that formulas with English-language words are easier to understand and debug than ones with sometimes-cryptic cell references, especially when those formulas get complicated.

To Identify Sections.   You may frequently need to select large chunks of your spread-sheet to do operations on all the cells in the selected area. One common use is spreadsheets with multiple areas you might want to print. Other possible uses include identifying rows or columns that you want to hide to view only summary information, ranges you are likely to want to copy to another worksheet, or ranges where you might want to make formatting changes to all of the cells. Report 6-2 is an example of a report showing two years of quarterly results. For every report you would want to print, the Print_Titles range is the left-hand column (A) and the top four rows (1:4), but I've created some named ranges to maximize printing flexibility.

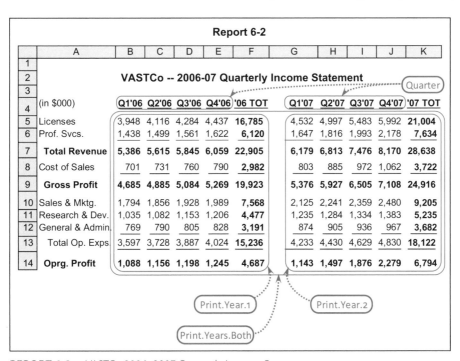

REPORT 6-2:   VASTCo 2006–2007 Quarterly Income Statement

In Report 6-2, *Print.Year.1* (cells B5:F14) includes all the cells that would be printed for 2006, *Print.Year.2* (cells G5:K14) does the same for 2007, and *Print. Years.Both* (cells B5:K14) includes both 2006 and 2007. Depending on what you'd like to print, any of these three ranges could be assigned to Print_Area. I've also created a range called "*Quarters*" to identify the columns containing the quarterly results. With these ranges I can easily produce Reports 6-3 and 6-4.

Report 6-3					
	A	B	C	D	E	F
1						
2	**VASTCo -- 2006 Quarterly Income Statement**					
3						
4	(in $000)	**Q1'06**	**Q2'06**	**Q3'06**	**Q4'06**	**'06 TOT**
5	Licenses	3,948	4,116	4,284	4,437	**16,785**
6	Prof. Svcs.	1,438	1,499	1,561	1,622	**6,120**
7	**Total Revenue**	**5,386**	**5,615**	**5,845**	**6,059**	**22,905**
8	Cost of Sales	701	731	760	790	**2,982**
9	**Gross Profit**	**4,685**	**4,885**	**5,084**	**5,269**	**19,923**
10	Sales & Mktg.	1,794	1,856	1,928	1,989	**7,568**
11	Research & Dev.	1,035	1,082	1,153	1,206	**4,477**
12	General & Admin.	769	790	805	828	**3,191**
13	Total Op. Exps.	3,597	3,728	3,887	4,024	**15,236**
14	**Oprg. Profit**	**1,088**	**1,156**	**1,198**	**1,245**	**4,687**

Report 6-4		
	A	F	K
1			
2	VASTCo -- 2006-07 Income Stmt		
3			
4	(in $000)	**'06 TOT**	**'07 TOT**
5	Licenses	**16,785**	**21,004**
6	Prof. Svcs.	**6,120**	**7,634**
7	**Total Revenue**	**22,905**	**28,638**
8	Cost of Sales	**2,982**	**3,722**
9	**Gross Profit**	**19,923**	**24,916**
10	Sales & Mktg.	**7,568**	**9,205**
11	Research & Dev.	**4,477**	**5,235**
12	General & Admin.	**3,191**	**3,682**
13	Total Op. Exps.	**15,236**	**18,122**
14	**Oprg. Profit**	**4,687**	**6,794**

REPORT 6-3: VASTCo 2006 Quarterly Income Statement

REPORT 6-4: VASTCo 2006–2007 Income Statement

Report 6-3, which shows only the quarterly and annual results for 2006, is created by setting Print_Area to be Print.Year.1. Report 6-4 shows the results for both years but with the quarterly results omitted. This report is created by setting Print_Area to be Print.Years.Both, but also selecting the Quarters range and doing a Hide Columns operation. (After printing, you can select these columns and perform the Unhide Columns operation to restore their visibility.) Also note that I remembered to change the report titles in row 2 so they accurately describe the contents. (Depending on how you've laid out your spreadsheet, you might instead need to do this in the Header/Footer section of Print Setup).

This suggestion is useful any time a single worksheet has a number of different print options. Your worksheet might print out in several pages, not all of which you want to print each time, or you might want to choose between printing detailed or summary information. I can assure you that you'll save lots of time and minimize clerical errors if you take advantage of named ranges to be smart about printing out your work.

Long-Term Payoff Tip #5: Use Named Formulas or Macros

If you are worried that having superhuman spreadsheet powers and capabilities will label you as a nerd, skip this section. But once in a while, knowing how to (dare I say it?) write computer programs can end up being a huge timesaver. Some situations where this skill can prove very helpful are:

- Your spreadsheet requires some extremely complex calculations, or has cells whose formulas are completely different, and these calculations and formulas depend on other values in the spreadsheet.

- Your spreadsheet depends on frequent, repetitive operations that are time consuming and error-prone to step through manually. (Examples are spreadsheets that roll up other spreadsheets, or printing multiple sections of a workbook.)

- You are developing spreadsheets where the main ongoing users will be others who not only aren't familiar with your spreadsheet architecture, but don't want to be. In these situations a custom user interface comes in handy. An example might be a budget model where each department manager is responsible for preparing his or her own departmental budget. The budget model might have complex operations, making macros helpful to the departmental users, and then you might need to roll up several different budget models.

Three ways you can write "programs" in Excel are named formulas (where you use Excel's naming capabilities to craft complex formulas), function macros, and command macros. Here are more details about each of these features:

Named Formulas. As an example, we revisit our trusty Gutenberg Printing Company pricing worksheet, which we first saw as Report 2-6. However, instead of using intermediate values as we did in Report 6-1 (see Long-Term Payoff Tips #3 and #4), we can achieve the same objective with named formulas as shown in Report 6-5.

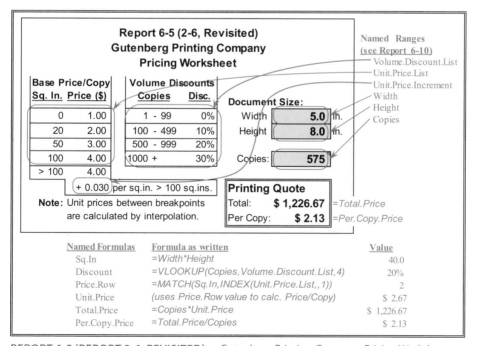

REPORT 6-5 (REPORT 2-6, REVISITED): Gutenberg Printing Company Pricing Worksheet

This worksheet again takes advantage of naming, but this time instead of having the names refer to cells or ranges of cells (as discussed in Long-Term Payoff Tip #4), they refer to formulas. These named entities, like Sq.In and Unit.Price, can be used in cell formulas just as you can use named ranges, which refer to cells or ranges of cells. The formulas themselves, and their values in the above example, are shown in red (except for Unit.Price, where the formula is too long and complicated to be meaningful in the example).

Macros.   To introduce you to macros, you must first understand that there are two kinds of macros: function macros and command macros. Function macros generate a single calculated value based on one or more input values, called "arguments."[2] You use function macros in much the same way you use named formulas. Command macros execute a sequence of Excel commands, which for the most part are the commands you have available in the command icon menus at the top of your Excel window. Both kinds of macros are written in a programming language called "Visual Basic," a widely used high-level programming language.[3] In this section, we will *not* focus on how to write macro code (there are plenty of books on the topic); instead we'll focus on situations where you might find macros useful.

Function Macros.   In our example, the XYZ Corporation has sales operations in its Americas, Europe, and Asia regions. Report 6-6 is a worldwide report on sales force performance and compensation. To the right of Report 6-6 is the description of the regional compensation plans. This description is laid out in a way that makes it easy for a reader to understand the plans, rather than arranging the data in an organized, structured array. This description does not necessarily need to reside in the same worksheet that generates Report 6-6. The compensation parameters are shown in the shaded cells.

As you can see from the table at the right of Report 6-6, the compensation methodologies differ significantly from region to region. In this case, I've written a function macro named "SalesComp," which requires as arguments (1) sales (column D in the above report), (2) quota (column C), and (3) whether the sales rep is "new" (either "Yes" or "No," in column F). The formula for calculating sales representative Unterberg's compensation is shown in *gray italics* and circled in red. It looks pretty straightforward, doesn't it? (I'll leave you to figure out the macro code on your own.)

Although it is at least theoretically possible to construct similar calculations using the named formulas described above, function macros have significant advantages in the following circumstances: (1) when the logic for doing the calculation is particularly complex, or (2) when you want to access a calculation from many different cells or worksheets and in many different ways. The SalesComp macro takes care of the calculation logic for you and the parameters underlying that logic, so all you have to do in your formula is provide the function arguments (i.e., sales, quota, and "new" status). If circumstances 1 and/or

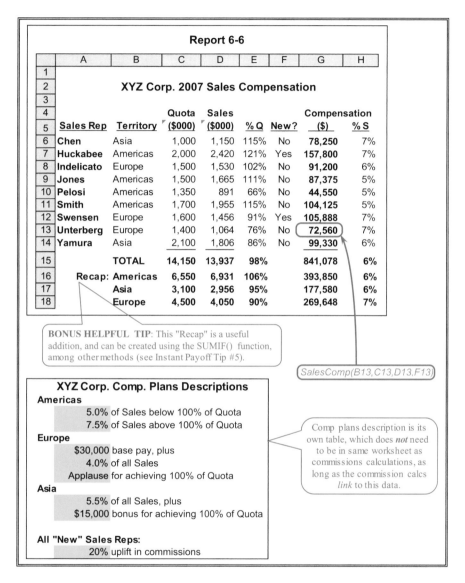

Report 6-6

	A	B	C	D	E	F	G	H
1								
2		**XYZ Corp. 2007 Sales Compensation**						
3								
4			Quota	Sales			Compensation	
5	**Sales Rep**	**Territory**	**($000)**	**($000)**	**% Q**	**New?**	**($)**	**% S**
6	Chen	Asia	1,000	1,150	115%	No	78,250	7%
7	Huckabee	Americas	2,000	2,420	121%	Yes	157,800	7%
8	Indelicato	Europe	1,500	1,530	102%	No	91,200	6%
9	Jones	Americas	1,500	1,665	111%	No	87,375	5%
10	Pelosi	Americas	1,350	891	66%	No	44,550	5%
11	Smith	Americas	1,700	1,955	115%	No	104,125	5%
12	Swensen	Europe	1,600	1,456	91%	Yes	105,888	7%
13	Unterberg	Europe	1,400	1,064	76%	No	72,560	7%
14	Yamura	Asia	2,100	1,806	86%	No	99,330	6%
15		TOTAL	14,150	13,937	98%		841,078	6%
16	Recap:	Americas	6,550	6,931	106%		393,850	6%
17		Asia	3,100	2,956	95%		177,580	6%
18		Europe	4,500	4,050	90%		269,648	7%

BONUS HELPFUL TIP: This "Recap" is a useful addition, and can be created using the SUMIF() function, among other methods (see Instant Payoff Tip #5).

SalesComp(B13,C13,D13,F13)

XYZ Corp. Comp. Plans Descriptions

Americas
  5.0% of Sales below 100% of Quota
  7.5% of Sales above 100% of Quota

Europe
  $30,000 base pay, plus
  4.0% of all Sales
  Applause for achieving 100% of Quota

Asia
  5.5% of all Sales, plus
  $15,000 bonus for achieving 100% of Quota

All "New" Sales Reps:
  20% uplift in commissions

Comp plans description is its own table, which does *not* need to be in same worksheet as commissions calculations, as long as the commission calcs *link* to this data.

REPORT 6-6:   XYZ Corp. 2007 Sales Compensation

2 are present, you're likely to find that constructing the calculation with named formulas is just too much work, and too difficult to decipher after the fact. In this case, writing a macro becomes worth the effort.

Command Macros. These are like actual computer programs that execute a sequence of Excel operations. Writing a command macro will end up being more efficient than executing the operations in these situations:

- You run the sequence often enough that the time savings from executing a single macro instruction justify the effort to write the macro.

- The sequence of Excel commands is clear and straightforward, but is so long that the odds are high that you'll make a clerical error.

- Some of the commands in the sequence are complicated and hard to remember.

- The spreadsheet is going to be used by other people who aren't as familiar with it as you are.

Report 6-7 is an example of a practical use of macros. The underlying spreadsheet is a complex business model, a workbook consisting of nine worksheets. Some of the worksheets contain modeling assumptions and some contain reports (see Long-Term Payoff Tip #7, about separating assumptions from calculated information). Printing out the desired portion(s) of the model can be a complex challenge. This is especially true when you might have a choice between printing out only the summary information, or the underlying detail as well. Moreover, for some reports in the model, you might want to print out annual summary information, quarterly summary information, or some or all of the monthly detail. For this spreadsheet I've written a macro that generates a dialog box designed specifically to address all of the spreadsheet's possible printing alternatives. This dialog box is the user's interface for printing out the desired portion(s) of the document. Report 6-7 shows the dialog box. The red-circled numbers I've added to Report 6-7 correspond to the numbered features listed here:

1. The organization of the dialog box corresponds to how the worksheets are organized in the workbook.

2. Where applicable, the user can select specific content within each worksheet.

3. The user simply checks the box for each report he or she wants to print.

4. Where applicable, the user has a choice of column formats (e.g., yearly, quarterly, monthly) for the selected report.

5. Drop-down lists show the user all possible input choices, and eliminate the chance of typos.

6. Areas showing a report's options are grayed out if that report is not selected.

7. This option allows a Print Preview of each report to be viewed by the user, who can then opt not to print the report by hitting Esc while previewing the report.

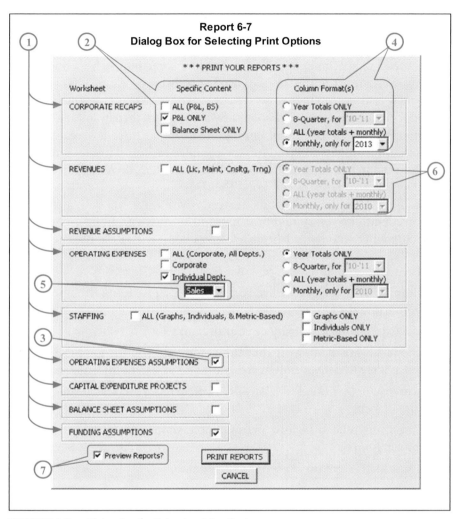

REPORT 6-7: Dialog Box for Selecting Print Options

Clicking buttons in a dialog box, and then clicking the "PRINT REPORTS" button, is *much* less laborious and error-prone than wandering throughout the worksheets, selecting and setting the Print_Area, and making the necessary changes to the report headings for each report again and again.

Dialog boxes are just one example of processes you might want to automate with a macro. And even dialog boxes have uses far beyond just selecting areas to print, such as helping users input data into a complex spreadsheet in a way that ensures the validity of the input data, or enabling people to input data in an intuitive and user-friendly way. There's no doubt that writing macro code can be a fair amount of work, but if the procedures it replicates are complex enough or used sufficiently often, writing a macro can be well worth the effort.

Long-Term Payoff Tip #6: Links: A Force That Can Be Used for Good or Evil

Every day, technology comes up with new ways for something to be connected to something else. One of the most important office software developments of the past 20 years has been the capability to insert one type of document (or presentation) into another document created by a different software product, thereby linking the two.

Although the myriad ways of linking the formulas in your spreadsheet to data in other documents can lead to very complex technical discussions, that's not my purpose here. I just want you to understand that *you have choices* about how and whether you link documents. The issues in this area don't lend themselves easily to examples or exhibits. Instead, I will leave you with a short list of the considerations you should bear in mind as you're deciding on how, and how much, to link your spreadsheets to other documents. Be sure to consider:

- The number of different users of a single spreadsheet
- How many other people are responsible for providing the underlying supporting data for your spreadsheet(s)
- The extent and complexity of your organization's network
- The reliability of your organization's network, and the approach that is most likely to deliver timely, reliable, and consistent information
- Your own technical skills, and how often you will be using the spreadsheet
- Questions related to how many people should have access to which information
- The sensitivity of the underlying information

Long-Term Payoff Tip #7: Make Different Types of Cells Visually Distinguishable and Physically Separate

Cells in a spreadsheet can have any number of different purposes, including:

- **Raw data**, which may be user-entered or extracted for other documents or systems
- **Underlying parameters**—values critical to the logic of your spreadsheet that are typically user-entered but don't tend to change much
- **Intermediate calculations** (see Long-Term Payoff Tip #3)
- **User inputs**—values the user might want to change each time the spreadsheet is used, in order to play "what-if" or calculate the results related to a specific situation

- **Calculated results**—the numbers that are what the spreadsheet was designed to calculate in the first place
- **Recaps** of more detailed information—useful when your spreadsheet has considerable detail, or has several levels of aggregation
- **Explanatory text** for any of the above

Recognizing the logical purpose of each cell or range of cells in a spreadsheet is an enormous help when you return to work on it later. If the distinctions aren't clear, it will almost certainly take you longer to understand your own logic and therefore to modify and debug your work. Even worse, you risk screwing up your spreadsheet. If, for example, you mistake an intermediate calculation cell or a calculated results cell for a user input cell and enter a constant value into that cell, you will introduce an error into your spreadsheet that you may never detect. (See my admonition to avoid constants in Long-Term Payoff Tip #3.)

To prevent problems like this, you will find it helpful to (1) group like types of cells together and (2) use text and other visual effects the help identify their purpose. Consider this example (Report 6-8) from our old friend, the Gutenberg Printing Company's price list. This particular spreadsheet has three of the above types of cells, with each group of cells circled in red.

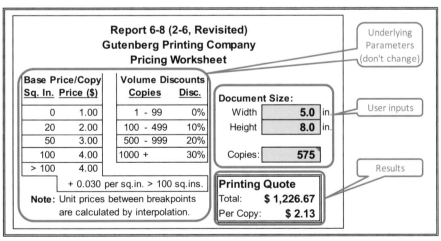

REPORT 6-8 (REPORT 2-6, REVISITED):   Gutenberg Printing Company Pricing Worksheet

The left half of the spreadsheet includes the unit price schedule and the volume discount schedule, that is, the *underlying parameters* that are unlikely to change from one use of the spreadsheet to another. To the upper right are the *user inputs* that identify the three distinguishing characteristics of each individual order. Note that these cells are in **boldface**, and are the only shaded cells in this worksheet, to show that these are the only cells the user should modify. In the lower right – the "bottom line," if you will– are the total and per-unit prices, whose calculation is the reason this spreadsheet exists. These values are also in **boldface**, and this area is further set off with a box with double-lined borders.

Moreover, if you have a really large spreadsheet that might be best organized as a workbook consisting of multiple worksheets, you might want to consider applying the above standard to entire worksheets, and not just to regions within a single worksheet. If you are building a complex model with lots of different possible user inputs, I make this recommendation especially strongly, because:

- It saves time and avoids confusion when your end-users need to go to only one place in the workbook to enter or change all their user inputs.
- You may find it effective for keeping the users honest. In some situations, users may be tempted, even if unconsciously, to play with the input values until the model comes back with the desired results. If this behavior is not what you want, keeping the user inputs and the calculated results in separate worksheets can block this temptation.

Long-Term Payoff Tip #8: Document Your Work!

Of all the tips in this chapter, this is the one that requires the most discipline and fortitude. It is also the one that has the least obvious benefit, especially compared to the time it takes to do it well, when you're under pressure to deliver a finished report. But be advised: few things are more time consuming *later*, when your spreadsheet isn't doing what you expected and youcan't figure out why on God's green earth you did what you did in the first place.

You have lots of choices for creating documentation for an Excel workbook, including:

- Using Excel's Comment capability to attach explanatory or descriptive comments to specific cells.
- Creating an additional worksheet in the same workbook, containing your narrative comments on the workbook design.
- Drafting a separate document as a detailed write-up.
- Writing handwritten notes on a hardcopy printout of the spreadsheet. File it and don't lose it.

All of these are perfectly acceptable approaches, and the right choice for you depends on factors like the complexity of the spreadsheet logic, the importance of each particular report, and how often you and others will be using the document in the future. Perhaps most important is *who* will be using the document. Your effort will depend on whether it's just you, people inside your department, or others outside your department.

I strongly suggest you write the document *while* you are developing the reports or very soon after, and while you are well-rested, sober, and otherwise lucid. Otherwise, the consequences can be as illustrated in this excerpt from one of the premier business journals of the mid-twentieth century:

From MAD Magazine. © E.C. Publications, Inc.

Long-Term Payoff Tip #9: Check Your Work!

We all know how important it is to deliver error-free work. But, in the same way most of us feel aversion to documenting our work (see Long-Term Payoff Tip #8), most of us would rather have a root canal than go through the tedious process of looking for errors in a spreadsheet, especially when we're pressed for time. So to give a little prodding to help you overcome this natural reluctance, I offer:

 Deadly Sin #11

Publishing a spreadsheet with a **basic error** that should have been **easy to detect**

We've been over this before: basic errors, especially when they're discovered by others long after distribution, have a way of affecting your reputation and your credibility much more than the significance of the error itself. In other words, the punishment doesn't fit the crime.

The good news is there are simple techniques you can employ to reduce the likelihood of an embarrassing mistake. And they don't generally involve spending significantly more time to make sure your work is error-free. Here are a few suggestions to reduce errors:

- **Use intelligent, sensible formulas**. Formulas that you and other users of your work can actually understand will go a long way toward avoiding errors. See Long-Term Payoff Tip #3 for more discussion and suggestions on this point.
- **Use checksums.** Often totals can be calculated in a number of different ways. Set up a place in the worksheet (it doesn't need to be in a printed area) where you calculate the total using one of these other ways and compare that total to the one you're printing out.

 Note

> **An example of checksums:** You are producing a summary P&L report that groups expenses by major functional area (e.g., Sales & Marketing, R&D, G&A), with results calculated from a complete copy of the general ledger that is stored in another worksheet in the workbook. Operating Income in the report is calculated as total revenues minus the individual line item expenses. The *checksum* is the net of all of the G/L activity for accounts that roll up to Operating Income. If the report's Net Income doesn't match the checksum, you've probably missed an account.

- **Get a fresh pair of eyes.** After a while, all numbers look the same, and they all look correct. Get a colleague or a friend (preferably someone picky and candid) to look over your work.
- **Look for numbers that don't make intuitive sense.** Some errors are not the least bit subtle. A formula that's just flat-out wrong will often give you numbers off by an order of magnitude, or numbers that are negative when they should be positive (and vice versa), or some other clue that something is not right. Find a comfortable place to sit and relax, and look at your report as if you just wanted to get the gist of it. Does anything look odd? (You should catch these mistakes because, if you don't, they're the ones your audience is most likely to find, and the ones that will make you look the most boneheaded.)

Long-Term Payoff Tip #10: Avoid Cool New Features

Once in a while, it's a good thing to be hidebound and set in your ways. When you encounter an amazing new feature in Excel, avoid the temptation to say,

"Wow, that's cool. Where can I start using it?" A more practical reaction is to think about what you need to accomplish, and *then* think about which software features do this for you. This approach makes it more likely that you'll use new software features only when they will be valuable to you, and less likely that you'll open your workbook months later and have no idea how your spreadsheet works.

The titles for Chapters 5 and 6 come from a famous slogan used by Fram Oil Filters in its TV commercials. They featured an auto mechanic earnestly telling viewers: "You can pay me now . . . or pay me later." This mechanic was saying that viewers could invest in a new oil filter now . . . or in a new *engine* later. Like that auto mechanic, I'm suggesting that small investments of your time will provide handsome rewards or time savings later. Some benefits you'll be able to realize instantly (the Instant Payoff Tips), and some you'll realize over weeks and months (the Long-Term Payoff Tips).

The secret to using these tips to your advantage is to practice them often and develop them into habits. This is true for all of the tips in both Chapters 5 and 6, but it's especially true for the Long-Term Payoff Tips in Chapter 6, which don't necessarily save you time when you create your spreadsheets but will when you *return* to them (and when you work on them with others).

Shaquille O'Neal, quoting Aristotle, put it aptly: "Excellence is . . . a habit." You achieve it by constant use, not simply by trying harder and staying calm when you're under pressure. The only way to ensure that your spreadsheets get your message across, and look good doing it, is to strive for clear and professional quantation *all* the time. As Aristotle also said, "We are what we repeatedly do."

NOTES

1. A different but eloquent characterization of this issue, from the perspective of database management, is Herzog's Law. This general principle is named after Oracle's IT Director in the 1980s, who first uttered it: "If data is stored in more than one place, it will be wrong in at least one place." Of course, the oft-cited Murphy's Law is the most general of the maxims that observe that bad stuff is certain to happen if it's given enough chance to happen.

2. As we first saw in Chapter 5, the "arguments" of a function are the values the function needs to know to calculate the value of the function. For example, for a function to calculate the total net price of a quantity purchase, the arguments would be the price for quantity 1 of the item, the number of items purchased, the discount from list price, and the sales tax rate.

3. For us older folks, Microsoft still enables macros to be written in "Excel 4.0 Macro Language," last fully supported in a 20-year-old version of Excel. The advantage of Excel 4.0 Macro Language is that it is fairly easy to learn and creates an intuitive connection between the macro program and the underlying Excel operations, but Visual Basic is a widely used general-purpose language that has uses far beyond Excel macros.

CHAPTER 7

Graphs: The "Cartoons" of Numbers

Never give a gun to a duck.

—An old hunters' saying

Graphs are a popular quantation tool with both presenters and audiences. They are easy to create, they "look professional," and they appeal to the visual side of our brains. But don't get swept off your feet. Graphs are like cartoons: at their best, cartoons can capture the essence of a complex issue in a concise, eloquent, memorable way. At their worst, they simply represent an entertaining look at a subject without communicating anything substantial.

Using graphs to present your quantation has a similarly bipolar potential. At their best, graphs are a succinct, effective way of getting key ideas across to your audience. At their worst, graphs don't say much and end up taking up a lot of space. Furthermore, they may put you in a bad light, as your audience comes to realize that your polished-*looking* presentation didn't educate them. Worse still, poorly executed graphs can cause your audience to question your professionalism and even your ethics, especially when they are part of graph-heavy presentations (that can themselves suggest to an audience that the presenter may be trying to snow them). This chapter will help you avoid these pitfalls by giving you practical tips for making your graphs clear and meaningful to your audience. It will also suggest approaches and behaviors to follow (and those to avoid) when using graphs in your quantation.

If you are looking for a how-to manual about which types of graphs to use in various situations, or how to tell what situation you're in, you won't find it in this chapter. A handful of other authors have done this beautifully, and I recommend you consult their works.[1] The focus of this chapter is on how to make your graphs clear and meaningful, *when you choose to employ them* in your quantation.

Note

A note on semantics: The words *chart* and *graph* have meanings that overlap, and they are often used interchangeably. Although *chart* is Microsoft Excel's word of choice to describe the visual objects discussed in this chapter, *chart* connotes a much wider range of visual objects (including tables). I much prefer *graph* because it has a narrower meaning that fits much better to the subject of this chapter.

Why Do People Use Graphs?

Understanding just when a graph is an appropriate, useful, or effective presentation of your quantation will go a long way toward making graphs a truly valuable part of your quantation strategy. Of course, there are many reasons for choosing graphs. Let's start with some *bad* reasons:

1. **Graphs are easy to create.** There's no need to lay out the information on the paper, figure out which data will appear in limited space, craft the row and column headings, format the numbers, add all the other visual elements in the table, and so on. And if you're using a "wizard" (more on that later), it's a real snap.

2. **Graphs "look professional."** This seems to be a belief held in many quarters. I find that ironic, since graphs are generally easier and less time consuming to assemble than well-designed tables presenting the same information. Perhaps this view is a throwback to the days before spreadsheet software, when high-quality graphs required the involvement of graphic artists, necessitating much advance planning and incurring significant expense.

3. **"I'm a visual person."** This commonly heard *mantra* is invoked by presenters and audience alike. No doubt, we all have different cognitive styles, strengths, and weaknesses. However, if the main reason for choosing between a graphical and a tabular presentation is nothing more than personal preference, personal preference in the absence of other rationale tends to lead to sloppy quantation.

Note

A word of advice: Even if you truly believe that you *are* a "visual person," think twice before saying this in public. Your listeners may instead be hearing you state that you don't understand how to process quantitative information or that you don't want to go to much effort. To those listeners, it's as if you were saying, "Don't give me too many big words to read."

There are actually some *good* reasons to use graphs:

1. **The "nuclear flyswatter."** You have one fundamentally important point and you want to make absolutely sure you drive it home.

2. **A complex situation.** The interactions between the numbers in your quantation are complicated, and the trends you want your audience to see don't jump out from a table of numbers.

3. **Quantity of quantation.** You have a large number of numbers to present, which you are reluctant to summarize (and your reasons are good ones). For example, it can be hard to present several years of monthly data in tabular form on one page in a way that your audience can assimilate quickly. (A good example of this occurs when you are trying to show whether seasonality exists in a revenue stream.)

4. **It's showtime.** You have a very large audience whom you don't know well, and you have very little time to deliver your message.

5. **The audience reads your graphs competently.** If the quantation you're presenting is presented often enough, even complicated data presented graphically can have the nuclear-flyswatter effect on your audience. An example of this might be the weekly sales forecast presented to the sales management team.

There are other situations where graphs are effective, of course, but the point is that your decision to use graphs in your quantation must be related to whether the graphs will actually help your audience understand the information better. If you remember this, your graphical presentations will be powerful indeed.

Help Your Audience

Little things can make the difference between a well-executed graph and one that accomplishes nothing. To give you a sense of this, we'll start with Report 7-1, Version A which is a graphical version of Report 2-4 from Chapter 2. But before you look ahead, follow these instructions:

1. Cover the exhibit with your hand or a slip of paper.

2. Uncover the exhibit, and study it. Take as much time as you like.

3. Re-cover the exhibit.

4. Tell a friend, or tell the mirror, what you learned about VASTCo from your study of Report 7-1, Version A. Be specific with your numbers. And keep the exhibit covered as you read on!

Now, with the graph still covered, let me ask some questions: Were 1999 revenues more or less than $1 million? Were 2002 revenues were more or less than $3 million? Was VASTCo more or less profitable in 2003 than in 2002? It's not so easy, is it?

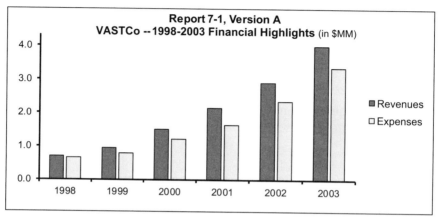

REPORT 7-1, VERSION A: VASTCo 1998–2003 Financial Highlights (in $MM)

About all you can tell from this graph is that both revenues and expenses are going up at a pretty nice clip. If you already have some involvement with VASTCo (as, say, an employee or an investor), did you really need to look at a graph to learn *that*? Don't be hard on yourself; it's virtually impossible for ordinary humans to get much out of reading a graph like this without a lot of visual help.

This is one of the fundamental problems with graphs: a graph may send a clear-as-day message to someone already intimately familiar with the numbers—like the presenter—but not say much at all to someone seeing the information for the first time. This is true of *any* report, but it's especially true of graphs because of the quick visual impact they are supposed to have.

If you're going to use graphs in your quantation, you must accept responsibility for making them easier to read and understand. Some of the features and techniques for achieving this include:

- Gridlines and tickmarks
- Data labels (callouts)
- Adding the data table itself
- Series lines
- Color and patterns
- Scaling the horizontal axis
- Adding a second vertical axis

Gridlines and Tickmarks.   It should be clear from Version A of Report 7-1 that without some "visual aids" it's very difficult to sight all the way across a page with any accuracy. Adding gridlines to your graph makes the task easier, as shown in Version B of Report 7-1.

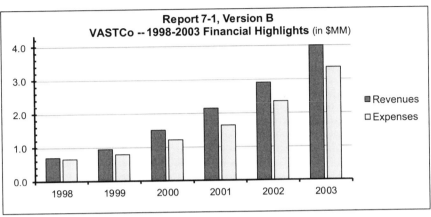

REPORT 7-1, VERSION B: VASTCo 1998–2003 Financial Highlights (in $MM)

With the gridlines, we now know the first digit for every number this graph is presenting. The gridlines also help us with visual interpolation so we can make a good estimate of the second digit. It can also help to add the minor tickmarks if it's really important for your audience to have a sense of the numbers themselves and not just the trends. (In Version B, there are tickmarks at each $0.2 million increment along the vertical axis.)

A couple of other thoughts about scaling your axis and including the gridlines:

- **Scale your axes intelligently.**[2] For Report 7-1, Version B, the vertical axis scale numbers are at every $1 million, a unit that will make intuitive sense to any reader, and has a frequency that is about right for the overall height of the graph. If, however, your graph showed numbers as high as, say, $20 million, you might want to have scale numbers every $2 million, or perhaps only every $5 million.

- **Not all visual elements are equal.** The gridlines are just helpers and aren't as important as data or visual boundaries. This is a subtle point, but note that the gridlines are thinner than the axes, and they are gray rather than black.

- **There can be vertical gridlines, too.** It's not necessary for Report 7-1, Version B, but occasionally you may find adding *vertical* gridlines to be helpful to your audience, too, so they can read the *x*-axis values more precisely. Vertical gridlines are most likely to be useful when the units along *both* the vertical and the horizontal axes are continuously measurable amounts (like dollars or units of production), rather than discrete values (like fiscal periods) or categories (like geographic regions or named people). The commonest examples of this are the "scatter chart" types of graph.

Data Labels (Callouts).[3] It is always possible to eliminate any uncertainty whatsoever by simply putting the numbers themselves on the report, as shown in Version C of Report 7-1.

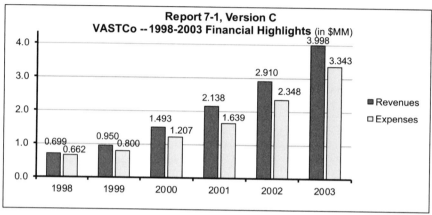

REPORT 7-1, VERSION C: VASTCo 1998–2003 Financial Highlights (in $MM)

Note that even though I've included data labels, I've still chosen to include gridlines. The whole reason for presenting a graph is to give the audience a *visual* sense of how the data are trending, and the major gridlines help immensely to communicate this (whether or not the data labels are present).

Another effective use of callouts is to highlight noteworthy *specific* data values. Report 7-2 is an example that compares U.S. home prices to general consumer prices for the entire twenty-first century (through October 2010). For

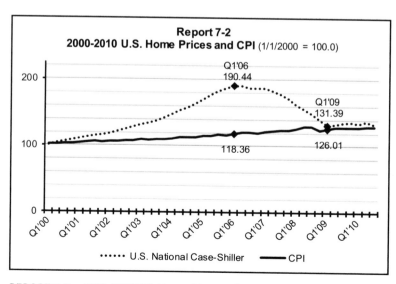

REPORT 7-2: 2000–2010 U.S. Home Prices and CPI (1/1/2000 = 100.0)

home prices I used the U.S. National Case-Shiller Home Price Index, a quarterly number that is the most widely-used measure of nationwide home prices, and for general prices the Consumer Price Index, reported monthly by the Bureau of Labor Statistics. Both statistics have been scaled so that the value of each index is 100.0 at January 1, 2000.

The specific values from quarter to quarter aren't really important. The numbers that *are* interesting are the results for the first quarter of 2006, when the Case-Shiller Index peaked at 190.44, and Q1 2009, when the Case-Shiller reached its lowest level since that peak (the lowest level in six previous years, and since). For Q1 2009, the Case-Shiller and the CPI were once again pretty close to each other, and in the six quarters since, the two indices have bumped along roughly in parallel, both showing very modest increases.[4] Does the entire graph look sort of like a bubble to you? Or maybe an anaconda swallowing a mule? That's the visual impression, but the reader's intellectual understanding of this information is significantly enhanced by adding callouts for only two of the specific data points in each series.

Adding the Data Table Itself. Data labels, as shown in Report 7-1, Version D, are a handy feature to know about, but sometimes there isn't enough room to fit all the numbers next to their graphical objects in a meaningful way. If this is the case, and you want your audience to see the actual numbers, why not just include the whole table? Report 7-3 is an example showing VASTCo's main income statement numbers over a five-year period.

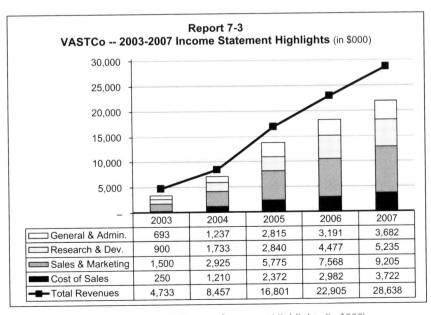

Report 7-3 VASTCo -- 2003-2007 Income Statement Highlights (in $000)	2003	2004	2005	2006	2007
General & Admin.	693	1,237	2,815	3,191	3,682
Research & Dev.	900	1,733	2,840	4,477	5,235
Sales & Marketing	1,500	2,925	5,775	7,568	9,205
Cost of Sales	250	1,210	2,372	2,982	3,722
Total Revenues	4,733	8,457	16,801	22,905	28,638

REPORT 7-3:   VASTCo 2003–2007 Income Statement Highlights (in $000)

To begin with, there are far too many numbers here for the graph to look good with data labels strewn all over the page. Moreover, numbers are usually easier to process when they're neatly organized into rows and columns. If you need to both present the numbers themselves *and* create a visual impression of the results, the approach in Report 7-3 is a good way to go.

Report 7-3 was created entirely within Microsoft's charting capabilities. (There is a feature enabling you to add the table within the chart itself.) This means that the numbers are positioned properly relative to the graph elements, and it's an easy capability to implement. But there's less layout flexibility. I would have chosen to present the information a bit differently: I would have used white space and text effects to group the numbers more intuitively, inserted a Total Expenses line just above the Total Revenues line, and most of all, I would have right-justified the numbers rather than centering them! But if these issues are important to you, you can always put the numbers into worksheet cells below the graph object—where you have more formatting options—and then print out the graph together with the cells you added.

There is an additional unrelated, but extremely useful capability shown in Report 7-3. Note that all of the expenses for each year are presented in a single stacked column, but Total Revenues are presented in a line graph format. Revenues and expenses are two different concepts, but it's clear that being able to compare *total* expenses (i.e., the sum of the four listed expenses, or the height of the stacked bar) to Total Revenues might be of great interest, since the difference between the two totals is, of course, VASTCo's operating profit. Using two different graphing styles in the same document can be very effective for this kind of purpose.

Series Lines. When your graph design makes it difficult to get a sense of the trends in any given series, series lines can help. Report 7-4 is an example in which we show five years of operating expenses broken out by the three components of operating expenses.

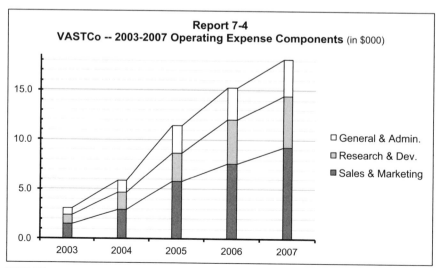

REPORT 7-4:   VASTCo 2003–2007 Operating Expense Components (in $000)

The total height of each stacked column is VASTCo's total operating expenses for the year. This is important information, but designing a graph to present this information also makes it more difficult to get a sense of the trends in R&D and G&A expenses, because the graphical elements for each of these series are now not in alignment from year to year—they're sitting on top of the S&M element, which keeps rising each year.

Using series lines is helpful here, because you can observe trends by sighting along each pair of adjacent lines to see whether they're diverging or converging, and generally by how much. In Report 7-4, we can see that all three expense components grew significantly from 2003 to 2004; all three components also grew in 2005, but S&M grew most dramatically. And G&A was flat in 2006 compared to 2005, which you can see because the series lines for the top and the bottom of the G&A column element are parallel from 2005 to 2006.

As a final comment on Report 7-4, note that even though I'm presenting much of the same information over the same time scale as in Report 7-3, the columns in Report 7-4 are narrower and the gaps between the columns correspondingly wider. This is because the series lines are an important element of Report 7-4, and this design change makes it easier for the audience to read the meaning of the lines and to compare the series lines between one pair of years and the next.

I'll conclude the discussion of series lines with an example where series lines would *not* be appropriate, and how this illustrates a fundamental principle of quantation. Report 7-5 shows the same information as Report 1-3 from Chapter 2. The products are listed in the same order as they were in Report 1-3.

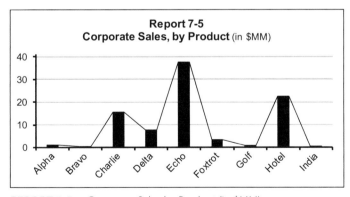

REPORT 7-5:   Corporate Sales by Product (in $MM)

The series lines add nothing here, *because there is no logical relationship between adjacent products in this graph*—that is, unless you are hypothesizing that there is a correlation between a product's revenues and that product name's order in the alphabetical list of products! Recall one of the most important principles of quantation, as stated in Chapter 4:

The Laws of Quantation

Your audience is entitled to presume that every number in a report is meaningful, and if data are omitted, it's because they are less meaningful.

This is the variant of that principle: your audience is entitled to assume that if data *are* presented, it's because they *are* meaningful. And in Report 7-5, the series lines aren't.

Now, you *might* be able to make a case for series lines in the following situation (see Report 7-6).

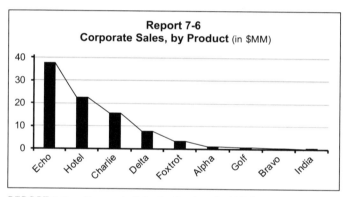

REPORT 7-6:   Corporate Sales by Product (in $MM)

Report 7-6 shows the same information as Report 7-5, except the products are presented in descending order of sales, rather than alphabetically. If you were trying to get a sense of whether there was a significant drop-off in sales between the top *X* products and the remaining products in the company's portfolio, series lines might help you.

Color and Patterns. We've discussed at length the importance and the value of *consistency* in your quantation. In Chapters 3 and 4, we discussed the use of visual effects, text effects, report layout, and other tactics to create a consistent look-and-feel for your quantation. Recall from Chapter 6 that "Use consistent formats" was the only tip that was both an Instant Payoff Tip and a Long-Term Payoff Tip. And in that chapter we discussed the importance of making different types of cells visually distinguishable. All of these points apply double to your graphs. First, the whole point of a graph is to create a powerful visual impression, so compared to tables, you need to pay special attention to anything affecting the visual impression. Second, with each new release of Excel and other spreadsheet products, it becomes easier and easier to add looks and features that at one time could be created only by sophisticated graphics professionals.

With this in mind, I encourage you to think carefully about the immense range of colors and patterns available when you produce graphs. Some suggestions you might consider:

- Use different types of colors for different categories of data in the same report, like expense items and revenue items.[5] For example, the characterization by TV newscasters of Republican-leaning states as "red states" and Democrat-leaning states as "blue states" is ubiquitous today, but it only came into common usage as recently as 2000. This shows you how powerful this kind of color imagery can be.

- Use different shades or patterns to distinguish different types of the same data, such as actual versus budget versus forecast, or license versus consulting versus technical support in a software company's revenues. You could go with different shades of the same color, or add patterns—like crosshatching or speckles—to elements of the same color.

- Develop a consistent approach to distinguish objects that are the actual data themselves from objects that make the data comprehensible—like axes, gridlines, callouts, series lines, and so on.

I caution you to be sparing with these features. If you're not careful, you'll have so many different color and pattern codes that no reader will be able to keep them all straight. Recall this admonition from Chapter 2: Avoid **creating** the **RANSOM** note Effect with your **rePORTS**!

Finally, bear in mind that your color-designed reports will not always be reproduced in color, especially if your audience is cost-conscious. So I leave this topic with:

Note

A suggestion about color: If the color scheme is an important element of the graphs in your quantation, *and* your reports have a wide distribution, then deliver **two versions** of your graphs, especially if you're concerned that not all of your recipients have access to color printers. Version 1 uses the color scheme you're so proud of, and Version 2 uses grayscale, taking advantage of different shades of gray and/or different fill and background patterns to create the same visual effects as your color scheme. (Even then, remember that some fill and background patterns don't look even remotely familiar when printed on particularly temperamental printers. So test before you send!)

Scaling the Horizontal Axis. We discussed the importance of proper scaling of your vertical axis, but scaling the vertical axis affects only how the axis looks and where the gridlines go, and doesn't affect the data points themselves. Scaling along the horizontal axis is an issue that comes up less often because, in many graphs, the horizontal axis just has categories or names (like Reports 7-5 and 7-6), or a continuous sequence of time periods (i.e., years, quarters, or months). But once in a while you will have more to think about. Version A of Report 7-7, which shows a project's completion percentage based on weekly reports, is an example.

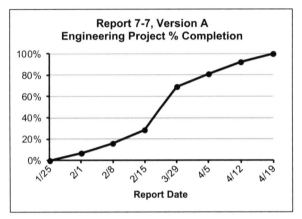

REPORT 7-7, VERSION A: Engineering Project % Completion

What happened here? Did the project team go bananas for one week? Take a closer look at the horizontal axis and you'll see that for the entry of March 29, there is a gap of six weeks between reports. Somebody went on vacation or just forgot to produce the weekly reports for a while. So let's take another look at Report 7-7, this time with spacing along the horizontal axis proportional to the time lag between the dates each forecast was produced. Version B of Report 7-7 tells a different story. Note that there is a marker on the graph line for every

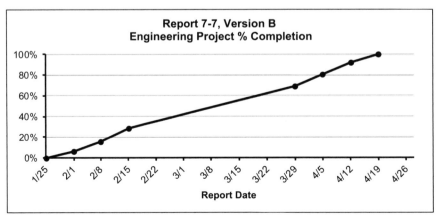

REPORT 7-7, VERSION B: Engineering Project % Completion

date a report was produced. A quick glance at the lines between the points suggests that, if anything, the project progressed a *little more slowly* between February 15 and March 29 than it did either before or after.[6]

Adding a Second Vertical Axis. You may occasionally encounter graphing situations where it's meaningful to compare the graphs of multiple different time series, but the different time series have different units of measure. As an example, consider Report 7-8, which compares home prices to the Consumer Price Index (like Report 7-2), but instead presents the actual average home price in dollars instead of as an index.[7]

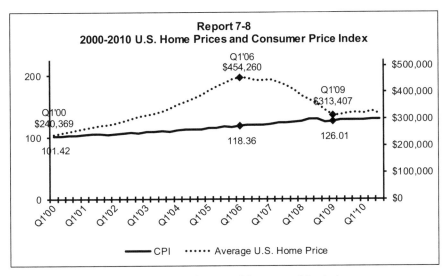

REPORT 7-8:   2000–2010 U.S. Home Prices and Consumer Price Index

Visually, the graph looks just like the one in Report 7-2 and makes the same visual points. A few things are worth noting, however:

- The callouts are still helpful. However, in Report 7-8 I've also added callouts for the first data point, at the far left. This wasn't necessary in Report 7-2, because the starting value for both series was 100.0.

- I dispensed with the gridlines. Unless you're very lucky, or deeply compulsive about details, it's difficult to make the gridlines meaningful for both vertical axes. As a result, as helpful as gridlines usually are, gridlines on a graph with both a primary and a secondary vertical axis may serve only to confuse the reader. For Report 7-8, it was more important to scale the right-hand axis so that both graphs started at the same point in Q1 of 2000. And without gridlines, the callouts are even more important.

- Although the dollar sign often adds an unnecessary character to a presentation, I've added the dollar sign to the home price series numbers to clarify the comparison versus the CPI numbers.

Now we come to an example where a second vertical axis is more problematic. As you often see in stock trading reports, Report 7-9 shows both closing price and average daily volume by month for Microsoft (MSFT) from 2007 through 2009.

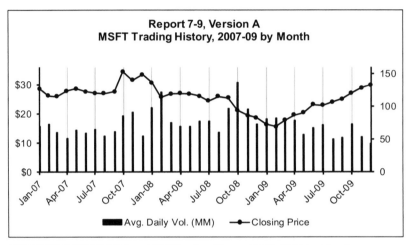

REPORT 7-9, VERSION A: MSFT Trading History, 2007–2009 by Month

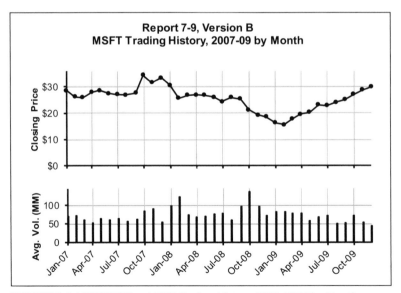

REPORT 7-9, VERSION B: MSFT Trading History, 2007–2009 by Month

Version A has a secondary vertical axis, just like Report 7-8. Price is on the primary (i.e., left) axis, with a dollar sign to distinguish the values from the trading volumes. Volume is on the secondary axis. Because price and volume are disparate measures, it's helpful to present them in different graph styles (price as a line graph and volume as a bar graph). Even so, I personally find this presentation confusing; it takes a few extra beats to figure out which graph is price and which is volume. Moreover, as in Report 7-8, the gridlines no longer help delineate graph values when there are two dueling axis scales. (However, note that I've used *vertical* gridlines to break the months into quarterly groups.) Fundamentally, the problem with this graph is that price and volume just aren't comparable enough to belong on the same graph.

A clearer presentation is shown in Version B, which happens to be the format used by most online stock tracking systems. Closing price and average daily volume are presented in separate graphs. The over-and-under layout means that both values for any given month are in vertical alignment with each other, and the vertical gridlines line up with each other exactly, so it's easier to match up a period's price with its trading volume. And since each graph has only one vertical axis, we can enhance readability by providing horizontal gridlines as well.[8]

First, Do No Harm

As we've discussed so far in this chapter, Excel (and other spreadsheet software products) offer an increasingly impressive array of tools and features to make your graphs more impactful and easier to understand. But don't go too far; not only are these tools getting increasingly impressive, they're also becoming increasingly easy to use. Before you know it, you'll find that you've added features that make your graphs look good at first glance but actually add no meaning to your quantation and make your graphs *harder* to understand overall. In the worst-case scenario, you may even make your graphs misleading. The rest of this chapter will focus on behaviors you should be very careful about (and sometimes avoid). These include:

- Don't be sleazy about the vertical axis.
- Avoid pie charts.
- Don't confuse the horizontal and vertical axes.
- Watch those wizards.
- Sometimes you don't want to focus on looks.
- Avoid fancy-shmancy effects.

Don't Be Sleazy about the Vertical Axis. Let's use a federal government spending example for a change. Report 7-10 shows U.S. total federal government discretionary spending over ten years. The ramp in spending looks pretty frightening, doesn't it?

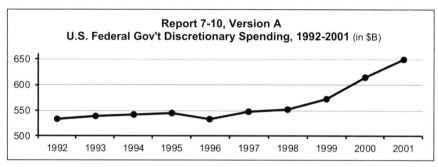

REPORT 7-10, VERSION A: U.S. Federal Government Discretionary Spending, 1992–2001 (in $B)

But hold on: during this ten-year period spending grew only a total of 22% (from $533.3B to $649.3B), or about 2% per year. If we redo the graph with a vertical axis scale that starts at 0, the growth looks a lot less visually impressive (see Report 7-10, Version B).

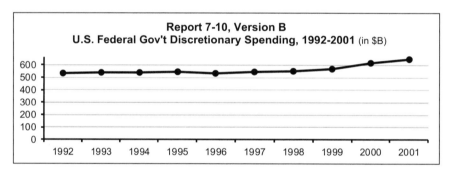

REPORT 7-10, VERSION B: U.S. Federal Government Discretionary Spending, 1992–2001 (in $B)

And just to show you that the effect can create the opposite impression, Report 7-11, Version A shows the profitability of a real U.S. public company. Can you guess the company?

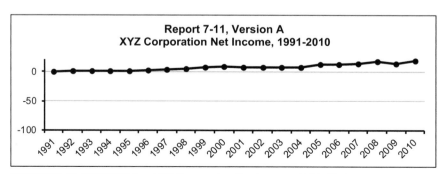

REPORT 7-11, VERSION A: XYZ Corporation Net Income, 1991–2010

A quick glance at the graph suggests *very* slow-and-steady growth. Well, this stodgy performer of a company is Microsoft! Oh, and the vertical axis shows net income in the *billions of dollars*. I guess I forgot to make that clear somewhere on the graph. Oops. Here's the same graph, this time with a zero baseline (see Report 7-11, Version B).

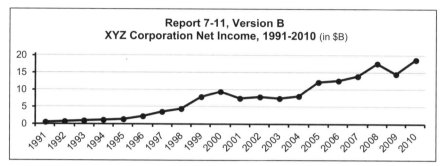

REPORT 7-11, VERSION B: XYZ Corporation Net Income, 1991–2010 (in $B)

Here are some reasons that you might start the vertical axis at a place other than zero:

1. You are trying to fool the audience into believing that a significant trend exists (or doesn't) when that's not really the case. (Examples: Report 7-10 for "exists," Report 7-11 for "doesn't exist")

2. You wish to bring out as much visual contrast as possible in the graph. (Example: Report 7-10)

3. The scale does not have a "natural zero." That is, unlike measures like revenues or expenses, the minimum plausible value is a number other than zero. Or perhaps there simply isn't any notion of a plausible minimum outside of the values themselves for the series you happen to be graphing. (Examples: profit, balance of trade, daily temperatures in Fairbanks, Alaska)

Of these reasons, only #3 is a *good* reason.

Reason #1 is obviously a sleazy tactic and is one of the oldest tricks in the quantation book.[9] In fact, it's so transparent and well-known that I haven't bothered to include it as a Deadly Sin.

Reason #2 is generally a well-meaning reason, but it's a bad reason nonetheless. First, if there is no significant upward or downward trend in the data, it should be more important to show that fact to your audience than to make your graph "pretty" or "interesting." Second (and this is much more important for your reputation), *your audience doesn't have any idea whether your motives were pure*. They can only guess at your reasons. Note that I cite Report 7-10 as an example of *both* reasons #1 and #2. All this brings us back to Bolten's Law (see Chapter 4), to which I now add:

The Laws of Quantation

Corollary #4 to Bolten's Law: If your audience is aware that a presentation tactic *could be* sleazy, they will conclude that it *is* sleazy. This perception applies to the presenter as well as to his or her content.

This is not a good thing. And it's certainly not worth risking your reputation just to create a little visual contrast in a graph.

Note

A suggestion: If you believe that there is a trend in the rate of change in a data series, but that trend isn't visible from an ethical graphing of the series itself, **then graph the rate of change in the series values instead of the series values themselves.** For example, if the revenue graph looks flat-ish, you might want to plot the annual growth rate instead.

Reason #3 deals with a fact of life: if no natural zero exists, then you don't have to start your vertical axis at zero. But you still have a choice about where to put the *horizontal axis*. I suggest you base your choice on whether zero is a *meaningful* number. Reports 7-12 and 7-13 are examples.

Report 7-12 presents a U.S. balance of trade history. For that series, most of us think of the zero as meaningful. After all, we use different words for balances of trade above and below zero (*surplus* and *deficit*, respectively). We take meaning from whether this number is positive or negative. Accordingly, I've chosen to locate the horizontal axis at a balance of trade of zero, so the reader can tell at a glance whether a data point shows a surplus or a deficit simply by observing whether the data point is above or below that axis. Note again that to

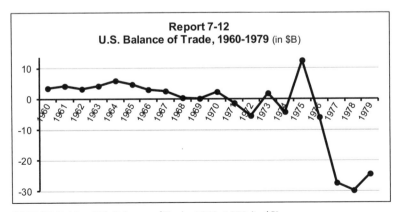

REPORT 7-12:   U.S. Balance of Trade, 1960–1979 (in $B)

make this task easier for the reader, I've made the axis heavier and darker than the gridlines parallel to it.

Report 7-13 is a different story. Whether the exact temperature is above or below 0°F has little significance other than anecdotal.[10] Since on this graph no one temperature has any particular significance, I've chosen to locate the horizontal axis where it usually goes: at the bottom.

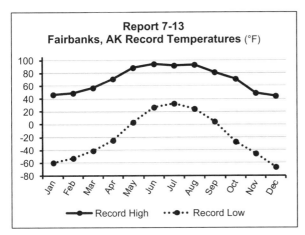

REPORT 7-13:   Fairbanks, Alaska, Record Temperatures (°F)

Avoid Pie Charts. As I've said before, one of the great risks of using graphs for your quantation is the possibility that they won't convey nearly as much information as you'd hoped. And no type of graph poses a greater risk of that than pie charts. Report 7-14 shows the VASTCo expenses breakdown that we also saw in Report 7-3.

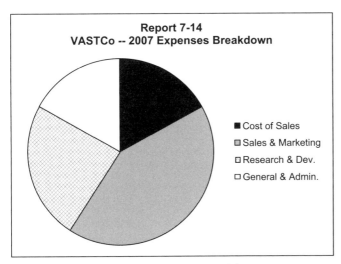

REPORT 7-14:   VASTCo 2007 Expenses Breakdown

Beyond the fact that Sales & Marketing was the largest VASTCo expense component, do you learn *anything* from this report? An extremely abbreviated list of its shortcomings would include:[11]

- There is no scale or other measure to help you estimate the magnitude of the numbers being presented.
- Even if you thought a scale would help, where would you put it?
- The pie wedges are difficult to compare to each other, because they lie at angles to each other.
- A pie chart's use of space is incredibly inefficient. Report 7-14 takes up as much space as any of the other graphs in this chapter, even though it shows only four data points. And you can't even read the magnitudes of the numbers.

Even worse, Report 7-14 shows the expense breakdown for 2007 only. There is no comparison to another year, or to budget, or to anything else, leading this report to commit Deadly Sin #7 (presenting numbers with no context whatsoever).

So let's fix that grievous context error in Report 7-15, by including pie charts for some other years, and doing a bit of housekeeping to address some of its other problems.

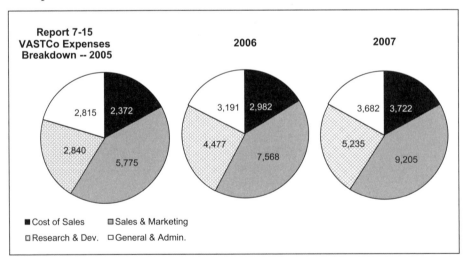

REPORT 7-15:   VASTCo 2005 Expenses Breakdown

Now we have a little context: we have three consecutive years of data, and even that I only accomplished by making each of the three pies much smaller than the one pie in Report 7-14 (although Report 7-3 presented *five* years of the same data and took up less space). We've also put callouts on the pie wedges, so at least the reader can see what the actual numbers are. (I'd argue that the callouts are the only worthwhile information in this report.) Unfortunately, just like Report 7-14, it's virtually impossible to make any comparisons between data points, especially when the two points you want to compare aren't even in the same pie. Moreover, these three equal-sized pie charts convey no sense of how expenses have grown over the three years. Now, you could make the size of each pie chart proportional to total expenses, but that would be a lot of work, *and* it would probably make Report 7-15 even *more* confusing! It's no wonder that Edward Tufte has said, "The only design worse than a pie chart is several of them."

All of this focus on an unaccountably popular presentation method wouldn't be so annoying if there weren't so many other ways of presenting the same information *much* more effectively in less space. So, I leave you with:

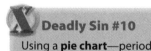

Deadly Sin #10
Using a **pie chart**—period

Oh, wait. I also want to offer:

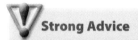

Strong Advice

Another word of advice: Please, please don't say, "I'm a visual person. Just give me a few pie charts." I've heard this request many times in my career. To some listeners, not only is it as if you were saying, "Don't give me too many big words to read," but it also says that your idea of a "big word" is one with more than two syllables or more than eight letters.

Don't Confuse the Horizontal and Vertical Axes. Consistency matters as much when presenting graphs as when presenting tables. Your audience gets used to information oriented in a certain way, not just because it's visually comfortable, but because it's easier to find important information quickly. Let's look at two more versions of Report 7-1, Versions D and E.

Versions D and E have, of course, identical specific design and formatting elements, except that the graph in Version E is rotated 90° from the graph in Version D.

Which one do you prefer? My strong preference is Version D, because Version E has two characteristics that I consider design flaws. First, in Version E, time is on the vertical axis, not the horizontal axis, and most readers (myself included) find this peculiar. (See Report 2-4 in Chapter 2 for a similar comparison involving *tables*.) Second, and more important, Version E isn't the intuitive way to read a graph. When we try to visually quantify a graphed number, or compare one value to another, we're more comfortable using a vertical scale at the *left* of the page, or seeing which graph element sits *higher* on the graph. Consider this: when using words, we say that one number is "higher" or "lower" than another, or that the revenues for a given year were "up" or "down" from the previous year. You wouldn't look at Report 7-1 and say, "I see that 2003 revenues were to the right of 2002 revenues."[12]

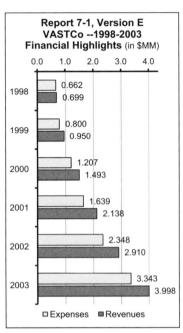

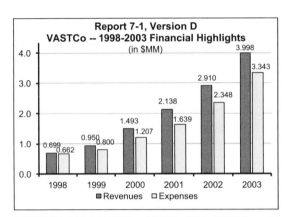

REPORT 7-1, VERSION D: VASTCo 1998–2003 Financial Highlights (in $MM)

REPORT 7-1, VERSION E: VASTCo 1998–2003 Financial Highlights (in $MM)

Taking this notion of what is *intuitive* even further, recall that from the time we first start learning to graph functions and relationships in school, we develop a sense of how causal relationships should be presented visually. For example, look at Versions A and B of Report 7-16, which graphs a sales representative's compensation plan, showing commission income versus revenues generated.

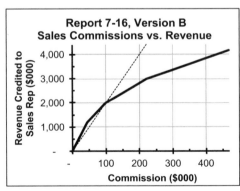

REPORT 7-16, VERSION A: Sales Commissions versus Revenue

REPORT 7-16, VERSION B: Sales Commissions versus Revenue

Report 7-16 graphs what is often referred to as an *accelerated* compensation plan, which means that the sales rep's commission rate increases when he or she meets certain revenue goals. Accelerated plans are an approach to compensation that is widely used in high-growth companies, especially in high technology, because they provide significant extra compensation for the most successful salespeople and are a powerful employee-retention tool. Versions A and B both graph revenues on one axis and commissions on the other; the only difference between the two versions is that the horizontal and vertical axes are switched. (The broken line shows commission income at a constant flat rate regardless of production, assuming the target commission of $100,000 for generating $2,000,000 in revenue.)

Most people would consider Version B *very* hard to read and understand. First, this is an accelerated compensation plan, with a clear intent to *reward* the biggest sales producers. So a curve that's flattening—instead of rising faster, like Version A—makes a dissonant impression on the reader. Moreover, from the time we first start learning algebra we are taught to graph the independent variable (that is, the variable whose value we don't control) along the horizontal axis and the dependent variable (that is, the variable whose value is driven by the value of the independent variable) along the vertical axis.[13,14] For these reasons, I offer the following admonition:

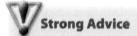

Strong Advice

When creating a graph where the values of **one or more variables** *depend* **on the value of an independent variable**, *always* graph the independent variable on the horizontal axis and the dependent variable(s) on the vertical axis.

Watch Those Wizards. Wizards are a great convenience, which is both their strength and their weakness. They definitely save you a lot of steps in the process of creating a graph, but the reason they save you so much time is that they make many decisions for you about how the axes are scaled, the color choices, the types of lines and other objects, and so on. Wizards can definitely make you more productive, but if you learn one thing from this chapter, I hope it's that there are lots of little decisions about how your graphs *look* that can have a big impact on how effective they are, *and you should make those decisions yourself.* So once the wizard has made all those little decisions, your own work should begin, starting with a thorough review of all those little decisions that the software made.

In this sense, wizards' effects on graphs are like the effects of scotch at a cocktail party. Using wizards can be pleasing, relaxing, and enjoyable. But at some point, when everything you see starts to appear wittier, more intelligent, and much better looking than real life, it's time to stop. Remember: real quantation professionals know when to say "when."

Sometimes You Don't Want to Focus on Looks.   When designing graphs, it's always tempting to gravitate toward visual impressions that are graceful, or elegant, or beautiful. Graphs that depict something visually pleasing make us believe that the graph is capturing the essence of the data. And more often than not, that belief would be right. With this in mind, consider Report 7-17, a histogram of a distribution of test scores.

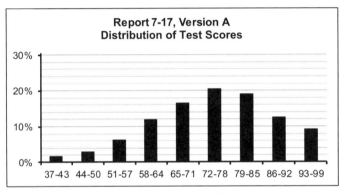

REPORT 7-17, VERSION A: Distribution of Test Scores

Note the categories 37-43, 44-50, and so on. Each one covers a seven-point range of test scores. By grouping things this way, the distribution of test scores forms a beautiful bell curve.

But is Version A the right way to present this information? Perhaps there are policy implications tied to certain scores. Suppose, for example, that 60 is a "passing score," and anyone scoring below that has to repeat the course. And perhaps the percentage of students scoring below 70 has government-funding implications. And perhaps the number of "A" students, as defined by a score of 90 or more, is also important.

Version A of Report 7-17 doesn't give us precise information about these issues, but look at Version B. Visually, this graph lacks the mathematical beauty of Version A, but it does provide precise answers to how many students scored below 60 and below 70, and how many scored 90 or better. Both versions of Report

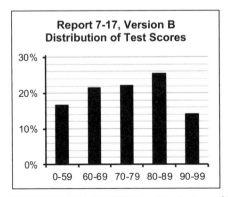

REPORT 7-17, VERSION B: Distribution of Test Scores

7-17 are valid ways of presenting the information. Version A will help us answer the question of whether there is a statistically valid distribution of student performance, and Version B will answer certain policy and fiscal questions. The right choice will depend on what you are trying to accomplish and who your audience is.

Avoid Fancy-Shmancy Effects. There is virtually no limit to the number of amazing visual effects that Excel lets you to add to your graphs. Are these effects worth the effort? Could they help your audience understand your quantation? As we consider this, let's again present Report 7-4.

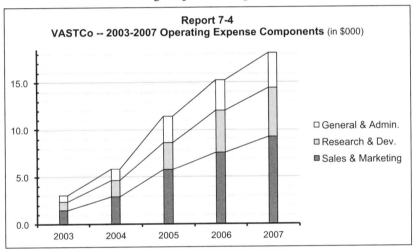

REPORT 7-4:   VASTCo 2003–2007 Operating Expense Components (in $000)

Report 7-18 is the same report with some 3-D effects to make it "look professional." It's got 3-D columns, shading, and walls for the box—the whole enchilada! Now tell me: is Report 7-18 easier to read and understand than Report 7-4? Frankly,

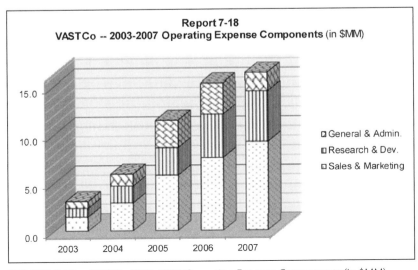

REPORT 7-18:   VASTCo 2003–2007 Operating Expense Components (in $MM)

I'd say that the fact that we now have 3-D columns makes it much harder to use the gridlines in the walls of the box to measure the values, especially since the columns are set away from those walls. And the series lines that were so helpful in Report 7-4 can't even be generated in a 3-D graph.

Don't get me wrong—it's terrific if you can make your graphs look polished and professional, with imaginative visual effects. But don't do it at the expense of making your quantation comprehensible and meaningful. Let me remind you of a Deadly Sin that applies as much to graphs as it does to any other form of quantation:

Deadly Sin #3

Using visual effects for any reason **other than clarifying, distinguishing, or adding meaning** to information

Any questions?

"Never give a gun to a duck," is a saying that has always made me chuckle. The image of cute little shotgun-toting ducks simply makes me laugh. The saying's deeper meaning may be debatable, but I choose to interpret it as a caution against putting weapons (or tools) in the hands of those not equipped to use them properly. The impressive array of graphing-related features in today's spreadsheet programs can be either a weapon or a tool; it all depends on how these features are employed.

As I hope you've observed, *Painting with Numbers* is about doing the little things that make a big difference in the effectiveness of your quantation. Little things are important to any type of nuanced communication, but they are especially important to quantation, and they are still more important when you are using graphs. This is because the purpose of graphs is to make quick, visual, and sometimes visceral impressions on your audience. Graphs are not usually something people ponder and linger over, so every little detail matters if it helps create the desired effect.

In this chapter we discussed the little details to make your graphs more effective, like including an appropriate scale on your axes, or adding gridlines to make the actual numbers easy to estimate, or showing the numbers themselves when greater precision is necessary. In addition, there are many little things the software allows you to do with graphs that may enhance the visual appeal of your graphs in a nonspecific way, but are likely to *hurt* your quantation rather than help it. In the hands of someone not thinking clearly about his or her quantation goals and how the audience is likely to process the information, these little things can make the resulting graphs harder to read and understand. They can distract from the underlying content and can inadvertently (or deliberately) mislead.

A simple rule of thumb is to avoid every new bell or whistle that doesn't enhance your quantation in some specific way. But that still leaves you plenty of options that will help your graphs be a very powerful addition to the way you present numbers.

NOTES

1. Edward Tufte, the patron saint of visual presentation, has written several books on the subject. The best known of them is *The Visual Display of Quantitative Information*. For a somewhat more practical, nuts-and-bolts view of graphing situations, I recommend the rather appropriately named Stephen Few, whose works include *Show Me the Numbers*. Both Tufte and Few conduct popular workshops as well (see their websites for more details). For a more lightweight take on the subject, you might enjoy the classic *How to Lie with Statistics*, by Darrell Huff, first published in 1954.

2. Scaling the vertical axis is something you will almost always have to consider. A thoughtful scaling of the horizontal axis comes up less often as an issue, but we discuss it later in this chapter.

3. *Data label* is the term used in the Microsoft Excel software. *Callout* is a term used in the graphic-arts industry, and has the same meaning.

4. If you look at the entire ten-plus years from the beginning of 2000, the Case-Shiller Index increased at a compound annual growth rate (CAGR) of 2.7%, while the CPI's CAGR was 2.4%. Those two numbers are awfully close to each other and suggest that, in the long run, home prices behave much like the other prices consumers face. This observation is completely obscured by the fact that the Case-Shiller's CAGR was 10.9% from Q1 2000 through Q1 2006, −11.6% (!) from Q1 2006 through Q1 2009, and 0.9% since then. The CPI's CAGRs for the same periods were 2.7%, 2.1%, and 1.8%, respectively. But compared to January 2000, both indices have ended up at pretty much the same place. These national results are still further obscured by the fact that there is great variance among the Case-Shiller indices for the 20 specific metropolitan areas that Case-Shiller tracks.

5. Be careful about relying on green and red for this distinction. Recall from Chapter 2 that a significant fraction of the population is colorblind, and the commonest form of colorblindness is the inability to distinguish between those two colors.

6. Version A of Report 7-7 was generated as a "line chart" and Version B as a "scatter chart." However, I could have created Version B as a line chart as well, and selected "Date axis" as the "Axis type" option in the "Axis Options" section of the "Format Axis" dialog box. Excel is capable of handling dates differently from other numbers, and of recognizing values that appear to be dates. Be that as it may, you will sometimes encounter graphs where it's important to think about how the horizontal access is scaled, just as you almost always have to with the vertical axis.

7. These are not the actual average U.S. home prices, but price levels I backed into from the Case-Shiller Index results, and which look reasonable and illustrate my point.

8. This MSFT trading data example is one of many situations where struggling to present two data series with different quantitative scales on the same graph just isn't worth the trouble, and you may be better off throwing in the towel and presenting two adjacent graphs. For a more exhaustive and scholarly review of the problems and considerations involving dual-scaled graphs, see Stephen Few's essay, "Dual-Scaled Axes in Graphs: Are They Ever the Best Solution?" available on his website, http://www.perceptualedge.com.

9. It features prominently, for example, in *How to Lie with Statistics*, published 55 years ago.

10. Legend has it that for his temperature scale Daniel Fahrenheit started by choosing 100° to be a human's body temperature, and 0° to be the coldest outside temperature he was aware of. What we learn from this is that (a) he was working with some hot people and (b) he didn't get around much. Anders Celsius chose for his temperature scale 0° and 100° to be the freezing and boiling points of water, respectively. Since the freezing point of water is a

temperature point we can relate to, you could perhaps argue that the Celsius scale does in fact have a *meaningful* zero. Taking this one step further, I'll mention the Kelvin temperature scale, in which a 1° difference is exactly the same heat difference as it is in the Celsius scale, but on the Kelvin scale, 273.15°K is the same temperature as 0°C, and 373.15°K is the same as 100°C. Zero degrees Kelvin (i.e., –273.15° C or –459.67° F) is the temperature that scientists call "absolute zero," and a negative temperature cannot exist on the Kelvin scale.So there actually is a temperature scale that does in fact have a *natural zero*.

11. For a more thorough, yet very readable, skewering of pie charts, see Stephen Few's essay, "Save the Pies for Dessert," available on his website, www.perceptualedge.com.

12. Versions D and E of Report 7-1 are what I would term "bar graphs," with Version D a "vertical bar graph" and Version E a "horizontal bar graph." For some reason, Microsoft Excel names the type of graph in Version D a "Column Chart" and the one in Version E a "Bar Chart." I believe that *bar graph* (or *bar chart*) is rather universal terminology for *either* type of graph, and that the Microsoft nomenclature leads many people, when asked to create a "bar chart," to make what I consider the wrong design choice. Moreover, Excel's default ordering of the Year axis in Version E put 2003 at the top and 1998 at the bottom, so I had to specify "Categories in reverse order" in Format Axis to present Version E as it is shown. The question is less clear when the time axis goes down the side of, rather than across, the page, but since our standard reading flow goes from left to right *and then from top to bottom*, I consider the Microsoft Excel default to be *reverse chronological order*. See the discussion of consistency in Chapter 4 for my opinion of *that* particular design choice.

13. Let's take a trip down memory lane (which I hope is nostalgic and not too painful) to Algebra I. Recall that the English translation of the equation, $y = f(x)$, is "y is a function of x." Put another way, the equation or formula represented by $f(x)$ describes how the value of y is determined by the value of x. The roles played by x and y are almost never switched. Graphing this equation then illustrates the range of possible values for y given a range of possible values for x, with x *always* measured along the horizontal axis and y measured along the vertical axis. This orientation is so strongly ingrained in us that many people go through life using the terms *horizontal axis* and *x-axis* synonymously, and likewise the terms *vertical axis* and *y-axis*.

14. The causal relationship is usually obvious, but please don't get the dependent and independent variables confused. Earthquakes are not caused by geologists accidentally jostling seismographs. And it isn't always wise to assert causality just because a correlation exists. Even if you discover that, say, the Dow Jones Industrial Average has always risen in years when a National Football Conference team wins the Super Bowl, think twice about betting the ranch on the stock market if the Redskins take it all. Go 'Skins!

CHAPTER 8

The Pitfalls of Presentations and PowerPoint

I took a speed reading course and read War and Peace *in twenty minutes. It involves Russia.*

—Woody Allen

When you a give an oral presentation, you are anything but anonymous. You are on the stage, live in front of an audience. Your audience can see you, talk to you, engage you (and harangue you if need be). As the presenter, you are directly and visibly associated with the information you have assembled, and your audience will view you as an expert, a trusted messenger, or someone with something important to say.

As such, giving an oral presentation is much more than getting your facts straight and your slides prepared. You must anticipate your audience's questions, help them understand the data, alleviate their confusion, and lead them through a decision-making experience in real time. And all these challenges are *heightened* when your presentation involves a significant amount of quantation. Furthermore, the most widely used software aids for oral presentations (e.g., Microsoft PowerPoint) have general limitations, and specific limitations when it comes to presenting numbers. To be an effective presenter of numbers, you must be aware of these limitations and gear your presentation to take them into account.

This chapter will focus on the issues that make numbers-related oral presentations difficult and challenging. In particular, we'll address how to cope with the physical constraints inherent in oral presentations, and key aspects of interacting with your audience that are especially important when presenting numbers. The pressure of a live audience, the high stakes, and the limitations of the software tools make oral presentations a unique challenge when presenting numbers, and they require that you know how to make your quantation clear and effective.

Why Do People Make Fun of Business Presentations?

A well-done oral presentation from a skillful presenter can be an amazingly persuasive, informative, and powerful experience. And yet, the "business presentation" is the single-most-ridiculed form of business communication. A quick online visit will turn up plenty of hilarious videos and slideshows, some made by professional comedians or trainers intending to lampoon the genre, and some serious presentations that are unintentionally and embarrassingly funny. Peter Norvik has published a delightful rendition of what the Gettysburg Address might have looked like had it been a stirring PowerPoint presentation instead of a stirring speech. Why in some circles, just mentioning the word "PowerPoint" will start people's eyeballs rolling.

Is all this ridicule deserved? *Of course it is!* There are many reasons for all this hilarity, but the ones most relevant to the art of quantation include:

- Presenting far more content than is reasonable given the time or the space available
- Unintelligible or meaningless numbers
- No correlation between the spoken words and the visual content of the slides
- Overuse of special effects, which the audience may see as an effort by the presenter to mask the fact that he or she:
  - Is delivering very bad news
  - Has a poor grasp of the subject matter
  - Is delivering no information whatsoever

Giving an effective presentation is a huge challenge, and even with the most number-heavy topics, the secrets of being effective involve more than just the numbers on the slides. The rest of this chapter details some realities of oral presentations and how to work with them to make your quantation as clear as possible.

Real Estate Is a Scarce and Precious Commodity

The best-known constraint of giving a presentation is a simple one: *there isn't much room on a slide.* As an example, here is Report 8-1, which is simply Report 2-2 copied into a PowerPoint slide. I've used a 20-point font, but I've included different font sizes in the shaded box to give you a sense of font size options.[1] To get a sense of what you would see if you were in the audience looking at this slide, hold the page about two feet from your eyes.

VASTCo Q3'06 Income Statement

(in $000)	Quarter Ended 9/06			Year-to-Date		
	Actual	**Budget**	**F(U)**	**Actual**	**Budget**	**F(U)**
Licenses	4,284	4,064	220	12,348	11,792	**556**
Prof. Svcs.	1,561	1,530	31	4,498	4,321	**177**
Total Revenues	**5,845**	**5,594**	**251**	**16,846**	**16,113**	**733**
Cost of Sales	760	667	(94)	2,192	1,899	**(293)**
Gross Profit	**5,084**	**4,927**	**157**	**14,654**	**14,214**	**440**
Sales & Marketing	1,928	1,915	(13)	5,579	5,517	**(61)**
Research & Dev.	1,153	1,167	14	3,270	3,312	**42**
General & Admin.	805	798	(7)	2,363	2,313	**(50)**
Total Oprg. Exps.	**3,887**	**3,880**	**(6)**	**11,212**	**11,142**	**(70)**
Oprg. Profit	**1,198**	**1,046**	**151**	**3,442**	**3,072**	**370**

(Font size annotations shown on slide: 24 points / 20 points / 18 points / 16 points / 14 points / 12 points)

10/25/06 10:53 AM   Report 8-1 (Report 2-2, Revisited)

REPORT 8-1 (REPORT 2-2, REVISITED):   VASTCo Q3 '06 Income Statement

Do you begin to see the problem? This report at its current size takes up the entire slide, so you can't make the words and numbers larger without jamming the rows and columns closer together. At the same time, the font size can't be made much smaller and still have the information be readable by everyone in a typical presentation room. So if you want to present a report with more columns or rows than the six columns and ten rows you see here, you may have a real problem.

Ignoring this constraint is the error that most frequently leads to lousy presentations. I can think of no more obvious Deadly Sin than uttering these words:

Deadly Sin #17

"I know most of you can't read the numbers on this slide, but . . ."

Please. Do yourself a favor: *never* put yourself in a position where you might think of saying this, and even then don't be tempted to say it. If you find yourself uttering this vile phrase, your audience may then be provoked to ask:

- "If you already knew that we couldn't read the numbers on this slide, why are you showing them to us?"
- "If you *didn't* know that we couldn't read the numbers, did you properly prepare for this presentation?"

- "Do you *want us* to be able to read the numbers? Do you *care* if we can't?"
- "Why are you wasting our time?"

In other words, this Deadly Sin is not just a presentation error; it says something about *you* and about your respect for your audience. And while responding to these questions is not how you may be wanting to spend your time, things could be even worse, because of:

The Laws of Quantation

Corollary #3 (general form) to Bolten's Law: The likelihood that your audience will express their concern about your motives for presenting information poorly is inversely proportional to the harshness of the conclusion they are in the process of forming.

The problem of font size can obviously apply to words as well. Who among us does not have painful memories of word slides jam-packed with unreadable paragraphs, or worse yet, having to sit through a presentation where the presenter had to resort to reading the slides aloud? With respect to quantation, however, bear in mind that the only experience more painful to an audience than having the words read aloud to them is having the *numbers* read aloud.

Avoiding Deadly Sin #17 is not always easy. It takes hard work, clear thought, and a lot of willpower to select the precise information that should appear in the limited space (and omit the rest). Here are a few tips that might help:

- Stick to the PowerPoint style and presentation guidelines for your organization, if such guidelines exist. If they don't, use the default font size and other software settings.
- If you can't fit all the desired content onto one slide, bite the bullet and add another.
- If you can't add more slides, find a better way to present the same information, perhaps by rearranging or boiling down the numbers. And you can always provide hard copy of the full detailed report as backup information.
- Rehearse the presentation, if possible *in the room you're actually going to be giving it in*. Have a colleague or a friend watch from the back of the room, so you will know for certain that your audience will be able to see your numbers.

Help Your Audience

An oral presentation is a unique form of communication, especially where quantation is concerned. There are many things that can prevent your audience from understanding the meaning of the numbers in your presentation: your time is limited; you have specific points that you want your audience to understand and you need to keep them focused on your agenda; your audience hasn't been able to absorb your materials in private and at their leisure; peer pressure may cause certain people to make distracting remarks, or to go down discussion paths that aren't helpful, or not to ask questions they *should* ask; and slide space is too limited to provide explanatory notes or other aids. The good news is that there are things you can do when preparing and giving a presentation that will make a huge difference in how clearly your audience gets your message. You can:

- Enable your audience to prepare for your presentation in advance.
- *Tell* your audience how to understand your quantation.
- Remember that the rules of quantation still apply.
- Use slide titles appropriately.
- Use key indicators.

Enable Your Audience to Prepare for Your Presentation in Advance. One of the principal differences between word slides and number slides is that words and sentences are instantly comprehensible, but it takes a few moments to absorb numbers. Furthermore, if further explanation is necessary with word slides, you can add a sentence or two to your talk or a couple of additional word slides, but adding more number data as backup slides will lead to a very dry (and data-heavy) presentation. For this reason, I strongly recommend that whenever possible you distribute the supporting reports to your audience beforehand.

But don't send out the slides themselves—just the reports! Most presentation coaches will tell you that sending out the actual presentation slides is a terrible idea, and I'm inclined to agree. An audience that already has all the slides in front of them is a distracted and inattentive audience: they're leafing through pages instead of listening to you, making comments and asking questions inappropriate for that moment in the presentation, and missing the impact of your most powerful statements. It may take some backbone to refrain from handing out the slides until after you've finished your presentation, but your presentation will go much better.

 Note

In well-run organizations, it's not unusual to have established standards for what is to be distributed before important meetings, and how far in advance. This imposes a useful discipline on the presenters, because it prevents frenzied last-minute cramming to be ready, and it allows audience members to get answers to questions ahead of time, instead of having to interrupt the flow of the presentation with their questions.

Tell Your Audience How to Understand Your Quantation. In Chapters 2, 3, and 4 we discussed a variety of tactics to ensure there are clues *on the report itself* that help your audience understand your quantation. Unfortunately, those tactics often can't be used on PowerPoint slides because there simply isn't enough room for extraneous words and artwork. If you are presenting quantation that needs some elaboration, my strong recommendation is to add a few sentences at appropriate times in your talk that start with something like, "Here's how to read this table: . . ." Some of the benefits that you will reap from this tactic are:

- Teaching the audience to understand your quantation becomes part of your presentation itself, rather than something each person does independently while you babble on with your talk.
- Everyone can have the same understanding of how to read the information because everyone is getting instructions from the same source: *you!*
- Adding these explanatory sentences will demonstrate to your audience that you are in complete control of your information and that you care that they understand the subject matter.

If you spend the extra 30 to 60 seconds you need to provide the instructions where necessary, you will be rewarded with better audience comprehension of your information and a stronger connection with your audience. You might want to include those explanatory sentences *every* time you give a quarterly or monthly presentation, and not just the first time. After all, you may have some new attendees in your audience, and you can't be sure the repeat attendees will remember from the previous time.

Remember That the Rules of Quantation Still Apply. One of the principal messages of *Painting with Numbers* is that there are *rules* to presenting numbers clearly and effectively. These rules are analogous to the rules of grammar, spelling, sentence structure, and paragraph organization, and they are necessary to follow if you want to be an effective writer or speaker. Chapters 1 through 4 are my effort to codify those rules.

With oral presentations, these rules are doubly important to follow, because in a live presentation (as opposed to a hardcopy or electronic distribution of reports) your audience has to understand the information much more quickly, Readability and clarity are still essential, but you don't have the space or time to devote to qualifying or elaborating. At the same time, though, because of those space and time limitations, following the rules of quantation (and avoiding the Deadly Sins) is *more* difficult in oral presentations and slideshows.

This topic doesn't need much more examination, but here is one example of what I mean: on a one-page printed report, you usually have enough room for two-, three-, or four-word row and column captions, so it's not hard to be clear about the meaning of each number. Not so on a PowerPoint slide, where every row and every pixel of column width are precious, and you often have to choose between shortening your captions and committing Deadly Sin #17 (that is, the Deadly Sin, mentioned earlier in this chapter, of making your slides unreadable). At the same time, it's critical that the numbers on your slide are laid out and grouped in a way that the report can be instantly understood. So, if we can take a trip down Memory Lane, I'd like remind you that when you are preparing your slides, it may take extra effort to avoid committing:

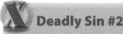

Deadly Sin #2

Basing column width or row height on the **length of the caption**

This is one area where the creative-yet-consistent use of intelligent, unambiguous abbreviations and acronyms can truly come in handy.

Use Slide Titles Appropriately.   Slide titles are the one element everyone in the audience is almost certainly able to see, regardless of the room size. For most of the default PowerPoint slide layouts, Microsoft allocates about 20% of the slide's area to the title alone. Moreover, the default font size for titles is 44 points,[2] compared with between 32 and 20 points for bulleted text (depending on the bullet level). If you stick to the default font sizes, the slide titles represent a great opportunity to drive home a point, so think carefully about whether and how you want to use the slide titles. (As we discussed in Chapter 3, "Words Matter.")

Opinions and practices vary widely when it comes to slide titles. Many presentation coaches are adamant that the title should be the central part of the slide's message; it should be a *sentence* that *tells* the audience what you want them to remember about the slide. Other coaches prefer a more neutral and abbreviated approach. Your choices run the gamut—here are some examples of titles one might consider for the slide we saw in Report 8-1:

Income Statement
VASTCo Q3 '06 Income Statement (this is the one I used)
Q3 '06 Results on Track with Q1 & Q2
We're Headed for a Blowout '06!

These examples show increasing levels of editorializing. The first one, "Income Statement," is a waste of valuable real estate. Any idiot can see that the report shown is an income statement, so the title should at least identify the company and the reporting period, as shown in the second example. The third example is an arguably factual assessment of how VASTCo is doing year-to-date (but a subjective opinion nonetheless), and the fourth example is an outright pep-talk.

The choice of title is more controversial for slides that primarily contain numbers. Some people feel that slide real estate is too scarce to pass up *any* opportunity to send a message. Others argue that, especially when presenting financial statements, it's the numbers themselves that should tell the story, not an author's statement at the top of the slide.[3] In some corporate cultures, directors and senior managers react negatively when they feel like they are being told how they should interpret the numbers, but in other corporate cultures, the opposite preference prevails. Good judgment and an assessment of your organization's culture should influence your approach to slide titles. But regardless of the path you choose, I have these suggestions:

- The more purely descriptive (as opposed to editorializing) your titles are, the more you should strive to minimize the number of words. If the title isn't part of the message content, then don't let it distract from the rest of the slide.

- Be consistent! Don't have a slide title that editorializes when the results are good, and simply describes the contents (e.g., "Income Statement") when they're not. Flip-flopping is amateurish and verges on being dishonest. It will not go unnoticed.

Use Key Indicators.   When time is short, any tactic that helps your audience understand the information more quickly is valuable. We've already discussed the practices of handing out the detailed reports beforehand, and using part of your talking time to teach the audience how to understand the numbers. One additional step you can take to help your audience evaluate the raw numbers is to include some additional metrics *on the slide itself.* I'm referring to key indicators, which we will discuss in detail in Chapter 10.

Consider Report 8-2, which contains the same information as Report 8-1 with some additional numbers (they're shown in *italics* to distinguish them). The additional metrics provide percentages—variances are shown as a % of Budget, and Operating Profit is shown as a % of Total Revenues.[4] Without tearing themselves away from your talk to reach for calculators or do arithmetic in their heads, the audience can now see that relatively small favorable variances (4.2% for Total Revenues and 0.9% for Total Operating Expenses) have led to an Operating Profit that is fully 16.8% better than the corporate plan.

The font sizes in Report 8-2 are basically the same as in Report 8-1, so there is no loss of visibility or readability because of the additional information. But it took a little work: I narrowed some of the columns, reduced the font size of the variance columns ("$$" and "%") to further distinguish them from the raw data columns, and added vertical borders to make it easier to distinguish the quarterly results from the year-to-date results. The 5 or 10 additional minutes I spent on formatting were well worth the effort because the result is improved readability.

VASTCo Q3 '06 Income Statement

(in $000)	Qtr End 9/06 Actual	Budget	F(U) $$	%	Year-to-Date Actual	Budget	F(U) $$	%
Licenses	4,284	4,064	220	5.4%	12,348	11,792	556	4.7%
Prof. Svcs.	1,561	1,530	31	2.0%	4,498	4,321	177	4.1%
Total Revenues	**5,845**	**5,594**	251	**4.5%**	**16,846**	**16,113**	733	**4.5%**
Cost of Sales	760	667	(94)	-14.1%	2,192	1,899	(293)	-15.4%
Gross Profit	**5,084**	**4,927**	157	**3.2%**	**14,654**	**14,214**	440	**3.1%**
Sales & Marketing	1,928	1,915	(13)	-0.7%	5,579	5,517	(61)	-1.1%
Research & Dev.	1,153	1,167	14	1.2%	3,270	3,312	42	1.3%
General & Admin.	805	798	(7)	-0.8%	2,363	2,313	(50)	-2.2%
Total Oprg. Exps	3,887	3,880	(6)	-0.2%	11,212	11,142	(70)	-0.6%
Oprg. Profit	**1,198**	**1,046**	151	**14.4%**	**3,442**	**3,072**	370	**12.1%**
Oprg. Margin	*20.5%*	*18.7%*			*20.4%*	*19.1%*		

10/25/06 10:53 AM   Report 8-2 (based on Report 8-1)

REPORT 8-2 (BASED ON REPORT 8-1):   VASTCo Q3 '06 Income Statement

First, Do No Harm

As we discussed in the previous chapter about graphs, each new release of presentation software includes more tools and features that can make your presentation easier to put together and have more impact. But also remember that these tools and features can occasionally detract from (rather than enhance) your presentations. Here are a few things to watch out for:

- Use great care with animation.
- Don't overuse all those great features!

Use Great Care with Animation. PowerPoint's basic animation features allow each object or bullet point on your slide to appear individually, from any direction, in many ways, with sound effects to boot, and then to disappear in equally exotic ways. And every new release of PowerPoint introduces additional animation capabilities. I've seen some PowerPoint presentations that felt more like a video game, with the presenter furiously clicking the mouse to fend off a bewildering array of attacks from alien fighter spaceships.

At the other end of the glitziness spectrum are those hard-line purists who feel that each entire slide is an integral unit of information, and that every mouse click should introduce a new slide in its entirety. Personally, I prefer a modest amount of animation, to the extent that it fits in with the flow of the presentation.

I'm a big fan of "bullet-level" animation, where each bullet on a word slide appears just as the presenter introduces that point so the audience can't read ahead. Also, for situations where you have a numbers slide that includes a one-sentence takeaway conclusion, it can be very effective to show the quantation *first*, and then bring in the text stating the conclusion. But remember, any time you use animation, it's especially important to be familiar enough with your slides that you speak to them in the same order that the slide elements appear.[5] Let me also state that *consistency* is important: if you're animating, every element of the slide should arrive in the same fashion (to do otherwise is confusing and distracting). And please leave the sound effects to the folks at Warner Bros.

Don't Overuse All Those Great Features! Even more so than Excel, PowerPoint is loaded with easy-to-use features that will make your presentation flashier and more professional. (Please note that those two adjectives don't mean the same thing!) The slide animation effects we just discussed are one example, but there is an infinitude of colors, fonts, and text effects to play with. And you also have the ability to insert artwork, photographs, and even video clips to your heart's content. So yet again, I remind you of:

Deadly Sin #3
Using visual effects for any reason **other than clarifying, distinguishing, or adding meaning** to information.

It's only natural to think of PowerPoint as theater and not just communication, but that just adds to the temptation to overdo things. Remember that your principal goal is to get your audience to understand you, to believe what you're telling them, or even to support you enthusiastically. Anything you do that doesn't directly further those goals may actually be destructive to your overall purpose.

Some Basic Truths That Go Double for Quantation

There are long lists of good habits and practices for making oral presentations, and the number of books on the topic would fill many shelves. I won't reinvent that particular wheel here, but we should discuss a few tips that have special significance where quantation is concerned, even though they also serve as universal truths about effective presentations. They include:

- Be familiar with the material.
- It's your presentation—manage it!
- Use the Stand-Alone Test.

Be Familiar with the Material. A very wise man once told me: "Take the pins out of a shirt before you try it on." That is an example of something so obvious, it's almost embarrassing to offer it as advice, but it is good counsel nevertheless. In that spirit, I offer you the following tip:

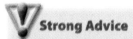

Strong Advice

Before you give an oral presentation, **be familiar with the material**. This advice applies to both the flow of the slides and the information content itself.

This suggestion is particularly relevant to PowerPoint presentations that include numbers, because it is often the case that the tasks of (1) compiling and analyzing the underlying information, (2) creating the presentation slides, and (3) giving the presentation are all performed by different people. In some organizations, the PowerPoint presentations themselves may be created by graphic arts professionals completely uninvolved with either compiling the information or making the presentations; this is especially true in larger organizations that feel strongly about presenting a consistent and unique corporate image. For these reasons, it is not always easy or natural to be familiar with the material.

If your presentation is mostly word slides, you can get the gist of the presentation simply by reading over the slides. This is less true for quantation, where the answers to questions like these don't always jump off the page: Which numbers are the important ones? Which numbers are unusual? What are the trends and patterns? Which trends and patterns are meaningful? As you ponder how to articulate the answers to questions like these, keep this in mind:

The Laws of Quantation

If *you* are the one giving the presentation, then it's *your* presentation. Its conclusions are *your* conclusions. Its quality is a reflection on *you*.

Please don't find yourself unable to answer some of the really picky questions about where your information came from. For example:

- **Accounting reports.** Are the numbers preliminary or final? Audited or unaudited?

- **Forecasts.** How long ago was the forecast prepared? This morning? Seven weeks ago? Who generated the forecast? Sales? Marketing? Finance?

- **Headcount.** Is the headcount from a report generated from the HR system or is it an estimate? Does the number reflect the total number of individuals or the "full-time equivalents"? In addition to permanent, full-time employees, does the number include part-timers? Temps? Contractors?

It's very possible that the answers to these questions will have no material impact on the audience's understanding of the numbers, or on the main points of the presentation. But *not knowing* the answers plants the seeds of doubt in the minds of your audience and can have an impact on your own credibility.

It's Your Presentation—Manage It! You may find yourself presenting to a large audience, or to people who are senior to you in your organization, or both. In those situations, getting your main messages across is critical. Consider it within your rights to politely but firmly keep your presentation on track to achieve that objective. This is true regardless of the type of presentation you're giving, but with respect to numbers presentations, recall from Chapter 4:

The Laws of Quantation

Bolten's Law of Discretionary Disclosure: If you present a number, your audience will ask about it.

Because you can't really control what parts of your quantation will provoke questions, you must be willing to refocus your audience on the relevant points if need be.

In the event that you find yourself being asked to give a 30-minute presentation in 10 minutes, do whatever you can to focus on the main messages: remove some slides, redo the presentation, negotiate, whine, enlist the support of powerful people to restore the original 30 minutes. But if quantation is involved, *never* say "No problem—I'll just talk faster." With word slides, you *might* be able to shorten sentences, or skip adjectives and definite and indefinite articles. But this will not work with numbers.

Use the Stand-Alone Test. Presentation coaches say one of the best things about oral presentations is that when a single message is delivered simultaneously in two different ways—both spoken and visually—the simultaneous effect of both is immensely powerful, and the impact is more than just the sum of the two individual methods.[6] Even so, when presenting numbers, it's important that the visual part of the presentation is intelligible and meaningful on its own. Words on a slide are likely to mean what they seem to mean. By contrast, *numbers* on a slide need to be carefully thought out and organized to ensure audience comprehension, so I offer this test as a useful tactic when your presentation contains a significant amount of quantation:

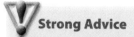

Strong Advice

The Stand-Alone Test: Does your presentation stand on its own two feet as a meaningful document? Is it comprehensible, and do the issues you consider most important stand out most prominently, even without your voiceover?

If your slides pass this test, then you can be confident that they will help you get your message across and do their part in supporting your talk.

To run this test you will need to enlist an assistant to review your slides. Ideally, the assistant should be a person not intimately familiar with the content of the presentation but *capable* of understanding it. Have this assistant go off alone and read the materials, and then come back and give you the gist of the presentation. If the assistant's gist matches up well with the messages you are planning to deliver, then your slides have passed the Stand-Alone Test.

The Stand-Alone Test has additional importance if your presentation slides are going to be handed out in hardcopy for the audience to keep after the meeting. This is especially true if your audience consists of customers or others outside your enterprise, because they're not likely to be able to seek you out afterward for clarification. Pay particular attention to your slide *headings* and whether they are doing the job they're supposed to; the headings are the elements your audience is most likely to notice when reviewing the slides later, and remember long afterward.

Woody Allen's comment at the beginning of this chapter is, of course, much more about speed-reading than it is about *War and Peace*. But it makes an apt comment here, because an oral presentation is very much the business equivalent of speed-reading. You, the presenter, take a large amount of data and condense it into some meaningful chunks of information. Your audience listens to your words, looks at your slides, and tries to get an understanding of what you are telling them, often taking away only the gist of what you've shown them or a few salient points to remember.

To further complicate things, oral presentations with a significant amount of quantation pose unique challenges to how you organize and present your information on PowerPoint slides, how you conduct yourself as a presenter, how you prepare for the presentation, and how you manage the presentation flow when giving the presentation.

(continued)

The principal limitation of PowerPoint presentations is simply the physical limitation of the medium, or how little space you have on one slide. It takes extra thought and effort to construct quantation that's still understandable and meaningful in spite of these space limitations. And not only is there limited space, but in most oral presentations the audience has only a minute or two to process the information on each slide. For these reasons, we discussed tactics to use before, during, and after your presentation to ensure that your audience is getting the most meaning from your presentation. And just like Excel and its graphing functions, PowerPoint offers an amazing number of features to spice up your presentation. It's important to use those features to your advantage, and not overuse them to the point where they actually detract from your audience's ability to get meaning from your presentation.

Finally, as in any communication medium, oral presentations are most effective when you conduct yourself appropriately and professionally when transmitting the information. For presentations that include a lot of quantation, it's especially critical that you have—and demonstrate—a strong grasp of the underlying subject matter, even if you weren't the one who developed the presentation in the first place. And while it may be daunting to take firm control of the presentation flow in the face of a very large or a very senior audience, managing your presentation well is one of the keys to a successful presentation.

Delivering a successful numbers presentation is a complex undertaking, requiring practice and skills far beyond what we've discussed in this chapter. But when done effectively it can be the most powerful and memorable form of business communication. If you can master the craft of quantation in your PowerPoint presentations, not only will you get the results you're looking for, but it will be an enormously positive reflection on you personally.

NOTES

1. Here is some arithmetic: The aspect ratio (i.e., the ratio of the width to the height) for PowerPoint slides is typically 4:3, basically the same as traditional computer screens and non-HD television images. So, for example, a slide presented on a screen 4 feet wide will be 3 feet high. Now, the "8H rule" states that the maximum viewing distance should not exceed 8 times the height of the screen, so viewers should not have to view our example 4'×3' screen from a distance of more than 24 feet. Moreover, the general rule of thumb is that the 8H rule works only for type that is at least one-fiftieth the height of the screen, which is roughly 11-point text on a PowerPoint slide. *And even then, the one-fiftieth standard will hold only for high-quality images.* Since the odds are good that some of your audience are sitting farther away from the screen than 8 times the image height, or some in your audience have imperfect eyesight, or your computer screen's image is not particularly high-resolution, or you're using a lightweight, low-powered projector, or the table on which the projector sits is a little wobbly, or one of many other conditions affecting projected image quality is present, using a font size smaller than 18–22 points is very risky. To support this point, I note that PowerPoint's default font sizes are 32 points for first-level bullets, stepping down to 20 points for fourth- and fifth-level bullets.

2. For titles that are too long to fit on a single line, Microsoft's default drops the font size to 40 points, so that two lines of text can still fit in the space allocated for the title; 40-point

type is still easy to read from a long way off, and it's hard to say much in a single line of 44-point type.

3. At a board meeting about a month after stepping into my first CFO position, I rose to the defense of my CEO, who was asserting that some report numbers were actually better than they looked. Afterward, an avuncular board member took me aside to admonish me that the CFO's job was to present the results factually and honestly, and the job of others to spin those numbers. These lessons—that numbers sometimes have to stand on their own, and that the CFO has a dual reporting relationship, both to the CEO and to the board of directors—have always stuck with me.

4. Recall from Chapter 3 that a useful convention when discussing profitability is to refer to the dollar amounts as *profit* and use *margin* when describing profitability as a percentage of revenue.

5. If you have multiple levels of bullets, PowerPoint allows you to select "first-level bullets," so that with each mouse click, a major bullet and all its sub-bullets appear together. This makes the animation effects less continuous and therefore less distracting, and your voiceover doesn't need to be as carefully synchronized with each bullet.

6. The presentation coaches will also tell you that to achieve this effect, the two messages must be slightly different in form, and not identical to each other. The impact of two *identical* messages given simultaneously is *less* than the sum of its parts. This is why, when giving an oral presentation, you should never simply read off the words or the numbers appearing on the slides. Not only is this a lame presentation style, it's cognitively ineffective.

Wrap-Up for Part II: The Tools

This chapter concludes Part II, which is a slight digression from the main ideas of *Painting with Numbers*: (1) that there are *rules* about how to put your numbers on the page, and (2) that how you treat your audience when presenting numbers is critical to getting your messages across. But this is an important digression. Any time you practice any craft, it's important to be familiar with the tools of that craft.

With quantation, knowing how to use the tools is critical for doing your work quickly and efficiently, since quantation is a craft all too often practiced under time pressure. Moreover, knowledgeable, careful, and imaginative use of the tools will add immeasurably to the effectiveness of your work. With these two objectives in mind, the subjects and the main themes of the chapters in Part II were:

- **Instant Payoff Tips for spreadsheets** (Chapter 5)—tips that will help you get your work done faster and more efficiently *every* time you sit down to create a spreadsheet

- **Long-Term Payoff Tips for spreadsheets** (Chapter 6)—Tips that will make your life (and the lives of those who use or inherit your spreadsheets) easier when you return to your original work weeks or months later

- **Graphs** (Chapter 7)—the right and the wrong reasons to use graphs instead of tables, and how to ensure that your quantation is clear and meaningful when you do choose to use graphs

- **Oral presentations and PowerPoint** (Chapter 8)—why presenting numbers in a presentation can be fundamentally different from other types of quantation, the strengths and limitations of PowerPoint, and how to use PowerPoint to maximum advantage

We now return to our regularly scheduled programming. "Part III: Real Mastery" will go back to the notion of understanding the craft itself, as opposed to using the tools needed to practice that craft.

To give you some context for where we are heading, "Part I: The Rules" focused on two levels of mastery: first, learning the principles of how to put numbers on the page (or the monitor, or the projection screen), and second, presenting quantation in a way that shows both understanding of and respect for an audience's needs and how they process information. Part III focuses on the third, and usually most difficult, level of mastery: understanding your own organization and its business practices as deeply as those who have line management responsibilities, so that your quantation is genuinely relevant and useful.

PART III

REAL MASTERY

PART III

REAL MASTERY

CHAPTER 9

It's Clear, But Is It Meaningful?

Price, quality, turnaround time . . . pick any two.

—Sign posted in many a print shop's scheduling department

Up to this point in *Painting with Numbers*, we've focused only on presenting *understandable* numbers: how to put them on the page and to deliver them in a way that your audience can grasp and appreciate them. Clarity in your quantation is important, but clarity alone is only half the job. To make your quantation *valuable and meaningful* to your audience, you need to have a sense of what decisions the people in your audience are facing, what problems they are facing, how they think about these decisions and problems, and your own ultimate goals in preparing your report(s).

Making your reports meaningful is vitally important to fulfilling your duty as a quantation professional. To accomplish this, you need to understand your organization and its mission deeply enough so that your understanding corresponds to the depth of your audience's understanding. You must also recognize that delivering good quantation is rarely a get-it-right-the-first-time endeavor. It is always an iterative process.

The War of the Adjectives

When you are preparing a report (or a whole reporting package), there are several adjectives you naturally would like to be true about what you prepare. You want it to be:

- Complete
- Accurate (or precise)
- Useful

Unfortunately, *all three of these adjectives are in conflict with each other.* All three of these adjectives are impossible to satisfy all at once. Here are just a few of the ways in which this battle plays out:

- **Your *data collection* time is limited.** You can choose to spend your available time collecting as much data as possible (*complete*), or making sure the data that you do collect are right (*accurate*).

- **Your *total* time is limited.** You can choose to spend your time ensuring the quality of the underlying data (*complete* and/or *accurate*), or on designing clear, effective reports to meet the needs of your specific audience (*useful*).

- **Your *audience's* time is limited.** You can focus your reporting package on telling them everything they need to know (*complete*), or on ensuring there will be no question about their confidence in the information (*accurate*), or on making it easy to quickly extract and understand the key points you are trying to make (*useful*).

- **Your audience is human, and so are their brains.** Your audience can *remember* only a finite number of data points from the information you are putting in front of them, so if you put *a lot* of data in front of them (*complete*), you can't have perfect control over *which* data they remember (*useful*).

- **Memory is a funny thing.** It's easier for the reader to remember a number rounded to the nearest million dollars (*useful*) than that same number shown to the nearest penny (*accurate*).

- **Perception is a funny thing.** Even though it's easier to remember a number rounded to the nearest million dollars (*useful*), people may associate careful work with a number shown to the nearest penny (*accurate*) and sloppy work with a number rounded to the nearest million dollars (and therefore neither *useful* nor *accurate*).

Striking the right balance between *complete, accurate,* and *useful* is tough. Indeed, negotiating between these three adjectives is the main reason that *designing a great reporting package is hard work.* If you don't think carefully about the balance between complete, accurate, and useful for your particular audience, your audience might not get what they need to get out of your reports, and then all your work collecting and presenting your information may be for naught.

At the same time, the *right* balance can cover a multitude of sins. Even if your package is more of a work-in-progress than you had hoped, if the design shows your audience that you are clearly thinking about their quantation needs in the way *they* would like you to, your audience may be surprisingly tolerant, and may also give you useful feedback for the next time you deliver the package.

Be sure to pay attention to this feedback, as it will help you figure out how to make good choices in the future.

A Quantation Professional

Like many skills, quantation is hard to master. It takes training, effort, perspective, a deep understanding of your organization's mission, a grasp of how and why your information is critical to that mission, and a certain amount of enjoyment of the craft itself. In addition to *acting like* a quantation professional, you must also *see yourself* as a quantation professional. And seeing yourself as a quantation professional, you must develop an understanding of your audience's business so you can respond to the issues and problems they are facing.

 **Strong Advice**

You may sometimes find it appropriate to *tell* your audience what reports they need. This can be a great way to start a dialogue that leads to meaningful and valuable quantation for that particular audience. This approach will work because you are the quantation expert with a clear sense of how to generate meaningful reports. But it will work only if you understand the business well enough to apply that skill properly, and the people you work with believe in your abilities.

This means that you should do some of the following things on a regular basis (if you don't already):

- Read your organization's annual report, strategic planning documents, and high-level marketing literature.
- Attend staff meetings (at least periodically) and planning sessions for the parts of your organization whose quantation you are responsible for.
- Have the occasional lunch or hallway conversation with people in your audience to learn more about their jobs and their perspective.

Seeing yourself as a professional and acting accordingly means you are less likely to deliver a reporting package and then find yourself saying:

 Deadly Sin #14

"Oh, is *that* what you wanted? We have all that information—all you had to do was ask."

When you say things like this, you are suggesting that *your audience* understands your job better than you do. You are also suggesting that you don't understand the jobs of your audience well enough to make sound decisions about what their quantation should look like. Worst of all, you are suggesting that your role is a passive one, waiting for information requests and acting only when you get a request. This Deadly Sin is not the kind of comment that a professional makes to his or her peers—at least not the kind of professional who wants to be afforded a modicum of respect.

Relating to Your Audience in a Constructive Way

Being a professional and relating to your audience *as* a professional involves some finer points that warrant discussion here. Suppose someone in your audience (a "commenter") offers a suggestion or criticism about one of your reports. Even if the comment is a surprise, resist the urge to commit:

Deadly Sin #15

"Gee, no one has ever had a problem with this report before."

At first glance, this response may appear to be a factual statement about your experience with audience feedback concerning this report, but put yourself in the place of the commenter and others within earshot, and consider what they might be hearing as subtext:

- "If there were a problem, someone would have pointed that out earlier."
- "I don't understand the business well enough to understand why you made that comment or suggestion."
- "To me, all audiences are the same. I see no reason to think different readers of this information have different needs."
- "You simply haven't put enough time and effort into studying my excellent report."
- "How dare you question my work?"

Leaving aside the unspoken messages you might be sending, here are all the reasons why you might have the perception that nobody has ever taken issue with your report:

- No one has ever bothered to look at your report. *Hence, you have received no comments.*
- Those who *have* looked at your report couldn't understand it but didn't bother to speak up. *Hence, you have received no comments.*

- People *have* commented on the report before, but you just don't remember, or you weren't in the room when the comments were made, or the comments were made to someone else (like your boss). *Hence, you have received no comments that you can recall.*

- Your quantation is perfect. *Hence, no intelligent person has needed to comment, and the commenter's critique is dead wrong.* This is possible, but highly unlikely.

There is a strong possibility that you are a victim of Corollary #3 to Bolten's Law,[1] namely that the harsher the conclusions your audience is forming, the less likely you are to be aware of them, and ignorance is never bliss in this case.

Put another way, audience silence is not quantation nirvana. I encourage you to get used to another dynamic: *the better the quantation you deliver, the more comments and suggestions you're likely to get.* This observation may seem counterintuitive, but it's accurate for two reasons:

1. The better your reports are, *the more likely it is that your audience will read them.* The more likely they are to read them, the more likely they are to think about the content. And the more likely they are to think about the content, the more likely they are to identify new information and changes to the existing reports they'd like to see. This is not a bad thing.

2. *There is no such thing as perfect quantation.* That's especially true when your reports are describing a dynamic and ever-changing environment, and your audience is diverse, with different people looking for different things from the same reports. Audiences also usually understand this, and therefore your professional image is more closely tied to how quickly and constructively you respond to feedback than it is to the quality of the quantation you deliver in the first place.

Let me leave you with this thought:

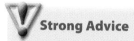

Strong Advice

Audience feedback about your reports is beneficial. Especially *before* you first deliver your reports, and after the first few times you deliver them, listen to any feedback and respond constructively. **A total absence of feedback is rarely a good sign.** Feedback ensures that you are on track with what your particular audience finds meaningful and valuable.

Good quantation is a process, not an event.

This chapter introduced "Part III: Real Mastery." In Part III, we take a step back from the basic techniques and skills of quantation and start to focus instead on what you need to do to make your information *meaningful* to your audience. In this chapter, we discussed:

- The **war of the adjectives.** When presenting numbers, you can focus your time and effort on making your quantation *complete*, *accurate* (or *precise*), or *useful*. All of these characteristics are wonderful, but they are often in fundamental conflict with each other. The right mix depends on your quantation objectives and your audience's needs, so choose wisely.

- **Quantation is a professional skill**, requiring a level of knowledge, experience, and perspective similar to the level of professional skill required of your audience members for their functional areas.

- **Responding to audience feedback constructively** and actively seeking feedback are essential to effective quantation. You should view the absence of feedback as a bad sign.

The remaining chapters of Part III of *Painting with Numbers* will discuss real-world quantation situations. As I've said before, this is not a cookbook. There are no spreadsheet templates in this book because I *can't* give you templates—I don't know enough about your organization and your various audiences to give you templates that will be meaningful often enough. Still, there are some additional topics that are important to understand once you've mastered the basics of quantation and are ready to hone your skills. With this is mind, we will cover:

- **Chapter 10, "53 . . . Uh, Is That a Lot?"**—how to use key indicators (that is, ratios and other metrics derived from the raw numbers in your reports) to give your audience a quicker, clearer sense of the main messages in your quantation

- **Chapter 11, "The One Report *Every* Organization Needs"**—how to design (and present) one particular management report called the "Natural P&L," which happens to be the one report that every organization is certain to need [**Note:** This chapter is where we do a very deep dive into a report's content, examining the layout of the rows, the appropriate column formats, and the business logic underlying the quantation choices.]

- **Chapter 12, "The Gaps in GAAP"**—a brief discussion of generally accepted accounting principles (GAAP) and some GAAP-related issues, with an eye toward how those issues relate to the subject of quantation in general, and why it's so critical to understand and reconcile the differences between GAAP financial statements and all the rest of the quantation that your organization depends on

- **Chapter 13, "Quantation: It's Not Just for Business Anymore"**—quantation applied to information about U.S. federal income taxes, to illustrate how effective quantation can help us understand public policy issues that are important to all of us

- **Chapter 14, "Quantation in Ordinary Life"**—a variety of examples of how quantation techniques can be applied to presenting numerical information in areas other than the ones we usually think of.

I encourage you to consider how the examples and discussion in all of these chapters relate to your specific situation. Remember that the goal of *Painting with Numbers* is to teach you to paint on your own. The goal is *not* to teach you to copy the work of others, but to be an artist in your own right.

NOTE

1. See Chapter 4 for the original exposition of this corollary, and Chapter 8 for its general form.

CHAPTER 10

53 . . . Uh, Is That a Lot?

*. . . so I buy things for $1.00 and then I sell them for $3.00, and
I'm fine as long as that 2% return keeps rolling in.*

—Punchline of an old joke about a very successful but innumerate busi-
nessman explaining the secret of his financial success

Numbers by themselves don't tell us very much. For example, #403 may have
been the number of your dorm room in college, and the 14th might have
been the day that you met your spouse, but aside from triggering memories
or connoting value, numbers by themselves aren't packed with meaning. To
understand the importance of a number, we need a context for understanding
it. We need something to compare it to. With respect to your quantation, this
means that your audience won't understand the significance of the numbers in
your reports unless they have other numbers for comparison. (We talked about
this in Chapter 4 as well.)

Your quantation paints a picture and tells a story about your organization.
But even if you have all the right numbers laid out in an easy-to-read manner,
you may need to boil things down even further and help your audience understand the meaning of the story (or at least make it extremely obvious). This is
where *key indicators* (KIs) come in.

All organizations run on key indicators, whether it's a business trying to
turn a profit, a hospital evaluating different medical treatments, a government
agency deliberating over whether to fund schools or better roads, or a baseball
team deciding who should bat in the leadoff position. All these organizations
need to make intelligent decisions about *effectiveness*, and key indicators allow
organizations to make their decisions with deeper insight as to what is happening inside the organization.

Key indicators are a critical ingredient of effective quantation, but to use key indicators properly, you need to consider the following:

- **What is a key indicator?** How do you construct a KI?
- **What makes a *good* key indicator?** What are the characteristics of the KIs that add real value to your audience's understanding of your information?
- **How do you present key indicators effectively?** Where do they belong on the page, and how can you use visual effects to integrate KIs with your basic information?

What Is a Key Indicator?

A key indicator is almost always a *ratio*, pure and simple. A ratio, of course, is one number divided by another number. A ratio is calculated by taking a *numerator* (or, as the theoretical mathematicians call it, "the thing at the top"), and dividing it by a denominator ("the thing at the bottom"). The KI's value is the numerator divided by the denominator.

Key indicators can be presented as a numbers or percentages. But independent of how KIs are presented, these ratios keep your audience from getting confused by the *scale* of the underlying numbers. For example, if VASTCo's profits are "only" half those of its main competitor, is that bad? Well, that depends on how large or small the competitor's revenues are. If there are 20 million people in the United States without health insurance (not the real number), is that bad? Well, 20 million is definitely a *lot* of people, but it's "only" about 6% of a nation with 320 million people.

Ratios also help your audience develop a perspective *over time* when the underlying numbers continue to change. For example, If VASTCo's profits for a year are 15% more than the year before, is that good? How does that compare to profit gains over the past few years? How does the figure of 20 million uninsured Americans compare to the number of uninsured people 30 years ago (when the U.S. population was just over 200 million)?

Every business runs on key indicators, and KIs are valuable in many other walks of life as well. Here are several categories of KI examples:

Business

Key Indicator	Numerator	Denominator
Growth Rate[1]	Change from the base period	Base period value
Profit Margin	Profits	Revenues
Sales Performance	Revenues	Number of employees
Budget Variance %	Actual sales	Sales quota

Not-for-Profit Institution

Key Indicator	Numerator	Denominator
Fundraising success	Funds actually raised	Fundraising goal
Fundraising efficiency	Expense of fundraising effort	Total expenses[2]
Institutional efficiency	"Achievement" metric (i.e., children vaccinated, pets rescued, trees planted, etc.)	Total expenses

High School District

Key Indicator	Numerator	Denominator
Cost per pupil	District operating costs	Number of pupils
Graduation rate	Number of graduates	Number of students who entered high school in that class
College success	Students accepted to at least one college	Students in the senior class
Administrative efficiency	Administrative expenses (cost of district HQ plus school administrators)	Total district expenses

U.S. Government

Key Indicator	Numerator	Denominator
Surplus (deficit) relative to GDP	U.S. government surplus(deficit)	Gross domestic product (GDP)
Spending growth	Change in spending versus base year	Base year spending
Income distribution	Taxable income of top 1% (or 5%, or 10%, etc.) of taxpayers	Total taxable income of U.S. taxpayers
Tax distribution[3]	Taxes paid by top 1% (or 5%, or 10%, etc.) of taxpayers	Total taxes paid by U.S. taxpayers

Baseball

Key Indicator	Numerator	Denominator
Won/lost %	Games won	Total games played
Batting average	Base hits	Official at-bats
Earned-run average	Earned runs allowed	"Complete games" pitched (i.e., total innings ÷ 9)

While key indicators are usually ratios, they don't *have* to be ratios. People might quibble over calling some of the items below "key indicators," but I assert that a KI can be any number calculated from the raw numbers that is used to help people understand those numbers. Here are some examples of key indicators that are not ratios:

Other Key Indicators:

Key Indicator	Explanation
Trend projections	Trend projections are estimates of future results calculated by applying a mathematical model to historical results. Examples include curve fitting, regression analysis, and exponential smoothing.
Compound annual growth rate (CAGR)	CAGR is one type of historical average growth rate. The calculation is more complex than simply dividing a numerator by a denominator, because the growth rate is calculated using the same mathematics used with financial instruments bearing compound interest.
Exotic indexes	Exotic indexes are special-purpose metrics that often involve extensive data gathering and mathematical algorithms known only to the provider. A good example of this is the Consumer Confidence Index published by the Conference Board. This index is widely used and relied on, but do *you* know how it's calculated?
Even more exotic calculations, like "seasonally adjusted" numbers	Seasonally adjusted statistics are manipulated (and I mean that in the most neutral sense of the word) so that period-over-period comparisons make sense. For example, in Europe, where many workers take vacation for an entire month in July or August, economic output statistics may need to be adjusted so that the distinction is clear between outputs that are lower because of employee vacations, and outputs that are higher or lower because of changing economic conditions.[4]

All of these non-ratio key indicators can be extremely valid for their intended purposes; however, ordinary humans rarely understand the underlying mathematics. Therefore, these types of key indicators have credibility and meaning only to (1) experts in the field and (2) non-experts who trust the information provider implicitly and without question. Unless your audience fits into one (or preferably both) of these categories, I would be careful when using these types of KIs.

Finally, note that you can even have key indicators on key indicators. For example, if you want to track whether employee productivity is improving, you would want to look at the *growth rate* of *employee productivity*, which you would calculate as the change in productivity from the base period to the current period, divided by the base period productivity.

Whether you are using ratios or specialized calculations, key indicators can help you understand your organization better and manage it better. There is no limit to the number of KIs that could be meaningful to your organization; the real skill is in selecting the KIs that truly shed light on your specific situation.

What Makes a *Good* Key Indicator?

There is a nearly infinite variety of possible key indicators you could include in your reports, so you need to think about which ones are really worth presenting to your audience. But first, it's important to establish some terminology. All of the numbers on your report are either "report numbers" or KIs. Report numbers are comprised of "raw numbers" and "calculated numbers." Here is an explanation of each:

Report Numbers

Number Type	Explanation
Raw numbers	Raw numbers come unmodified from somewhere else, such as your accounting system, the budget (which might be an actual "system," or maybe just another spreadsheet someone else is maintaining), the sales forecasting system, the human resources system, or even just your best guess.
Calculated numbers	Calculated numbers are calculated within your spreadsheet from the raw numbers. Typical calculated numbers are the subtotals and totals of the rows and columns (e.g., Total Revenue, Total Expenses, Operating Income) .

Now that you're familiar the with distinctions between key indicators and report numbers, let's dive into a deeper understanding of KIs.

Recall that the purpose of key indicators is to make the information you're presenting more understandable and more meaningful. But the information you're presenting won't be understandable and meaningful unless the KIs *themselves* are understandable and meaningful. For this to happen, your audience needs to:

- Know how the key indicator was **calculated**.
- Understand the key indicator **intuitively**.

Knowing How the Key Indicator Was Calculated.   Remember, it's really simple: a key indicator is calculated from a *numerator* and a *denominator*. Most likely, you are considering adding a KI to a report that is already showing at least one of the two components of the KI, either the numerator or the denominator. In fact, the first lesson in presenting key indicators is that *both the numerator and the denominator must be visible on the page.* Why do I say this?

- **Audience comfort.** It is *comforting* for the audience to know the origin of *every* number in the report. For the raw numbers, it should be clear that they came from a properly maintained system (like the accounting system) and not just from the presenter's estimates and modeling assumptions. The audience should be able to easily figure out how the calculated numbers were derived. And since a KI results from a calculation, *this means enabling the audience to see both the numerator and the denominator.*

- **Provoking valuable discussion.** Full disclosure encourages intelligent and useful conversation. Everyone may agree that "productivity" is an important key indicator for the organization to track. But what's the right numerator? Total revenues? Product revenues? Or just revenues from new customers? How about the denominator? Total employees? Full-time equivalent headcount? Should the headcount include only permanent employees, or contractors and temps as well? If both the numerator and the denominator are clearly identifiable, you can be sure that the right choice for each will be fully discussed.

- **The audience sing-along.** Every audience has a few people (and they're often the most astute ones) who take out a calculator just to make sure they understand where the calculated numbers and key indicators came from. Basically, they're dialing the "audience comfort" factor up a notch. But don't throw up your hands and groan; these folks might help you catch an inadvertent mistake in a spreadsheet formula, so show some respect!

Understanding the Key Indicator Intuitively.   With a key indicator, what you're really trying to do is create an *aha!* moment. The perfect KI delivers the same message that a whole lot of numbers might also deliver, but with much less reader time and effort and lower demands on reader experience and skill in reviewing quantation. To achieve this effect, however, the choice of the KI has to make intuitive sense to the reader. Put another way, a good key indicator is the mathematical expression of a well-phrased English question. Consider these widely used KIs:

- **Productivity.** In most organizations, the single largest expense is employee costs (compensation, benefits, office costs, etc.), so it's critical to get the most out of every one of those expensive employees. "Productivity" KIs, in all their variations, are asking, "How much revenue are we getting from an average employee?"

- **Budget variance %.** Dollar variances are important, but they don't necessarily tell you where your biggest management issues are. A 2% overrun on salaries may be a larger total dollar amount than a 100% overrun on tradeshow expenses, but from a budget management standpoint, the tradeshow issue may be more pertinent. Percentage budget variances are asking, "Which line item results show the biggest differences from what we were expecting, in proportion to our expectations?"

A Simple Example

With all this in mind, Report 10-1 is a simple example of a report presenting key indicators. You've seen the report numbers in this exhibit several times before.

Report 10-1						
VASTCo -- 1998-2003 Financial Highlights						
($ in 000)	**1998**	**1999**	**2000**	**2001**	**2002**	**2003**
Revenues	699	950	1,493	2,138	2,910	4,733
Expenses	662	800	1,207	1,639	2,348	3,343
Oprg. Profit	37	150	286	499	562	1,390
Oprg. Margin	5.3%	15.8%	19.1%	23.3%	19.3%	29.4%
Avg. Headcount	8.0	9.2	12.0	15.7	18.9	26.0
Revenues/Avg. HC	87.4	103.3	124.4	136.2	154.0	182.0
Oprg. Exps./Avg. HC	82.8	87.0	100.6	104.4	124.2	128.6

REPORT 10-1: VASTCo 1998–2003 Financial Highlights

Does this report meet the criteria for good key indicators? Let's double-check: (1) every report number needed to calculate each of the KIs is present on the page, and (2) since the notion of *productivity* is well-understood by most people as some notion of output or effort per person, you can assume the concepts of Revenues per Employee (Avg. HC) and Expenses per Employee (Avg. HC) will be intuitively clear to most readers.[5] So, the answer is *yes*.

The rest of this chapter will focus on the placement and visual appearance of KIs, but *always* start with (1) an approach that ensures that your audience can see exactly how the KIs were calculated, and (2) KIs that will make sense to your audience. If you don't, you will simply face the time-sapping wrath of Bolten's Law.

How Do You Present Key Indicators Effectively?

Where do key indicators go on the page? There's really no right or wrong answer, but intelligent placement does help the readability and comprehensibility of your report. The principal rule to keep in mind is that KIs should always appear *after* the numerator and the denominator so that readers can see all the report numbers needed to calculate a KI *before* they see the KI itself. So, if the numerator and the denominator are in the same column, the KI should appear somewhere below both of them in that same column. If they both are in the same row, the KI should appear to their right.

Reports 10-2 and 10-3 are two examples of how to present KIs that involve adding *rows* to a report.

Report 10-2
VASTCo -- 2004-06 Income Statements

($ in 000)	2004	2005	2006
Licenses	6,797	12,365	16,785
Services	1,660	4,436	6,120
Total Revenues	**8,457**	**16,801**	**22,905**
Cost of Sales	1,210	2,372	2,982
Gross Profit	**7,247**	**14,429**	**19,923**
Sales & Marketing	2,925	5,775	7,568
Research & Dev.	1,733	2,840	4,477
General & Admin.	1,237	2,815	3,191
Total Oprg. Exps.	5,895	11,430	15,236
Operating Profit	**1,352**	**2,999**	**4,687**
Avg. Headcount	80.0	150.0	160.0
Emplye. Productivity	**105.7**	**112.0**	**143.2**
Gross Margin	**85.7%**	**85.9%**	**87.0%**
Operating Margin	**16.0%**	**17.8%**	**20.5%**

Report 10-3
VASTCo -- 2004-06 Income Stmts.

($ in 000, % of Tot. Revs.)	2004	2005	2006
Licenses	6,797	12,365	16,785
	80%	74%	73%
Services	1,660	4,436	6,120
	20%	26%	27%
Total Revenues	**8,457**	**16,801**	**22,905**
	100%	100%	100%
Cost of Sales	1,210	2,372	2,982
	14%	14%	13%
Gross Profit	**7,247**	**14,429**	**19,923**
	86%	86%	87%
Sales & Marketing	2,925	5,775	7,568
	35%	34%	33%
Research & Dev.	1,733	2,840	4,477
	20%	17%	20%
General & Admin.	1,237	2,815	3,191
	15%	17%	14%
Total Oprg. Exps.	5,895	11,430	15,236
	70%	68%	67%
Operating Profit	**1,352**	**2,999**	**4,687**
	16%	18%	20%

REPORT 10-2: VASTCo 2004–2006 Income Statements

REPORT 10-3: VASTCo 2004–2006 Income Statements

In Report 10-2, there are only three key indicators: Employee Productivity, Gross Margin, and Operating Margin. You'll note that they are grouped together at the bottom of the report in boldface so that they're easy to find and review. (Remember, the best place to put the important stuff is around the edges of the report.)

In Report 10-3, there are ten key indicators presented as percentages interspersed throughout the report. Interspersing the KIs throughout the report is a good choice for this particular report, because the reader is likely to use each KI in conjunction with its corresponding report number. Note that the KIs below Total Revenues are included here, even though their value will always be 100%, just to give the reader a clue that every KI is calculated as percentage of Total Revenues.

Let's look at a couple of examples of reports where the key indicators show up as *columns* in the report. In the first example (Report 10-4), we see the same report numbers as we saw in Reports 10-2 and 10-3, but this report shows KIs measuring year-over-year growth. Presenting these key indicators to the *right of* (rather than below) their related report numbers is a natural choice. Think back to our discussion in Chapter 3 of the reader's natural flow, and why the time axis should be presented horizontally across the page rather than vertically down the page.[6] As the reader scans across the page looking at a line item's results over time, he or she can use the KIs for additional perspective on that progression without having to drop down to the next line and then back up.

Report 10-4
VASTCo -- 2004-06 Income Statements

($ in 000)	2004 $$	Y/Y %	2005 $$	Y/Y %	2006 $$	Y/Y %
Licenses	6,797	75%	12,365	82%	16,785	36%
Services	1,660	93%	4,436	167%	6,120	38%
Total Revenues	**8,457**	**79%**	**16,801**	**99%**	**22,905**	**36%**
Cost of Sales	1,210	384%	2,372	96%	2,982	26%
Gross Profit	**7,247**	**62%**	**14,429**	**99%**	**19,923**	**38%**
Sales & Marketing	2,925	95%	5,775	97%	7,568	31%
Research & Dev.	1,733	93%	2,840	64%	4,477	58%
General & Admin.	1,237	79%	2,815	128%	3,191	13%
Total Oprg. Exps.	5,895	91%	11,430	94%	15,236	33%
Operating Profit	**1,352**	**-3%**	**2,999**	**122%**	**4,687**	**56%**

REPORT 10-4:   VASTCo 2004–2006 Income Statements

Report 10-5 is another example presenting key indicators to the right of related report numbers. You've seen these report numbers a couple of times now, but I've added a KI here for % Variance.

Report 10-5
VASTCo -- 2006 Income Statement, Actuals thru Q3 & Outlook for the Year

($ in 000)	Year-to-Date thru Q3		Var. F(U)			Outlook for Full Year		Var. F(U)	
	YTD Tot.	Budget	$$	%	Q4	06 TOT.	Budget	$$	%
Licenses	**12,348**	11,792	556	4.7%	4,500	**16,848**	16,000	848	5.3%
Services	**4,498**	4,321	177	4.1%	1,620	**6,118**	5,940	178	3.0%
Total Revenues	16,846	16,113	733	4.5%	6,120	22,966	21,940	1,026	4.7%
Cost of Sales	**2,192**	1,899	(293)	-15.4%	765	**2,957**	2,600	(357)	-13.7%
Gross Profit	14,654	14,214	440	3.1%	5,355	20,009	19,340	669	3.5%
Sales & Marketing	**5,579**	5,517	(61)	-1.1%	2,019	**7,598**	7,510	(88)	-1.2%
Research & Dev.	**3,270**	3,312	42	1.3%	1,191	**4,461**	4,542	81	1.8%
General & Admin.	**2,363**	2,313	(50)	-2.2%	825	**3,188**	3,138	(50)	-1.6%
Total Oprg. Exps.	**11,212**	11,142	(70)	-0.6%	4,035	**15,247**	15,190	(57)	-0.4%
Operating Profit	**3,442**	3,072	370	12.1%	1,320	**4,762**	4,150	612	14.8%

REPORT 10-5:   VASTCo 2006 Income Statement, Actuals through Q3 and Outlook for the Year

The choice to include this key indicator was informed by the report itself. Budget variances are worthy of attention because they are *either* large in terms of total dollars, or large in terms of the percentage difference from the budgeted amount. Putting the "$$" and the "%" variances side by side helps the reader look for both possible reasons for concern at the same time.

Please note these additional points about this report:

- **There are no underscores in the % Variance columns,** because those columns should not be summed. Put another way, the % Variance of a subtotal or total number (like Total Revenues) is *not* the sum of the % Variance numbers of the line items rolling up to that total.[7] This is a common spreadsheet formula error usually caused by just copying formulas or formats from one column to another. Be careful.
- **Negative percentages are denoted by a minus sign rather than parentheses.** This is Excel's default approach, perhaps because it takes up less space than parentheses and a % sign together (e.g., –45% vs. (45%)).

There is a delicate balance between adding enough key indicators to make the report numbers meaningful and cluttering up your report. Still, there are times when the KIs are sufficiently useful that it's worth really pulling out the stops to highlight and emphasize them. To do this, you can always use the visual effects we discussed in Chapter 3. Report 10-6 is an example of a report in which each report number has *two* KIs: percentage of revenues, and Y/Y% growth.

Report 10-6
VASTCo -- 2004-06 Income Statements

($ in 000)	2004	Y/Y %	2005	Y/Y %	2006	Y/Y %
Licenses	6,797	75%	12,365	82%	16,785	36%
	80%		74%		73%	
Services	1,660	93%	4,436	167%	6,120	38%
	20%		26%		27%	
Total Revenues	**8,457**	79%	**16,801**	99%	**22,905**	36%
	100%		100%		100%	
Cost of Sales	1,210	384%	2,372	96%	2,982	26%
	14%		14%		13%	
Gross Profit	**7,247**	62%	**14,429**	99%	**19,923**	38%
	86%		86%		87%	
Sales & Marketing	2,925	95%	5,775	97%	7,568	31%
	35%		34%		33%	
Research & Dev.	1,733	93%	2,840	64%	4,477	58%
	20%		17%		20%	
General & Admin.	1,237	79%	2,815	128%	3,191	13%
	15%		17%		14%	
Total Oprg. Exps.	5,895	91%	11,430	94%	15,236	33%
	70%		68%		67%	
Operating Profit	**1,352**	-3%	**2,999**	122%	**4,687**	56%
	16%		18%		20%	

REPORT 10-6: VASTCo 2004–2006 Income Statements

Can you see the presentation choices in this report? Here's a list of quantation objectives and the choices in Report 10-6 that support those objectives:

- **Natural reading flow.** When we consider year-over-year changes, we look at the report number for one year and then move rightward to see the next year's number, so the key indicators for Y/Y% change are immediately to the right of each report number. The KIs for % of Total Revenues present each line item as a percentage of that year's revenues, so those KIs appear in the same *column* as the raw numbers from which they're derived.

- **Easy-to-find information:**
  - The report numbers are in a normal font size, and the key indicators are in a *smaller font size and in italics.* The reader can find the report numbers easily, but still spot the KIs. Also, to make the year easier to find, the "Y/Y%" column caption is set slightly lower than the year caption.
  - White space and cell borders have been used to make it easy for the reader to associate each key indicator with its respective report number. Note that adding two sets of KIs triples the number of numbers in this report, so it is important to use white space to avoid the "Where's Waldo?" effect.

- **Clear information.** Report numbers that are boldfaced have boldfaced key indicators.

Let's not forget to get help from our friend, the *word*. One of the most useful reading aids you can provide your audience is a one-page cheat-sheet briefly listing all the key indicators in the reporting package, along with how each KI is calculated and how the reader might interpret different values of that KI. This cheat-sheet can go a long way toward helping your audience make sense of complex information. Report 10-7 is an example based on Report 6-2 (although I'm not showing the cheat-sheet on a separate page here).

Report 10-7
VASTCo -- 2004-06 Income Statements

($ in 000)	2004	2005	2006
Licenses	6,797	12,365	16,785
Services	1,660	4,436	6,120
Total Revenues	**8,457**	**16,801**	**22,905**
Cost of Sales	1,210	2,372	2,982
Gross Profit	**7,247**	**14,429**	**19,923**
Sales & Marketing	2,925	5,775	7,568
Research & Dev.	1,733	2,840	4,477
General & Admin.	1,237	2,815	3,191
Total Oprg. Exps.	5,895	11,430	15,236
Operating Profit	**1,352**	**2,999**	**4,687**
Avg. Headcount	80.0	150.0	160.0
Employee Productivity	**105.7**	**112.0**	**143.2**
Gross Margin	**85.7%**	**85.9%**	**87.0%**
Operating Margin	**16.0%**	**17.8%**	**20.5%**

Key Indicators:

Employee Productivity = Total Revenues (for period) ÷ Average Hdcnt (during period)

Gross Margin = Gross Profit ÷ Total Revenues

Operating Margin = Operating Profit ÷ Total Revenues

REPORT 10-7:   VASTCo 2004–2006 Income Statements

Some of the distinctions I've drawn in this section of the chapter are subtle. But I want to stress two points I've made before:

1. ***Everything* has meaning.** All of your presentation decisions—columns versus rows, visual effects, what gets underscored, your choice of key indicators—send signals about the meaning of your information and what you want your audience to focus on. Remember:

The Laws of Quantation

Your audience is entitled to presume that **every number in a report is meaningful**, and if data are omitted, it's because they are less meaningful.

2. **You have choices.** The wide range of reasonable choices you have at your disposal can help you put your own personal stamp on your quantation and show your audience the depth of your understanding of the subject matter. This is especially true with key indicators.

A Note on Precision

The precision of your key indicators (that is, how many digits you present) is also a choice you need to make. (And if you don't make a choice, Excel will do it for you—sometimes with strange-looking results.) The best guideline I can give you about precision is to base your choices first on how your quantation will be used by your audience. Within that broad guideline, here are some factors you'll want to consider:

- **The precision of the underlying report numbers.** If you've ever heard the saying, "Measured with a micrometer, marked with a pencil, and cut with an axe," you understand that there's no point in presenting key indicators with more significant digits than the number of significant digits being presented for the numerator or the denominator.[8] Please note that "significant digits" does not mean the same thing as "decimal places." For example, in Report 10-7, Employee Productivity has four significant digits (143.2 is the number for 2006). Average Headcount (160.0) also has four significant digits because the tenths digit is significant even if it's zero. Total Revenues (22,905), however, has five significant digits even though it has no decimal places and the last three digits are truncated.

- **What the key indicators are being used for.** In high-volume, low-margin businesses (like grocery store chains), margin differences of hundredths of a percent may be extremely important. In the enterprise software industry, that kind of precision may have no value whatsoever. Think about whether the number of decimal places you are choosing will be useful to your audience.

- **The variability of the key indicators and of the underlying report numbers.** Sometimes you might want to consider adding an additional digit of precision to a KI that doesn't fluctuate much. If, for example, profit margins have hardly changed for five years, presenting a sequence of 11.0%, 11.1%, 10.8%, 11.2%, and 11.0% may have more credibility than five consecutive "11%" numbers. But again, please remember that you shouldn't under any circumstances present more significant digits in a KI than are justified by the levels of precision of the numerator and denominator.

Note

A digression on compensation plans: When you provide employees with the backup calculations for incentive compensation payouts (which you should *always* do) it is wise to present enough digits so that variations in the digits *not* presented will not affect employee payment by more than a few dollars. A "rounding error" to the employer may be seen as real money to the employee, who certainly wants to feel that the employer isn't being casual about compensation. This is a matter of respect for and sensitivity to your audience.

A Note on Dashboards

No discussion of key indicators would be complete without at least a passing mention of dashboards, one of the hottest management reporting buzzwords of recent years. A *dashboard* is a brief summary report, often a half-page or less, that combines the most important report numbers, plus key indicators. This chapter's first exhibit, Report 10-1, is a good example.

Report 10-1
VASTCo -- 1998-2003 Financial Highlights

($ in 000)	1998	1999	2000	2001	2002	2003
Revenues	699	950	1,493	2,138	2,910	4,733
Expenses	662	800	1,207	1,639	2,348	3,343
Oprg. Profit	37	150	286	499	562	1,390
Oprg. Margin	5.3%	15.8%	19.1%	23.3%	19.3%	29.4%
Avg. Headcount	8.0	9.2	12.0	15.7	18.9	26.0
Revenues/Avg. HC	87.4	103.3	124.4	136.2	154.0	182.0
Oprg. Exps./Avg. HC	82.8	87.0	100.6	104.4	124.2	128.6

REPORT 10-1:   VASTCo 1998–2003 Financial Highlights

Dashboards are a great idea, in principle. They are, after all, a reflection of several central premises that I've already emphasized:

- Key indicators are immensely valuable.

- Important information can get lost if it is buried in the middle of too many numbers.

- Different audiences need different information, different audiences may look for different main points from the same information, and different audiences may use data differently.

- The ideal report fits on one page, or even just a fraction of a page.

So, if dashboards are such a great idea, why did I follow it with a passive-aggressive phrase like "in principle"? And why am I expressing concern about dashboards *in this book*? Let's start with a little background: dashboards have become popular recently, as business software vendors have touted the ability of each individual user to get a summarized and customized view of the information critical to him or her. The ability to generate reports like this has been made easier because of business software applications now residing "in the cloud." Previously, generating numerous individualized, customized reports was extremely difficult to do because complex, proprietary, and customized software applications were under the internal control of finance and IT departments. In this new world of application software, I have two concerns about dashboard proliferation:

- **Addressing the symptom and not the disease.** Much of the demand for dashboards comes from line managers frustrated by the inadequacies of the organization's standard reports. Those inadequacies are in turn the result of these complex internal business systems under the control of employees to whom effective quantation does not come naturally.

- **The "Tower of Babel" effect.** One of the principal benefits of effective quantation is to create a "common language" throughout the organization so that everyone can have a thorough understanding of the organization's main objectives and a general understanding of every department's main objectives. The risk posed by proliferating dashboards is that each user instead identifies his or her own important numbers and designs his or her own KIs. (See Chapter 11 for a lengthier discussion of the value of creating a common language and ways to help create one.)

If these concerns are not addressed, the organization with dueling dashboards will be no better off than it was before. On the other hand, dashboards can be immensely effective if they are a central, coherent, and integrated part of the organization's overall quantation strategy.[9]

Key indicators are an essential part of how every organization makes decisions, and therefore, they are an essential element of effective quantation. Here is a recap of the main points regarding KIs:

- A key indicator is almost always a *ratio* of two numbers.

- Your audience needs to understand where a key indicator comes from. This means that:
  - Your audience needs to understand the methodology underlying the calculation.
  - Any report with a KI should include both the numerator and the denominator used to calculate it.
  - Both the numerator and the denominator should appear before the KI in the reader's normal reading flow.

- Key indicators need to make *intuitive* sense to your audience.

- Where you place key indicators on the page and how you treat them visually depend on several factors, including:
  - How many KIs you're presenting
  - How important the KIs are relative to the "report numbers"
  - How the KIs should fit into the reader's natural reading flow

Knowing how to use key indicators properly will distinguish you as a skilled quantation professional. KIs enable you to connect with your audience by giving them a synthesized, summarized view of the numbers. And offering them the *right* KIs demonstrates that you understand your audience as well as the enterprise of which you are all a part. Moreover, providing KIs is an *act of kindness and team play*, because you are giving your audience information that they would otherwise have to generate on their own.

What makes people successful in business (or in any other enterprise) is the ability to set clear, understandable goals, measure progress against those goals, and stay focused on the end results. There is considerable lore and legend about the successful but hard-driving and cold-hearted executive who "manages strictly by the numbers," as if being numbers-focused goes hand-in hand with being uncaring and inhumane. This is nonsense, of course, since a need for objective measurement of one's surroundings and a great concern for fellow humans are completely unrelated traits. Knowing the numbers always comes in handy, just as being aware of *any* important details is smart and useful. But staying focused on *goals* is what's truly important, and in quantation, this means understanding *key indicators*.

NOTES

1. Recall from Chapter 1 that the change from one period to another is always the amount for the later period (e.g., 2004) minus the amount for the base period (e.g., 2003), so that increases over time are positive numbers and decreases are negative. And when calculating growth *rates* (i.e., % changes), the denominator is always the base period amount. For example, if sales grew from $60 in the base period to $100 in the following period, the change is $40 ($100 minus $60) and the growth rate is 67% ($40 divided by $60). If you used the later period amount as the denominator, you would get 40% ($40 divided by $100). As you can see, the difference can be large, so please don't make this fairly common logical mistake.

    Another note on the arithmetic: You can save an arithmetic step by calculating the ratio as the later period value divided by the base period value, and then subtracting 1 (or 100%). For example, in the calculation earlier in this footnote, you could calculate the growth rate as

    $$\$100/\$60 - 1 = 1.67 - 1 = 0.67 \text{ (or 67\%)}$$

    Both approaches yield the same number.

2. As with many of the possible numerators and denominators on this list, there is plenty of discretion here. For example, "Total expenses" could mean exactly that (the *total* expenses incurred by the organization for everything it does, including fundraising) or it could mean operating expenses, which would exclude expenses for fundraising and other activities not directly related to the institution's stated goals.

3. Comparing "income distribution" to "tax distribution" is an interesting study and would give people a fairly clear idea of whether the top earners are paying their "fair share" of taxes. Equally interesting would be how the comparison changes over time. Suppose, for example, the share of taxes paid by the top 5% has gone up by 12% over the past five years (this is a fictitious example). Is that good? Well, it depends on whether their share of *income* has gone up by that much!

4. Of course, economists are fond of saying, "Seasonally adjusted, the Great Lakes never freeze."

5. A few other points to note about this exhibit: (a) The note in the upper left is "($ in 000)"; previous exhibits had "(in $000)." This is to communicate that only the dollar amounts in this report are presented in thousands (not the Average Headcount figure). (b) The headcount number presented is the *average* during the year, because that's a more appropriate denominator for the KI than the headcount at any single point in time (like the beginning or ending date for the period). If you don't have an easy way to determine the running average headcount throughout the period, using the average of the beginning and ending headcounts will usually be fine. And since that average might not be an integer, it's appropriate to present it out to one decimal place. (c) I have chosen to present the per-employee KI results to one decimal place (that is, to the nearest $100). This is a judgment call on my part, which I made because the per-headcount KIs are an order of magnitude smaller than the total dollar numbers at the top of this report (which do not have any decimal places).

6. Please note that I've violated my own rule—that a report must present both the numerator and the denominator needed for each KI—for the 2004 Y/Y% numbers. To avoid violating my rule, I would have had to choose between (a) including the "report numbers" for 2003 (which perhaps were not of interest to the audience) and (b) simply not presenting the Y/Y% numbers for 2004. I chose the best alternative.

7. Recall the "digression" in Chapter 2 about the mathematical meaning of an underscore. However, if you do want to play along to understand this point intuitively, note that the Variance % of a *total* is the *average* of the component Variance % numbers, *weighted*

by the relative size of each component's Budget amount. Feel free to try this with a calculator!

8. Most likely, in your accounting system all of your numbers are precise down to the nearest penny. For example, your accounting system might show revenues of $3,712,605.44 and operating profit of $575,312.89. But if your report presents revenues and operating profit of 3,713 and 575 (both in $000), *do not* present an operating margin of 15.496203%; 15.5% (or perhaps even 15%) will almost certainly suffice, and all those extra digits will distract the reader from the important digits.

   Moreover (and I hope I am not alarming the accounting "true believers"), recall from Chapter 1 that *precision* and *accuracy* are not the same thing. In large organizations, every significant accounting number is the result of dozens or even thousands of judgment calls and estimates. It all evens out over time, but in the short run, presenting accounting information down to the last penny and asserting that presentation is "more accurate" is just absurd.

9. Much of the recent buzz about dashboards has been focused on those composed primarily of charts and graphs as opposed to tables. The visual impression of an array of graphic objects like dials is no doubt where the term *dashboard* comes from. However, my comments apply equally to dashboards that present information graphically or in tables.

CHAPTER 11

The One Report *Every* Organization Needs

When you ask a question, a CFO tries to answer the question he thinks you asked. A controller tells you what he does for a living.

—An anonymous wise, but blunt, person, when asked to explain the difference between a chief financial officer and a controller

"The balance sheet"—this is the response you'll get if you ask a group of accountants and auditors to choose the most important financial statement of any organization. And they have a point. The balance sheet is certainly an important report. It tells you the financial condition of an enterprise *right now*, as well as the state of its assets and liabilities, and who actually owns it. The balance sheet tells you whether the organization is solvent, and it affirms the financial condition of the enterprise *as of a specific date*.

The balance sheet is certainly important, but to most people involved with managing an enterprise, the main use of financial statements is to help them understand how the organization is *performing*, not just to provide a snapshot of how it *is* or *was* at a single moment. After all, management is about *doing*, not about *being*. Reports that describe this flow of revenues and expenses over a period of time are called *income statements*,[1] and because these reports are so widely important, we'll devote a whole chapter to designing a specific type of income statement. But before we dive into the design of this report, please understand that there are many flavors of income (or *P&L*) statements:[2]

Name of Report(s)	Focus	Description of the Report's Line Items
Functional P&L	**Who** is responsible	Line items identify roles played within the organization, such as "Sales & Marketing" or "Research & Development." Frequently, each line item reflects the span of management control of a single manager. (Most of the VASTCo reports shown so far in this book are this type of report.)
Geographic P&L **Product Line P&L** **Line of Business P&L**	**Where** responsibility lies	Line items identify geographical areas, products, major lines of business, or other "slices" through the organization.
Natural P&L **Management P&L** (these terms are used interchangeably)	**What** is generating revenue and **what kinds** of expenses are being incurred	Line items identify specific *categories* of revenues or expenses in the way that we are naturally inclined to organize them.[3] For example, revenue categories (for a software company) might include Licenses, Maintenance (or Technical Support), and Professional Services (consulting, training, etc.). Expense categories might include Salaries, Benefits, Travel & Entertainment, and Office Costs.

The focus of this chapter is the Natural P&L—the *what* report. I consider it the single most important and widely useful report for an organization because:

- **It's decision-focused.** Any of the above reports will give you a sense of where things are going well and where there are problems, but only the Natural P&L provides insight into what might specifically be *causing* the problems.

- **It's usable across the entire enterprise.** A well-designed Natural P&L can be used throughout the organization. If every entity within the organization receives and uses the same basic report design at all management and functional levels, then everyone will use the terminology in that report in the same way. This means that when, say, a sales manager has a conversation about "office costs" with the assistant controller, there will be no confusion or misunderstanding.

These points will be addressed in depth in this chapter. As this chapter's title asserts, the Natural P&L is the one report format that's critical to *every* organization, whether it's a business, a not-for-profit organization, a government entity, an academic institution—you name it. If you can design a report that works for your organization, it will be a demonstration that you truly have a deep understanding of the underlying business model and the critical issues it faces. Still, designing such a report—one that can be used *throughout* the organization, and one that can play a key role in how the organization is *managed*—is easier said than done, so I'm devoting an entire chapter to the principles that underlie that design.

A Sample Natural P&L, and What Makes It a Good One

Let's start with an example of a Natural P&L for VASTCo. I want to stress that VASTCo is a software company, and so a well-designed Natural P&L for a company in a different line of business will look very different. And even for a software company, there are other equally effective ways to design such a report. Remember that we are *not* in the template business here. However, the same design principles (which will be enumerated shortly) will always apply.

Consider Report 11-1, the report for VASTCo's Worldwide Sales organization,[4] and focus on the choice of *categories*—that is, the captions down the left side of the report.

Report 11-1
VASTCo Worldwide Sales & Marketing -- 2006 Q3 Natural P&L

(in $000)	Quarter Ended 9/06			Year-to-Date		
	Actual	Budget	F(U)	Actual	Budget	F(U)
REVENUES						
Licenses	4,284	4,064	220	12,348	11,792	556
Maintenance	905	857	49	2,564	2,377	187
Consulting & Training	655	673	(18)	1,934	1,945	(10)
Total Revenues	**5,845**	**5,594**	**251**	**16,846**	**16,113**	**733**
Cost of Sales	760	667	(94)	2,192	1,899	(293)
Gross Profit	**5,084**	**4,927**	**157**	**14,654**	**14,214**	**440**
OPERATING EXPENSES						
Salaries	598	632	34	1,752	1,821	69
Commissions	422	383	(39)	1,194	1,103	(90)
Bonuses	19	19	(0)	61	55	(6)
Benefits	123	115	(9)	363	331	(32)
Contractors/Temps	77	77	(1)	223	221	(2)
Office Costs	150	153	3	430	441	12
Travel & Entertainment	179	172	(7)	446	497	50
Professional Services	62	57	(4)	201	166	(35)
Marketing Programs	222	230	8	703	662	(41)
Recruitment & Relocation	42	38	(4)	100	110	10
Other	33	38	6	106	110	4
Total Operating Exps.	**1,928**	**1,915**	**(13)**	**5,579**	**5,517**	**(61)**
Operating Profit	**3,156**	**3,011**	**144**	**9,076**	**8,697**	**379**

REPORT 11-1:   VASTCo Worldwide Sales: 2006 Q3 Natural P&L

Report 11-1 is a Natural P&L. To understand it better, let's look at eight characteristics that make it useful. It has:

1. One page!
2. Decision-focused line items
3. Appropriate dollar amounts, neither too big nor too small
4. Intuitive organization of the line items
5. Understandable categories, meaningful to all users
6. Plain-English terminology
7. Consistent look-and-feel
8. Key results equal to the corresponding numbers in the accounting system (or an explanation why not)

Let's discuss each of these eight characteristics in more detail.

1. One Page!

Recall from Chapter 2 that you can fit up to about 30 lines in a report with landscape orientation (about 45 lines for portrait orientation, but I usually prefer landscape). Report 11-1 has 21 lines, so if you add just a couple of additional lines and a few key indicators (see Chapter 10), you'll be getting pretty close to that physical limit. In a typical moderately large enterprise, the chart of accounts[5] in the accounting system will have between 100 and 200 separate accounts. If this is the case for your organization, it's clear that in order to map each of these accounts onto one of the lines in your Natural P&L, you'll need to make some thoughtful choices.

I have heard many reasons why some particular Natural P&L just *had* to use more than one page, but I have yet to hear a *good* reason. And we've come too far together to start shrinking fonts or taping pieces of paper together *now* (see Deadly Sin #9, Chapter 4). As I've said before, if you can't fit your report onto one page, the problem is almost certainly with your report design.

2. Decision-Focused Line Items

Let's face it: the principal reason (some would say the only reason) for management reporting is *to help managers make better decisions*. Good management reporting has to organize information in a way that clearly identifies problems or issues and perhaps even suggests a course of action. Suppose, for example, you are a sales manager whose department's revenues are behind plan and a senior manager or corporate director asks you what you plan to do about it. "Generate more revenues" is not going to be a career-enhancing response, because it doesn't suggest any understanding of the underlying problem, or thoughts about the *specific* actions you're considering to address that problem. A well-designed report, where each line item has a different set of *driving factors* influencing success or failure, can really help here. Understanding which factors need management attention is a critical first step toward fixing your problems.

Revenues. As a first example of how a well-designed Natural P&L can help suggest solutions, let's consider the categories rolling up to Revenues in Report 11-1, and some of the drivers that might influence results in those categories for a typical software company:

Line Item	Driving Factors
Licenses	• New customers signed up • Enterprise-wide adoption of products already sold to existing customers • License pricing • Discounting and other sales management practices
Maintenance	• Annual maintenance renewal rates • Maintenance pricing
Consulting & Training	• Size of "installed base" (i.e., cumulative license sales) • Services pricing • Rate at which customers identify new applications for existing products • Relationships with third-party service providers

If revenues are lagging (or exploding) in any of these categories, any one of the factors driving revenues for that particular category might explain the results. For example, if Licenses and Consulting & Training were on track but the Maintenance results were lagging, a manager could focus his attention on the two factors driving that revenue category. He or she might ask, "Are there product and support issues causing more customers to cancel their annual maintenance services? Are pricing practices different from what was planned?"

With this kind of information in a straightforward, easy-to-read report, a manager responsible for the category can zero-in on decisions relevant to the problem at hand. But if all the manager knew was that "Revenues" differed from expectations, he or she would have no clue about the correct action. In other words, designing the Natural P&L involves a balancing act between reports that are concise and simple enough that the audience can easily understand them, and reports that provide enough detail so that single line items will suggest a limited and fairly specific set of actions.

Compensation Expenses. You have the same opportunity to provide reports suggesting management actions when it comes to expenses. Let's take a similar look at the first four categories under "Operating Expenses" (i.e., the ones that we normally think of as falling into the general category of compensation-related expenses). The driving factors include:

Line Item	Driving Factors
Salaries	• Total headcount • Merit and promotional raise practices • Turnover (to the extent that it means replacing employees either more or less highly compensated)
Commissions	• Structure of commission plans • "Override" plans for people indirectly related to the sales process (e.g., sales management, pre-sales support, customer services, marketing, channels) • Distribution of results across the sales force (i.e., where there are disparities in compensation levels, or where "accelerated" plans provide for even higher commission rates for overachievers)
Bonuses	• How widespread bonus plans are across the entire employee base • Target bonus amounts • Corporate results that the bonuses may be linked to • How strict or lenient managers are about scoring bonuses (where the plans have subjective elements)
Benefits	• Tax rates • How carefully vacation time is tracked and recorded • Enterprise policies and practices regarding health-care coverage, vacations, retirement plans, and morale-building activities

The dollar amounts are often large—it's not unusual for a software company to see as much as 70% of its expenses fall into these four categories. This is yet another reason why grouping them all into a single "Compensation" category is a terrible idea. First, as you can see above, variances in each of these four expense categories suggest a completely different set of actions. Moreover, the *people* responsible for the actions differ widely: line managers can have a significant influence over the salaries in their organizations; commissions in many enterprises are set by senior sales management working closely with finance; Bonuses are typically the purview of senior management working closely with the compensation committee of the board of directors; and benefits are often based on company-wide policies driven by the human resources department.

 Note

Blame and responsibility are *not* the same thing. It's useful to provide management reports designed so as to separate revenue and expense categories that can be affected by management decisions from those that can't. If possible, design your Natural P&L so that each category line item primarily consists of either expenses that are controllable by the manager or ones that aren't, rather than a mixture of the two.

Miscellaneous Thoughts on Decision-Focused Line Items. Here are some other examples of category distinctions you will want to consider:

- **Commissions versus Bonuses.** The first inclination of many people might be to lump the two together on the grounds that both are types of variable incentive compensation. But commissions and bonuses are not the same. Commissions are tied to revenue production, and bonuses are driven by enterprise, departmental, or individual performance. These two types of incentive compensation are usually determined and administered by very different decision processes and by different people in the organization. In many organizations, both involve significant dollar amounts and are therefore worthy of their own line items. It's good practice to keep these two lines separate.

- **Contractors/Temps versus Professional Services**. Note that I have chosen to present both of these lines, even though both reflect compensation to people who are not employees. In this reporting scheme, payments to people retained to do work that would normally be done by employees, like temporaries hired to do the work of employees on vacation or leave of absence (or work needed because the employee has transferred or left, or the job search is taking longer than expected) are coded to an account rolling up to Contractors/Temps. Payments for work *not* typically done by employees, like audit and tax preparation, outside legal fees, and management consulting services, are coded to an account rolling up to Professional Services. This distinction requires more than one account for recording outside professional services and therefore some coding judgment by the accounting department, but it's a distinction I recommend making, because the results in these two line items often have significantly different management implications. (See Report 11-2 for more discussion of this point.)

- **Recruitment & Relocation.** Note that this item is near the bottom of the list of categories and is not presented near the compensation-related items. This is because I don't consider Recruitment & Relocation to be an expense directly related to headcount. It's an expense driven by the number of employees you *hire*, not by the number of employees you *have*. From a management perspective, the distinction is important; if an organization has employee turnover, it may incur significant Recruitment & Relocation expenses. In this way, a well-designed report can highlight the expense of unexpected or unwanted turnover.

Decision-focused line items are what make a well-designed Natural P&L useful in its broadest sense. If your report includes the proper line items, management will know where problems are and will have the appropriate clues for fixing them.

3. Appropriate Dollar Amounts, Neither Too Big Nor Too Small

To understand what I mean by *appropriate* in terms of dollar amounts, let's turn to the culinary arts. When chefs are creating a dish with multiple major ingredients, they are taught to cut each of those ingredients into pieces of roughly comparable size, even if the ingredients differ in texture or consistency. This is because the resulting dish will be more pleasing to the eye and easier to eat, and all of the ingredients will cook more evenly (if the dish is cooked). Now, some might say it's a little risky to use the word *cooking* in a discussion of financial statements, but I'm trying to make a point here: *the same principle applies to the design of the Natural P&L.* If you're mapping the results from possibly 100 or more accounts in your accounting system into a dozen-or-so lines on your Natural P&L, you will have lots of choices, and you'll want to slice it into pieces that are *juuuust* the right size.

For numbers that are really small, the decision is obvious: In a one-page summary report for a multimillion-dollar enterprise, is it important to present a line item that routinely amounts to only a few hundred dollars? Probably not—why would your audience care? Moreover, presenting extraneous, unimportant numbers distracts your audience's attention from the larger, more important numbers. And don't forget Bolten's Law of Discretionary Disclosure (see Chapter 4), which observes that you can't control what your audience will focus on. If there's anything worse than giving unnecessary information to your audience, it's having to discuss it with them.

But the opposite situation—one line item dwarfing the other numbers—can also be a problem. Although this obviously can be true only for one single line item in your report, when the "Snow White and the Seven Dwarfs" effect occurs, you may find that one number is so large compared to all the other lines in the report that the audience just doesn't bother to focus on anything else in the report. For most enterprises, by far the single largest expense line will be Salaries, which can sometimes run to 50% or more of total expenses. You can't do much about that, but don't compound the problem by lumping Salaries together with Bonus, Commissions, Benefits, and Contractors/Temps to create a single humongous "Compensation" category.

Here are a couple of observations about why this goal of balance is admirable but it's not always easy for your Natural P&L reports to achieve:

- One of the great things about the Natural P&L is that a single report design can be used companywide, across all function areas, and from the overall corporation down to the individual department. However, it's inevitable that some of the line items you present won't be relevant in the reports for some of the entities within the organization. For example, the expenses included in the Marketing Programs category (e.g., advertising, public relations, trade shows, collateral material) are frequently incurred only by the departments with marketing responsibilities, and frequently it's only sales departments that will incur Commission expense.

- The "Other" category is there for completeness, that is, to make sure there is a place to include every expense, including those that shouldn't reasonably be included in the more precisely named categories.[6] Ideally, numbers in the "Other" category should routinely be very small. After all, you rarely hear a manager say, "Our 'Other' expenses are out of control."

The point to keep in mind is that each of the Natural P&L line items you create (other than "Other") should be material to the *overall enterprise*.

4. Intuitive Organization of the Line Items

Of the eight characteristics listed here, this one might be the subtlest, but understanding this principle is critical to delivering reports that are coherent and understandable—especially to those in your audience who work in functional areas other than accounting and finance. After all, how often in *Painting with Numbers* have we observed that the *little things* can make a big difference in how easy it is for your audience to understand your quantation? As we discussed in Chapter 3, when it comes to the words that are part of your quantation, not only is it important to get them *right*, but often it's important to put them in the *right order*. When you're designing the Natural P&L, you have wide discretion about the layout of the information on the page—you're not bound by the formalities of generally accepted accounting principles (GAAP) or any other rules. Take advantage of this freedom!

For the organization of the line items in the Natural P&L shown in Report 11-1, I've chosen the following ordering logic:

1. **Revenues** are at the top, a convention used in almost every type of income statement. Within Revenues:
   - The "License" category comes first. This category is first not just because it's the largest of the revenue categories, but because selling licenses is the core activity of virtually every software vendor. It's what VASTCo does for a living.
   - The other Revenues categories follow, because they are activities in support of generating and supporting those license revenues.
2. **Cost of Sales** categories are immediately below revenues. These are expenses incurred solely because a license was sold or a service was rendered. So far, the line-item organization I've described is conventional for most types of income statements. But note that because the Cost of Sales categories are adjacent to the Revenues categories, we are able to present

the difference as Gross Profit (a figure that is meaningful to many types of enterprises), before we get to the Operating Expenses.

3. **Operating Expenses** categories are next. These are expenses that are driven by the general operations of the enterprise and (at least in the short run) are not affected by the amount of revenues generated. Within Operating Expenses:

   - From top to bottom, the categories are arranged in order of how directly they tend to vary with headcount.

   - The "Salaries" category is at the top. Not only is it the expense most directly correlated with headcount, but like Licenses it's almost certain to be the largest item in its group. Recall that, if possible, you should put the largest numbers where they're the easiest to find, and that's typically around the edges (top, bottom, left, or right).

   - As we move toward the bottom of the report, we get to expense categories that tend to have no correlation with headcount, like Professional Services (outside lawyers, audit & tax, consultants, etc.) and Marketing Programs. The Other category, which ideally should have the smallest numbers, brings up the rear.

The advantage to this ordering logic is that it makes intuitive sense and, as a result, readers can easily find and home in on the line items of greatest interest to them. All of the expenses directly related to paying people are at the top, and the categories that are less directly related and generally less classifiable are at the bottom. Also note the use of white space, indented captions, and text effects to further visually organize the information.

Another advantage to a thoughtful organization of the line items is that you can use the layout itself to generate additional information useful to management. To understand what I mean by this, consider Report 11-2. It's identical to Report 11-1, except that I've added two subtotal lines (which I've circled in red): Total Compensation Expense and Total People Expenses. The expenses totals are progressive, so that People Expenses equals Compensation Expense plus Contractors/Temps plus Travel & Entertainment plus Office Costs, and Operating Expenses equals People Expenses plus the remaining four categories.

Think of Compensation Expense as the portion of VASTCo's expenses paid directly to employees (or on behalf of them, when you include Benefits). And People Expenses are the costs VASTCo incurs *because they have employees*: not only do they have to be compensated (Compensation Expense), but they need to be replaced when they go on vacation or change jobs unexpectedly (Contractors/Temps), they have to be housed and equipped (Office Costs), and they may have to leave the office to perform some of their responsibilities (Travel & Entertainment). It's not hard to see that understanding these expense groupings can play a role in some very significant management decisions.[7] It also brings additional focus to

Report 11-2
VASTCo Worldwide Sales & Marketing -- 2006 Q3 Natural P&L

	Quarter Ended 9/06			Year-to-Date		
(in $000)	Actual	Budget	F(U)	Actual	Budget	F(U)
REVENUES						
Licenses	4,284	4,064	220	12,348	11,792	556
Maintenance	905	857	49	2,564	2,377	187
Consulting & Training	655	673	(18)	1,934	1,945	(10)
Total Revenues	**5,845**	**5,594**	**251**	**16,846**	**16,113**	**733**
Cost of Sales	760	667	(94)	2,192	1,899	(293)
Gross Profit	**5,084**	**4,927**	**157**	**14,654**	**14,214**	**440**
OPERATING EXPENSES						
Salaries	598	632	34	1,752	1,821	69
Commissions	422	383	(39)	1,194	1,103	(90)
Bonuses	19	19	(0)	61	55	(6)
Benefits	123	115	(9)	363	331	(32)
Total Comp. Expense	**1,163**	**1,149**	**(14)**	**3,369**	**3,310**	**(59)**
Contractors/Temps	77	77	(1)	223	221	(2)
Office Costs	150	153	3	430	441	12
Travel & Entertainment	179	172	(7)	446	497	50
Total People Expense	**1,570**	**1,551**	**(18)**	**4,468**	**4,469**	**1**
Professional Services	62	57	(4)	201	166	(35)
Marketing Programs	222	230	8	703	662	(41)
Recruitment & Relocation	42	38	(4)	100	110	10
Other	33	38	6	106	110	4
Total Operating Exps.	**1,928**	**1,915**	**(13)**	**5,579**	**5,517**	**(61)**
Operating Profit	**3,156**	**3,011**	**144**	**9,076**	**8,697**	**379**

REPORT 11-2:   VASTCo Worldwide Sales: 2006 Q3 Natural P&L

the decision to separate out payments to people who are not employees into payments that roll up to the Contractors/Temps line and payments that roll up to the Professional Services line (see characteristic #2, "Decision-Focused Line Items").

One important guideline you should follow when ordering line items is:

Strong Advice

The ***first* operating expense line** in your Natural P&L should be **Salaries**, regardless of the rest of the layout you choose for your report. The Salaries line should not include any other expenses—not even other compensation-related expenses.

This is a wise choice because, first, salaries will be by far the largest single expense item for most enterprises, so the Salaries line deserves this place of honor (Natural P&L characteristic #3). Second, to keep important line items truly decision focused, you don't want your audience's assessment of the Salaries expense to be clouded by the possibility that other types of expenses (such as incentive compensation and benefits) have been included in the value of this line item (characteristic #2). Salaries are also *intuitively* understandable. Of all the expense categories, Salaries is the one that will come to mind first for most people—and not only is Salaries a big number, it's about the *people* (characteristic #4). Finally, *salaries* is both a word and an expense concept that *everyone* understands (characteristics #5 and #6).

5. Understandable Categories, Meaningful to All Users

You are creating a single report design that will be meaningful to people at all levels and in all functional areas in your organization. Every line item you choose to present should be either directly relevant to your audience's responsibilities or of general relevance to anyone trying to understand your enterprise's activities. Most of the line items shown in Reports 11-1 and 11-2 should be understandable to any reader, like Salaries, Benefits, and Travel & Entertainment. Even though a term like *marketing programs* might not be quite so universally understood, anyone involved in the software industry understands that this general category of expenses is critical to the enterprise's success and represents a material expense worth recognizing in the Natural P&L.

At the same time, the distinction among the expense subcomponents within the "Marketing Programs" category (advertising, public relations, trade shows, collateral materials, etc.) is usually of interest only to people in marketing. To everyone else, they are all simply different approaches to making your enterprise known in the industry and to the general public. For that reason, even if some of them may be of comparable magnitude to some of the other line items in the Natural P&L, any further breakout of Marketing Programs expense into its components is best left to backup reports prepared specifically for marketing staff.

6. Plain-English Terminology

One person's clear terminology is another's incomprehensible jargon. Remember that you are designing a report for everyone with any sort of significant responsibility in the organization, not just the accountants and not just the techies. Whereas most people knowledgeable about the software industry understand that lead generation is the objective of the marketing programs, the term *marketing activities* may be more meaningful than *lead generation* to people less familiar with industry terminology. And although the term *MBO* (management by objective) has become synonymous with *bonus* (e.g., "My MBO was 40% last year."), it's still an acronym. It's imprecise terminology, it's jargon, and not everyone will understand the term. The word *bonuses* is unambiguous.

7. Consistent Look-and-Feel

Consistency is critical to effective quantation. The topic even has its own section in Chapter 4. Taking a consistent approach and creating a consistent look-and-feel are essential to delivering useful and meaningful Natural P&L reports. In addition to the reasons we've discussed in previous chapters, here are some advantages of consistency that are specific to the design of the Natural P&L:

- **You are creating a common language for your enterprise.** A well-designed report will be widely used throughout the organization. If everyone receives and uses the same basic report design, then everyone will use the terminology in that report in the same way. This means that when a sales manager discusses "office costs" with the assistant controller, there should be no confusion or misunderstanding. *Please note that this is an opportunity for your reporting to drive how people use words and terminology, and not the other way around. This can be a very powerful benefit of well-designed reports.*

- **You minimize report generation effort.** In a typical medium-sized enterprise with, say, 1,000 employees, it would not be unusual to generate a total of 100 to 200 Natural P&Ls enterprise-wide in each reporting period. Keeping track of slight differences among this pile of reports can be a huge administrative challenge. You're much better off with the same standard report format for every manager, plus a few standard reports to meet anticipated need for backup detail (such as the detailed report on Marketing Programs discussed earlier), and occasionally having to be responsive to ad-hoc requests for additional detail in specific situations.

8. Key Results Equal to the Corresponding Numbers in the Accounting System (or an Explanation Why Not)

We now come to the final and most technical of the eight characteristics of a well-designed Natural P&L. With respect to the principal numbers in your Natural P&L, either:

1. The numbers must equal the corresponding numbers in your enterprise's accounting system, or
2. You must provide (or at least have available on request) a report reconciling the differences.

This is not a glamorous task, but it is critical not only to the comprehensibility of your quantation, but also to your credibility as a professional. Remember that your Natural P&L reports are an *extract* from your organization's accounting system. To create this extract, numbers in the accounting system roll up to designated lines in the Natural P&L report, as discussed in the next section of this chapter. The mapping of the accounting numbers onto your reports can very easily be incomplete, either by accident or by design.

Unequal by Accident. A company's chart of accounts is a living, breathing document, as is its list of departments, product lines, and other dimensions along which accounting transactions can be coded. As these new accounts or other classifications are created, you may find yourself with a Natural P&L report that doesn't reflect all of the accounting transactions in your system if you don't check back regularly. *So, pay attention!* Not paying attention means that you may publish erroneous information, and the errors may be easy for your audience to detect. For example, in a public traded company, the Total Revenues or the Operating Profit in the Natural P&L for the entire company could be easily compared to the corresponding numbers in the company's quarterly earnings announcement—a report that is almost certainly generated directly from the accounting system. Recall from Chapter 6:

Deadly Sin #11

Publishing a spreadsheet with a **basic error** that should have been **easy to detect**

The last thing you want is your audience catching mistakes that you should have caught yourself.

Unequal by Design. You may occasionally be dealing with certain types of accounting transactions that will make the Natural P&L harder (rather than easier) for your audience to understand if you include them. One example that comes to my mind is accounting entries to impute compensation expense as stock options are granted.[8] In the world of accounting and finance, reports that produce numbers different from those produced using generally accepted accounting principles (GAAP) are called *pro forma* reports. *Pro forma* reports are sometimes controversial because while the presenters' stated intention is to make the information more meaningful to the audience, the skeptics will assert that the real purpose of the *pro formas* is simply to present financial information in a better light than the GAAP reports do. One way to protect yourself from that sort of suspicion is to provide (or have available on request) a backup report reconciling and explaining the differences between the two reports.

Even if the reports that differ are intended solely for internal management consumption (which is usually the case for the Natural P&L reports), this sort of reconciliation can be extremely useful. First, it is always a bad habit to publish numbers that don't have a firm, objective, verifiable footing. Making sure that you yourself know where these numbers come from is an act of self-preservation. Moreover, some of the people in your audience will be aware of other published reports and will be curious about the differences, and for those people it's best to have an answer ready.

Mapping the Chart of Accounts

As we discussed earlier, the Natural P&L is an excerpt from the information in your organization's accounting system. The chart of accounts (CoA) is a listing of the finest detail you can extract from the accounting system. In a properly designed Natural P&L, every item in the CoA related to income and expenses[9] should have a line in the Natural P&L onto which it should be mapped (or "rolls up to," if we're using accounting department terminology). Report 11-3 is an example of a typical spreadsheet showing the mapping of the CoA onto the line items of a Natural P&L report (the squiggles indicate the omission of many rows of data).

Report 11-3
Chart of Accounts Mapped to Natural P&L Line Items

Chart of Accounts		Natural P&L Lines	
No.	**Description**	**No.**	**Description**
3010	License Fees - Up-front	101	Licenses
3015	License Fees - Monthly	101	Licenses
3110	Software Maintenance Fees	102	Maintenance
3210	Consulting Fees	103	Consulting & Training
3220	Training Fees	103	Consulting & Training
3230	Other Professional Services	103	Consulting & Training
4010	Media and Documentation	201	Cost of Sales
4015	Third-Party License Fees	201	Cost of Sales
5010	Salaries	301	Salaries
5020	Commission Expense	302	Commissions
5030	Bonus Expense	303	Bonuses
5100	Payroll Tax Expense	304	Benefits
5125	Health Insurance	304	Benefits
5640	Entertainment	403	Travel & Entertainment
5710	Advertising - Marketing	502	Marketing Programs
5720	Advertising - Recruitment	503	Recruitment & Relocation
5730	Public Relations	502	Marketing Programs
5810	Bank Fees	504	Other
5820	Dues and Subscriptions	504	Other
5830	Insurance	504	Other
5840	Training	304	Benefits
5850	Relocation Expenses	503	Recruitment & Relocation

REPORT 11-3:   Chart of Accounts Mapped to Natural P&L Line Items

The two left-hand columns list the accounts in the accounting system's CoA. The two right-hand columns show how each account is mapped onto the line items in the Natural P&L shown in Reports 11-1 and 11-2. Please also note the following:

- My own preference is to assign a line number to each row of the natural P&L (e.g., 101 for License revenue, 302 for Commissions) and in a separate reference table store the names of the rows. This makes data entry easier, since you need only input the row numbers in the shaded cells of Report 11-3 (the line names shown in the rightmost column are calculated using one of the Lookup & Reference functions discussed in Chapter 5). This approach also means that if I want to change the description of a line item (e.g., from "Salaries" to "Salary"), I need only make the change to the reference table instead of making sure that the correction is made to every account in the CoA that rolls up to that line item.

- The number ordering of the CoA does not have to match the rows in the Natural P&L. Every company's chart of accounts is different. Its numbering scheme is based on the needs and preferences of that company's accounting staff, and you may change your mind about how the accounts map onto the Natural P&L line items. For example, you might decide that account 5830—Insurance should roll up to Office Costs instead of Other.

- The rows in Report 11-3 can be sorted on any of the four columns. The information can be sorted by either CoA account or Natural P&L line item, and either numerically or alphabetically, depending on the preferences and needs of the user.

You may or may not find this exercise fascinating. But mapping your line items to your CoA need be done only once and then revisited periodically as new accounts are added to the CoA (or as you review your management reporting). Take a positive attitude, and let me leave you with this thought:

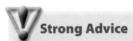

Strong Advice

Regardless of your position and responsibilities, I encourage you to **be familiar with your organization's chart of accounts**. If you are in **accounting or finance**, that familiarity will enable you to design useful reports. It also helps ensure that your organization's accounting system is designed to capture information that management needs, and that your organization records accounting transactions properly and consistently. If you are in **other functional areas**, familiarity with your CoA will help you understand how the accounting system can provide the information you need to do your job. It will enable you to speak the same language as the accounting and finance professionals you work with.

Generate a Natural P&L from a Spreadsheet, or from the Accounting System?

There are two principal ways of generating a Natural P&L report: you can generate the document from within the report-writing capabilities of your accounting system, or you can download the accounting information into a spreadsheet and generate the report using Excel or some other spreadsheet software. To do this, you will need to have some knowledge about using Excel as a database (see Instant Payoff Tip #5 in Chapter 5). In many organizations you will have a choice, with the key considerations including:

Issue	Spreadsheet	Accounting System
Skill Required	Ordinary spreadsheet knowledge (other than download from accounting system).	Knowledge of enterprise's accounting system, and familiarity with system's report-writing capabilities in particular.
Formatting Flexibility	The full formatting capabilities available for any document generated by a spreadsheet.	Depends on power and flexibility of accounting software's report writer module (high-priced accounting systems generally have significantly better report writers).
Use Flexibility	Accounting data and report numbers accessible by any other spreadsheet (e.g., summary reports, planning and budgeting models).	Report can generally be used only as a report, and not used by or linked to other documents.
Control/ Reliability	Additional process is needed to ensure that additional accounting transactions have not been recorded since the download to the spreadsheet.	Reports will always reflect the current state of the accounting system.
Security/ Unauthorized Access	May require additional IT work, if the same level of security is required as is required for accounting system.	Same security and access controls as apply to any user of the accounting system.

Now Let's Talk about the Columns

So far, we've talked only about what should be in the *rows* of a Natural P&L report (i.e., the line items whose names appear along the left side of the report and the content in each of those lines). Well, the *columns* matter as well. Here are some of the choices you can make for the content of each column:

- **Type of number**—actual, plan/budget, or forecast/outlook
- **Time period**—year, quarter, month (or week, day, century, decade, etc.)
- **Key indicators**—growth rate, $ variance, % variance, % of revenues, and so forth

As you ponder these choices, let me offer you some guidelines:

1. **One page!** You went to so much effort to make sure the *rows* of your report fit on one page. Don't let that effort go to waste because you have too many columns.

2. **Different audiences, different needs.** Consider the range of possible audiences for different flavors of the natural P&L. For example, line managers who constantly monitor their organizations' performance will want monthly results. The board of directors, who typically meet only quarterly, may not be interested in monthly results.

3. **Relatively few column layouts.** You can almost certainly meet the information needs of the majority of your audience with just a handful of column formats. Moreover, sticking to a small number of different layouts will help you to achieve "goodness" characteristic #7 (consistent look-and-feel)—the "common language" that is so valuable to your organization. Three to five different layouts should be just fine.

4. **Precision as appropriate**. You can present your results to the nearest penny, or in thousands, or even millions. But don't provide more precision than necessary for each report's particular use. Recall from Chapter 1 that the precision decision is not necessarily just a harmless matter of personal preference: the more digits you inflict on your audience, the harder it is for them to find and recall the important amounts. Moreover, the more digits you present, the harder it may be to fit the report onto one page (see guideline #1 above!).

With these thoughts in mind, here is a set of column formats[10] (see Reports 11-4, 11-5, 11-6, and 11-7) that are sufficient for many organizations (for space reasons, I show only the first row of content).

Report 11-4												
VASTCo Worldwide Sales -- Rolling Monthly Natural P&L (thru Aug 2006)												
(in $000)	Sep-05	Oct-05	Nov-05	Dec-05	Jan-06	Feb-06	Mar-06	Apr-06	May-06	Jun-06	Jul-06	Aug-06	Total
REVENUES												
Licenses	1,382	835	1,072	1,421	987	1,263	1,698	1,029	1,317	1,770	1,071	1,371	**15,215**
↓	↓	↓	↓	↓	↓	↓	↓	↓	↓	↓	↓	↓	↓

REPORT 11-4:   VASTCo Worldwide Sales: Rolling Monthly Natural P&L (through August 2006)[11]

Report 11-5											
VASTCo Worldwide Sales -- Month/QtD/YtD Natural P&L (Aug 2006)											
	Month Aug '06				Quarter-to-Date Aug '06				Year-to-Date Aug '06		
			Var F(U)				Var F(U)				Var F(U)	
(in $000)	Actual	Budget	$$	%	Actual	Budget	F(U)	%	Actual	Budget	$	%
REVENUES												
Licenses	1,842	1,748	95	5%	4,284	4,064	220	5%	**12,348**	**11,792**	556	5%
↓	↓	↓	↓	↓	↓	↓	↓	↓	↓	↓	↓	↓

REPORT 11-5:   VASTCo Worldwide Sales: Month/QtD/YtD Natural P&L (August 2006)

Report 11-6									
VASTCo Worldwide Sales -- Natural P&L, YtD and Full-Year Outlook (Aug 2006)									
	Year-to-Date thru Aug '06					Outlook for Full Year 2006			
			Var. F(U)		RoY	Actual			Var. F(U)	
($ in 000)	Actual	Budget	$$	%	Fcst.	+ Fcst.	Budget	$$	%
REVENUES									
Licenses	**12,348**	11,792	556	4.7%	4,500	**16,848**	16,000	848	5.3%
↓	↓	↓	↓	↓	↓	↓	↓	↓	↓

REPORT 11-6:   VASTCo Worldwide Sales: Natural P&L, YtD, and Full-Year Outlook (August 2006)

Report 11-7 VASTCo Worldwide Sales -- Natural P&L 8-Quarter Outlook (2006 & 2007, as of Aug '06)											
	←——————— 2006 ———————→						←——————— 2007 ———————→				
	Q1	Q2	Q3	Q4	2006	Y/Y	Q1	Q2	Q3	Q4	2007	Y/Y
(in $000)	Actual	Actual	Actual	Fcst.	TOTAL	% Chg.	Budget	Budget	Budget	Budget	TOTAL	% Chg.
REVENUES												
Licenses	3,948	4,116	4,284	4,500	16,848	36.3%	4,532	4,997	5,483	5,992	21,004	24.7%
↓	↓	↓	↓	↓	↓	↓	↓	↓	↓	↓	↓	↓

REPORT 11-7:   VASTCo Worldwide Sales: Natural P&L 8-Quarter Outlook (2006 and 2007, as of August 2006)

Please note that the basic report design (that is, the row captions down the left side of the page) is identical for each of the above reports. Keeping the design consistent will help build a common language for discussing operations and financial results throughout the organization. At the same time, the different column formats are intended to meet different management needs and to be useful to different levels of managers. For example:

- **Line managers.** Line managers will probably find that the "Rolling Monthly" format (Report 11-4) will help them understand recent revenue and expense trends in detail, and the "Month/QTD/YTD" format (Report 11-5) measures progress toward their annual targets (as reflected in the Budget numbers).

- **Senior managers.** Senior managers who are most focused on overall results against objectives will probably find the "Month/QTD/YTD" format (Report 11-5) the most useful, and the "YTD and Full-Year Outlook" format (Report 11-6) valuable for determining how well board of directors and stockholder expectations are likely to be met (not to mention the report best suited for measuring progress toward their annual incentive compensation). The "Rolling Monthly" format (Report 11-4) will at times be useful for day-to-day management, and the "8-Quarter Outlook" format (Report 11-7) should be a principal tool for managing the planning and budgeting process.

- **Board of directors.** Board members will probably find the "Month/QTD/ YTD" format (Report 11-5) the most detailed report they will need. And given that the board has a long-term stewardship role, the "8-Quarter Outlook" format (Report 11-7) should be one that they review regularly (and may even make the "YTD and Full-Year Outlook" format (Report 11-6) unnecessary, since both reports provide an outlook for the current year).

Let's wrap up this discussion with a few additional detailed observations about these various column format choices:

- The "Month/QTD/YTD" format shown in Report 11-5 is similar to the layout of Reports 11-1 and 11-2 that we used as the basis for discussion of report design. The key differences are the inclusion of the monthly columns in addition to the quarter-to-date and year-to-date columns, and the addition of the *percentage* budget variance to all three groups of columns.

- The "YTD and Full-Year Outlook" format shown in Report 11-6 has fundamentally the same column layout as Report 10-5, which introduced percentage budget variance as a meaningful key indicator.

- In both Reports 11-6 and 11-7, note the use of *italics* to distinguish future results (either forecast or budgeted) from the actual and budget numbers for past periods, which are shown in plain text. This use of text effects to distinguish different types of numbers was first introduced in Chapter 2 (see Report 2-5, as well as its revisitation in Report 4-1). It is also a useful spreadsheet design technique (as we discussed in Chapter 6 in Long-Term Payoff Tip #7).

- The column format of Report 11-7 is a "living document"—that is, the mix of columns labeled "Actual," "*Fcst.*," and "*Budget*" has to be changed each quarter. Since most enterprises begin planning in earnest for the upcoming year sometime during the third fiscal quarter, my recommendation is that this report should always have between two and five quarters of "Actual" results. So, after Q1 and Q2, this report would include the actual results for all four quarters of the prior year, and the outlook for the remainder of the current year. But starting with the report that includes Q2 actual results, the columns for the prior year should be dropped and the columns for the upcoming year added. Taking this approach imposes a useful discipline on the enterprise planning process.

- Note the use of *key indicators*, particularly year-to-year growth rates and percentage budget variances, to add meaning and context to the raw report numbers.

The main idea infusing this chapter is that *you can produce great quantation only if you have a thorough and sound understanding of your organization.* This means you must understand your organization's business, its operations, and its challenges and objectives, because the Natural P&L designs that will be most valuable for your organization will be unique to *your* organization. As you design your Natural P&L, consider the following questions:

- What are the management problems your audience faces, and their principal objectives?

- How can the information you provide help your audience identify problems and make good decisions?

- How can you provide a *complete* picture, but still one that presents relevant information and minimizes the less critical information?

- How do the answers to the above questions differ among your audience— across functional areas and from top to bottom in your organization?

- How can you take advantage of the design of your organization's accounting system, especially as reflected in its chart of accounts, to deliver the information its people need? What updates or revisions are necessary?

- How can your quantation help create a common language for your organization, so that everyone has a similar understanding of your essential business issues, and communication is crisp and unambiguous?

Most of this chapter focused on strategies for selecting and organizing the *line items* (that is, the captions down the left side of the page) of the Natural P&L. But we also discussed an overall strategy for creating and maintaining reports, and how different column formats for the same report design can address different management purposes (as well as meet the needs of different people in the organization).

We also identified eight characteristics common to all well-designed Natural P&L reports. If your reports meet these criteria, you can be confident that the management information you are presenting is valuable. And by making sure you understand your organization and its business, you can establish yourself as a key player of your organization's operational success.

APPENDIX 11 A

A Sermon to the Accounting Purists

Accounting is a complex, technical, and sometimes arcane discipline. But as hard as the job is, *the hallmark of real professionalism is to make a difficult job look easy to others.* One main idea to keep in mind is that management reports like the Natural P&L are for managers. As such, they should *insulate* their audience from the accounting complexities, especially if reducing complexity is necessary to make the information meaningful.

To understand this idea, let's look at one of the more exotic accounting topics (at least to non-accountants): *depreciation.* When you design a Natural P&L for your organization, I strongly recommend that you avoid presenting depreciation[12] as a single, stand-alone line item, and I also suggest avoiding use of the word *depreciation* in your reports. To some in your audience it is jargon, causing you to run afoul of characteristic #6 (Plain-English terminology). You don't want your audience to do a quick glance down the left side of the page, and start to worry that they won't understand your information.

But a more important problem associated with presenting depreciation expense in a Natural P&L is that it shifts attention away from matters of real importance for the majority of your audience. Including depreciation as a line item sends a loud signal that a Natural P&L has not had appropriate care in its design, and that the audience's needs are not being properly addressed.

Consider the following highly simplified example, in which a company has three types of capital equipment: (1) office equipment (i.e., computers, copiers, office furniture, etc.), (2) a fleet of cars for use by the company's sales force, and (3) a very expensive tradeshow booth. Capital equipment can be either purchased outright or rented from a third party, and the company has used both methods. The expense for purchased equipment is the monthly depreciation over its useful life, and the expense for rented equipment is simply the rental payments as shown in Report 11A-1.

Report 11-8
Different Ways of Reporting the Cost of Capital Equipment

Equipment Type	PURCHASED			RENTED	
	Original Cost ($)	Useful Life (Mos.)	Monthly Depr'n ($)	$/Mo.	TOTAL
Office Equipment	759,600	36	21,100	10,750	31,850
Auto Fleet	1,035,000	60	17,250	25,360	42,610
Trade Show Booth	364,800	48	7,600	–	7,600
TOTAL	**2,159,400**		**45,950**	**36,110**	**82,060**

REPORT 11A-1: Different Ways of Reporting the Cost of Capital Equipment

Assume for a moment that the following is true for the Natural P&L design shown in Reports 11-1 and 11-2 from earlier in this chapter: (1) the cost of Office Equipment rolls up to the "Office Costs" category line of those reports, (2) the Auto Fleet expense is included in the "Travel & Entertainment" category, and (3) the Trade Show Booth is a Marketing Programs expense. Also assume for simplicity that the above items are the *only* expenses in their categories. Then the Office Costs, Travel & Entertainment, and Marketing Programs expenses for the month would be $31,850, $42,610, $7,600, respectively, as shown in the "TOTAL" column at the far right of Report 11A-1.

Another possible Natural P&L design might be to show category line items for Depreciation and Equipment Rental, and to show the expenses in the "TOTAL" row at the bottom. In a Natural P&L report designed like this, Depreciation and Equipment Rental expenses would be $45,950 and $36,110, respectively. People with a strong background in accounting are often inclined to choose this design, because tracking and accounting for fixed-asset purchases is a significant and complex accounting task in many enterprises.

Is the decision to categorize these expenses into Depreciation and Equipment Rental a reasonable or useful choice? The answer is an unequivocal *no*! How much the company spends on Office Costs, on Travel & Entertainment, and on Marketing Programs is important management information required for decision making. The question of how the assets were *paid for*—which is reflected in the levels of depreciation and equipment rental expense—is of secondary importance. Moreover, the purchase-versus-rent decision is highly centralized in most companies. It's the responsibility of a small group in the company's treasury department and of little interest to anyone else.

We won't go into this level of detail on other accounting issues, but suffice to say that there are plenty of situations where the way you report to meet the needs of operating managers is different from the way you report to meet the needs of the accounting department, and is different from how a publicly traded company must provide information to its stockholders. Some examples from my own personal experience include:

- **Direct versus indirect labor.** In many companies, accounting properly for cost of goods sold is critically important. The distinction between direct and indirect labor reflects this issue by separating the compensation of employees whose cost is included in cost of goods sold from that of employees whose cost is an operating expense. However, for many managers and other consumers of business information, salaries is salaries is salaries, and the treatment of some salaries as "direct labor" and some as "indirect labor" appears arbitrary and confusing. This is another area where strict compliance with generally accepted accounting principles (GAAP) may not lead to the most useful management reports.

- **Expensing stock options.** Today's GAAP rules require companies to value stock options granted and run that valuation through the income statement as an operating expense. Every company required to provide GAAP-compliant financial statements needs to have a serious discussion about whether and, if so, how this expense should be reflected in its *internal management* financial statements (like the Natural P&L).

In some cases, making the reporting changes needed to give managers meaningful information will have no impact on the important top-line (i.e., revenues) or bottom-line (i.e., profits) results. In situations where there *is* an impact, it's essential that management keep proper track of the differences in the report results. This is one area where Natural P&L characteristic #8 [Key results identical to the corresponding numbers in the accounting system (or an explanation why not)] becomes important.

A key point in this Appendix is to reinforce the fact that quantation, like all other types of communication, has rules and best practices you need to understand in order to communicate clearly and effectively. Moreover, *how* you communicate and present information sends messages to your audience about you personally, and about your relationship with your audience. If the way you present numbers marks you as an accounting/finance professional who is knowledgeable about your business, understands your audience's needs, and is otherwise worthy of respect, that's a good thing. But it's entirely another thing if the way you present numbers marks you as a "bean-counter" (in the most unflattering sense of that term) with no real grasp of what your audience needs or how you can help them understand your information. So (with a nod to David Letterman) here are *the top-six dead giveaways that the Natural P&L was designed by a bean-counter*:

6. One or more expense lines (other than "Other") each routinely account for less than 2% of total expenses, or one or more revenue lines each account for less than 5% of total revenues.

5. One expense line routinely accounts for more than two-thirds of total expenses. (I would have said 50%, but in many organizations salaries alone reach that number easily.)

4. The report contains one or more line items requiring more than the most basic familiarity with the rules of GAAP to understand them.

3. "Compensation" is a single huge line item, with Benefits (as well as Bonuses, Commissions, and Contractors/Temps, if applicable) mushed together with Salaries rather than broken out separately.

2. The report does not fit on one page.

   . . . and the number-one dead giveaway that a Natural P&L was designed by a bean-counter . . .

1. *The line items are ordered alphabetically!*

You could think of this list as a sort of Natural P&L–specific version of the Deadly Sins of Presenting Numbers. If you are an accountant delivering management reports that fit any of the above descriptions, please go back to the drawing-board. Start by reviewing the eight characteristics of a well-designed Natural P &L listed in this chapter, and redesign your report. You might also want to test-market your report design with key members of your audience for clarity, comprehensibility, and meaning. And if you are a manager *receiving* reports flawed in these ways, don't be afraid to say something. Speak up—after all, management reports are for *managers*.

NOTES

1. There is yet a third report in the "tripod" of financial statements: the cash flow statement, which differs from the income statement because an understanding of when an enterprise generates revenues or incurs expenses in an economic sense, and an understanding of when checks actually come in or go out the door, are not the same thing. The relationship between these three key financial statements—balance sheet, income statement, and cash flow statement—is so strong that it's usually possible to derive large chunks of each one from the other two. Yes, double-entry bookkeeping is a beautiful mathematical model! This is one reason why accounting fraud is almost impossible to get away with, a point we'll discuss further in Chapter 15.

2. A note on semantics: As we discussed in Chapter 3, the terms *income statement* and *profit and loss statement (P&L)* are often used interchangeably, since both convey some notion of inflows and outflows. But *income statement* has a more specific meaning, because it generally ties to the enterprise's *overall* operating, pretax, or net income, whereas a P&L can be any report with revenues offset by expenses, without the requirement to include *all* inflows and *all* outflows of that organization. For that reason, I will use the term *P&L* for the remainder of this chapter.

3. Quicken users will recognize that Intuit uses the word *category* in the same sense as I do here. Pre-loaded Quicken categories include items like Auto Repair, Life Insurance, Vacation, and

Taxes. But then the terminology diverges: for example, in large business-oriented accounting systems, these classifications are called *accounts*, whereas in Quicken, *accounts* are places where you keep your money, like checking and brokerage accounts. As we discussed in Chapter 3, precision in our use of *words* is critical to meaningful quantation. In my career, I've seen much confusion result from casual, imprecise, and contradictory uses of the word *account*.

4. You might notice that the organization in Report 11-1 appears immensely profitable, showing, for example, actual Operating Profit of $3,156,000 on Revenues of $5,084,000 for the quarter. But note that this report is for VASTCo's Worldwide Sales & Marketing department (or group of departments), an organization where the credit goes for *all* of VASTCo's revenues, but only the expenses related to sales and marketing personnel. Some departments getting similar reports will show no revenues at all. The idea here – as we will discuss in this chapter – is to design a single report layout that every manager in the company is familiar with.

5. The chart of accounts (CoA) is the complete list of accounts used by an organization. For each account in the CoA, the list typically includes the account number (a three- to five-digit number used for coding accounting transactions), the account name (e.g., Salaries, Health Insurance, Meals, Lodging, Rent, etc.), and perhaps a brief description of the account. The Quicken equivalent of the chart of accounts is the Category List (type Ctrl-Shift-c in Quicken to view it). Later in this chapter, we'll go over some tips for mapping the accounts in the chart of accounts onto the line items of your Natural P&L.

6. All kinds of unclassifiable, cats-and-dogs expenses have a way of creeping into the accounting system. Bank fees, dues and subscriptions, and the all-important library overdue charges are examples of accounts created by hyper-diligent accounting staff. They are a favorite topic for accounting humor, to the extent that such a thing exists.

7. You can take the same approach to revenues. If, for example, VASTCo had a number of significant revenue categories in addition to Licenses—say, maintenance, consulting, training, outside seminars, and technical documentation—it might make sense to present them all individually but present a "Support Services" subtotal.

8. See Chapter 12 for a longer discussion of the particularly sticky situation resulting from the application of recently promulgated rules of generally accepted accounting principles (GAAP).

9. The CoA will also have other accounts, such as Cash, Accounts Receivable, Accounts Payable, and Paid-In Capital, that roll up to line items on the balance sheet. Also, to be strictly correct, most management reports like the Natural P&L reflect only the *operating* results of the company. The CoA will include other accounts, frequently referred to as "below-the-line" or "non-operating," for income and expenses not directly related to company operations, such as Interest Income, Interest Expense, Extraordinary Items, and Tax Provision.

10. In the early versions of the Oracle Financials product, the report writer software used the terminology *row sets*, *column sets*, and *content sets*. Each "row set" the user created was the set of line items that created a specific report. (An example might be the Natural P&L shown in Reports 11-1 and 11-2, and discussed in this chapter.) Each "column set" was one particular layout of columns, plus the time period to run the report for. The "content set" was the unit within the organization for which the report was run. (Examples of content sets might be a single department, a division or other group of departments, or the entire corporation.) Each report to be run was thus simply the selection of a row set, a column set, and a content set from the library of available choices.

11. In Report 11-4, note the use of cell borders to group the three months of each calendar quarter. However, this particular feature of Report 11-4 does require revising the cell borders each month. Alternatively, you could omit the cell borders denoting quarters, thereby avoiding the need to revise them each month. Either approach is acceptable, and both are preferable

to simply leaving borders after the third, sixth, and ninth months, since the intuitive visual grouping of months in each *calendar* quarter is lost in two months out of three. This "small detail" of report design is especially relevant in enterprises where the calendar quarter is a meaningful period of time, or where results often show seasonality within each quarter.

12. If you are not an accountant by training (but are reading this Appendix nonetheless) and are not familiar with the accounting meaning of the term *depreciation*, here is an explanation: depreciation is the method used to account for purchased assets with useful lives longer than a single accounting period. (The term often used for these assets is *capital equipment*.) Suppose, for example, a business pays $60,000 in cash for a delivery truck that is expected to have a useful life of five years. At the time of purchase, cash is reduced by $60,000 and "fixed assets" are increased by that amount on the company's balance sheet—there is no impact at all on any income statement. However, for each of the five years starting when the truck is first put to use, the income statements (such as the Natural P&L) reflect an expense of $12,000 for depreciation on the truck (or $1,000 per month for 60 months). The purpose of this is to match the expense of the truck to the periods in which the company benefits from its use. This *matching principle* is central to the accrual-basis accounting that is used in all *well-run* organizations. Forgive my lack of subtlety as I note that most government entities use cash-basis accounting rather than accrual-basis accounting.

CHAPTER 12

The Gaps in GAAP

In examining our books, Mr. Mathews promises to use generally accepted accounting principles, if you know what I mean.

© William Hamilton/ The New Yorker Collection/ www.cartoonbank.com

Generally accepted accounting principles (GAAP) is the set of rules governing all aspects of the financial statements that companies publicly traded in the United States are required to provide to their stockholders. As a quantation professional, if you don't have to understand GAAP financial statements already, there will come a time when you will. However, as important as GAAP financial statements are to the efficient functioning of the U.S. capital markets, they are the tip of the business-quantation iceberg. GAAP financial statements comprise a minuscule fraction of the mass of numbers-based data, reports, plans, and analysis that managers depend on to run their businesses. Also, there is much in GAAP that is antithetical to the basic themes in this book. The rules of GAAP stress consistency, mathematical accuracy, and presenting information in tightly prescribed formats. Whereas these can be important goals, they are frequently less important (and occasionally *much* less important) than the other goals of effective quantation discussed in this book.

Much of this chapter will be devoted to a handful of detailed, but *nontechnical*, discussions of GAAP-related issues from my own career experience. We'll conclude with a brief discussion about how to reconcile the GAAP approach to financial statements with your mission to produce useful quantation.

Rules-Based versus Principles-Based

(Note: I've written this chapter in a way that presumes a basic knowledge of GAAP. If you lack that familiarity, the Appendix to this chapter will provide enough background for the topics raised here.)

GAAP is usually characterized as a rules-based system as opposed to a principles-based system. A rules-based system sets out specific, objective requirements for compliance. A principles-based system lays out general guidelines that are based on ultimate objectives. In a rules-based system, those responsible for compliance are expected to follow the rules precisely. In a principles-based system, those responsible for compliance with the system (such as a corporation responsible for complying with accounting standards) are permitted to use some judgment about what is compliant. As an example of the two types of systems, suppose you are the parent of a teenager and you are seeking to establish an agreement on your child's social life. A principles-based agreement might look like this:

1. You must be home at a reasonable hour every night.
2. Schoolwork should almost always take precedence over your social life, especially on school nights.

A rules-based agreement on the same topic might look like this:

1. You must be home by 6:30 P.M. on typical school nights.
2. On school nights when you are not having dinner at home, you must be home by 8:00 P.M.
3. If you are doing your homework at the library or at a friend's house on a school night, you must be home by 10:00 P.M. Staying at a friend's house to do homework must be confirmed by a phone conversation between the parents of both of you.
4. You must be home by 11:30 P.M. on weekend nights (i.e., Fridays and Saturdays) and on other nights when school is not in session the next day.

5. On weekend nights where the activity is more than a half-hour's drive from home *and* you are in a group of four or more people, the curfew is extended to12:30 A.M.

6. To break any of the above rules, you must get the approval of one parent at least one day in advance.

The advantages and disadvantages of each approach are pretty obvious. Principles-based systems have guidelines that are simple and easy to articulate and can be applied to *any* situation. Rules-based systems minimize arguments and ambiguity. The advantages and disadvantages of being able to use judgment (principles-based systems) or rely on very specific rules (rules-based systems) vary according to the specific situation and according to the wisdom and intelligence of the people responsible for complying.

Of course, no system of accounting regulations can ever be considered purely rules based or purely principles based. But the fact that there are 25,000 pages of GAAP regulations strongly suggests that GAAP is fundamentally rules based. And a close reading of GAAP writings on any of the major accounting issues it covers will remove any doubt that the central approach is based on providing detailed rules.

Where Is All This Headed?

In recent years, there has been a strong movement to bring U.S. financial statements back to more of a principles-based footing. That movement has arisen because the rules of GAAP have become increasingly complex as the world has gotten more complex, and this complexity has sometimes led to incomprehensible rules and pronouncements. Moreover, the world's increasing complexity h made it virtually impossible for the rule-makers to keep pace with the chan and to publish rules that are applicable to every possible situation. (We'll dis a couple of examples of this in what follows.)

The alternative accounting standard getting the most attention now is the International Financial Reporting Standards (IFRS), ie maintained by the International Accounting Standards Board (ard rule-making counterpart to the U.S.'s Financial Accounting Stanges, (FASB), the organization responsible for GAAP. In sheer num sig- IFRS is about one-tenth the size of GAAP and is generally c stan- nificantly more principles-based than GAAP. IFRS is the a by the dard used in over 100 countries, and the current plan be mpliant Securities and Exchange Commission is for U.S. compan debate de- with IFRS by 2014. focuses on This principles-based-versus-rules-based (IFRS-ver serves mention here because much of the discussion *why* you are presenting numbers, not just *how* to present them. In that context, a strictly rules-based approach to most quantation is doomed to be inflexible, incomprehensible, and ultimately unsuccessful. However, even within the context of the GAAP–IFRS debate, a somewhat different set of standards and criteria must apply to the statutory requirements regarding how publicly traded companies and other organizations report their financial results to their stakeholders. It's important to understand how these reports relate to, interact with, and are different from all the other quantation (like the internal management reports discussed in Chapter 11). This is certainly important if you are a professional accountant whose principal responsibility is generating standards-compliant financial statements. But it's also true if you generate other types of quantation, or are simply a consumer of this information. In this sense, it is critical for you to understand not just the *limitations* of GAAP, but the great *importance* of GAAP-driven financial statements, and how your own responsibilities relate to them.

"Expensing" Stock Options

(If you need a general explanation of stock options, see the Appendix to this chapter.)

One of the most hotly debated accounting topics in recent years has been whether to treat stock options as compensation, and therefore reflect them as an expense in the company's income statement. Historically, most companies chose not to expense[1] stock options, but beginning with the implementation of Statement of Financial Accounting Standards No. 123 (FAS 123) in 2006, all public companies were required to expense them.

Within the accounting debate, there were many people (especially academics and some vocal members of the investment community) who felt strongly that stock options are a form of compensation. They also felt strongly that that some notion of the value of the options granted should be reflected in the income statement—and therefore the profitability—of companies granting stock options. accounting implications were powerful: for a number of the companies had initial public offerings in the decade or so before FAS 123 became the adopting FAS 123 would have meant reporting higher expenses, and lower and retained earnings—by several hundred million dollars (and several of dollars in a few cases).

opposing view (most vocally expressed by the management of startups venture capital community) was that GAAP-compliant financial *already* properly reflected the impact of stock options on share- Moreover, opponents expressed concern that the adverse ac- quences of expensing stock options would be so severe that a chilling effect on the willingness of early-stage companies tions, and therefore a chilling effect on the entrepreneurial spirit that has made the United States such a powerful engine for creating high-growth new businesses.

Both sides of the argument were partially right. Yes, of course stock options are compensation. You are giving an employee something of value in lieu of salary or bonus, and it has the potential to have significant dollar value to the employee. That is the very definition of compensation. And yes, the implementation of FAS 123 has had some chilling effect on option grants. Some companies chose to offer restricted stock grants and other stock-related benefits that have a less dramatic impact on their financial statements.[3]

But both sides also missed some important points, and that is why this topic deserves mention in this book. First, and most important, those favoring expensing stock options didn't completely grasp just why it is that investors read financial statements, and one of the prerequisites for generating meaningful, useful quantation *is understanding what the audience is going to do with the information.*

The single most important thing an investor needs to understand about a company is its future *cash-generating* ability, and a good starting point to estimate this ability is the company's historical income statements. Unfortunately, including the expenses related to stock option grants in the income statement makes it *harder*, not easier, to develop that estimate, because (1) granting the option has a significant expense consequence, but no cash flow consequence at the time of the grant; (2) this consequence is actually *positive* when the option is exercised (as the employee purchases the shares); and (3) the current year's income statement reflects expenses related to grants of options made in *prior* years that are still outstanding, making the financial results just for that year even harder to understand. So while expensing stock options properly reflects the economic consequences of granting the options, it's a practice that doesn't necessarily provide investors what they need.

Second, both sides of the stock options debate underestimated the level of awareness and common sense of both companies and investors. They underestimated the ability of companies to focus on the management and motivational benefit of stock options (and to ignore the accounting consequences), and they underestimated the ability of investors to understand the underlying economic substance of a company regardless of the accounting methodology used. I say this because following the implementation of FAS 123:

- The impact on stock prices was minimal as companies converted their financial statements over to compliance with FAS 123. In other words, the revised financial statements contained little new information justifying investor action.[4]

- Although some companies did stop granting stock options because of the dire accounting consequences, many did not. Stock options are still a highly popular method of compensation and motivation, especially among pre-public startups.

■ Securities analysts found that their investor clients were asking them to provide *pro forma* income statements, which had the impact of the expensed stock options backed out. Several analysts I've spoken with reported that well over half of their readers preferred the *pro forma* statements over the original GAAP statements, suggesting that the *pro forma* statements better meet investor needs.

As we discussed in Chapter 9, it is often the case that as the quantation expert, you need to tell your audience what information they need and how it should look. But these observations about the aftermath of FAS 123 suggest that consumers of information, and of numbers in particular, frequently know more about what they want than we give them credit for. If that is the case, it is wise to listen to your audience!

Software Revenue Recognition

(If you need a general explanation of revenue recognition, see the Appendix to this chapter.)

Another hotly debated topic of recent years has been how to account for software revenue, and it's a relevant topic here, because it highlights how *complexity* can have a destructive effect on quantation. With most businesses, revenue recognition issues are pretty clear-cut. No so with software licenses, which are often intangible products that have minimal or no marginal cost associated with producing additional units. A few of the many questions that can muddy the clarity of software revenue recognition include:

■ If you sell a bundle of products and services that includes not just the software license, but annual maintenance, documentation, user training, consulting services, and other elements, how much revenue should be attributed to each element? And when can revenue for each of those elements be recognized?

■ For a product that exists only as bits on a chip or "in the cloud," when can the product be said to have been "delivered"?

■ If the customer is expecting certain enhancements in future releases of the software, should any revenue be recognized before those enhancements have been delivered? If so, how much?

■ If application software, such as accounting or manufacturing control software, needs integration work by the customer or outside consultants before the finished system can be put into use, should the software license revenue be recognized when the software is delivered or when the finished system is implemented?

- If the software is being provided to a reseller that will in turn be selling software to as-yet unidentified end-users, under what circumstance can the software vendor recognize revenue on delivery to the reseller?

- If a software license comes with a warranty, can revenue be recognized when the software is delivered (with an appropriate reserve taken for warranty obligations)? Or should revenue recognition be deferred until the warranty period ends?

These are obviously extremely complex questions, and they became increasingly important topics as the software industry attracted more and more investor interest in the 1980s and 1990s. *If clear, precise accounting rules were to be the resolution for addressing these questions*, it was increasingly evident that the existing GAAP literature was not adequate to answer them. So around 1997, the Financial Accounting Standards Board published a rather lengthy GAAP pronouncement focused specifically on software revenue recognition. More, equally lengthy pronouncements have followed to clarify points of confusion, correct for unintended results, and close loopholes.

The results have been mixed. On the positive side, accounting practices across the entire software industry have become more uniform, so one company's financials can be more easily compared to another's. Moreover, the introduction of more strictly prescribed, and generally more conservative, GAAP rules has meant that fewer software companies have run into legal problems or other controversies resulting from their accounting practices.[5] But the implementation of these increasingly complex accounting pronouncements has had some unintended consequences:

- The revenue reported sometimes doesn't make intuitive sense to people who are not deeply knowledgeable or expert in GAAP. In fact, for some transactions that a businessperson would consider reasonable, software license revenue can *never* be recognized![6]

- Software revenue recognition has at times become a mathematical exercise divorced from the underlying economic or business reality of the transaction.

- Software vendors now need to devote considerably more staff and other resources to the revenue recognition process.

- Software revenue recognition has become an increasingly lucrative segment of the auditing business of large accounting firms, all of which have developed layers of audit staff with software revenue recognition expertise. (Cynics might question whether this was an unintended consequence.)

- The increasingly arcane, or at least increasingly lengthy, accounting rules have resulted in accounting treatments more open to interpretation, and that has actually *hindered* reporting consistency across companies.

From the perspective of investor relations, a practical consequence of the recent GAAP software revenue recognition rules is that investors have shifted their reliance from the income statements (where reported revenue is the top line), to the cash flow statements (which tend to be less affected by differences in accounting rules). Investors have also increasingly asked vendors to provide "non-GAAP" metrics, such as backlog, bookings, new customer counts, and average total deal size. Overall, this is not a bad thing, but it's a shame that the motivation for these requests is that the GAAP reports do not suit investor needs.

This lengthy, confusing tale illustrates another important idea that is central to developing effective quantation, namely, *that valid and desirable objectives* ("consistent," "all-encompassing," "meaningful," "useful," and "clear and simple") *are sometimes in direct conflict with each other.* (See "The War of the Adjectives" in Chapter 9.) In this case, the desire to provide cheating-proof, unambiguous software revenue numbers has led to accounting rules that are incredibly hard to understand and expensive to comply with, and reported results that don't always make intuitive sense from a practical business perspective. And if the accounting experts can't win the War of the Adjectives, know that you are not alone in your battle with this quantation paradox.

The good news is that this decades-long turmoil over software revenue recognition has been a significant factor driving the movement to steer U.S. companies away from a rules-based system like GAAP and toward a more principles-based system like IFRS.

Tying GAAP to Internal Management Reports

GAAP financial statements, and the kinds of GAAP-related issues we've discussed in this chapter, matter a great deal to investors and are important to be aware of, but they are just the tiny tip of the quantation iceberg that organizations depend on to manage themselves and stay afloat. In order for an organization to operate effectively, it's critical that managers throughout the company have a sense of how the information they use to manage themselves as an organization is related to the information used by internal and external shareholders to evaluate the company's success (i.e., the GAAP financial statements). And it's equally critical that those responsible for preparing the GAAP reports can communicate with the rest of the company's management in ways meaningful to them.

Quantation plays a critical role in this interrelationship. Recall from Chapter 11 that characteristic #8 of a well-designed Natural P&L is key results equal to the corresponding numbers in the accounting system (or an explanation why not). Report 12-1 is an example of a report designed to achieve this objective.

Report 12-1
VASTCo -- Comparison of 2006
Internal and GAAP Income Statements

(in $000)	Internal 2006 Total	← Adjustments → COS[1]	Options[2]	Rev. Rec.[3]	GAAP 2006 Total	Net Impact
Licenses	16,785	–	–	(1,720)	15,065	(1,720)
Services	6,120	–	–	54	6,174	54
Total Revenues	**22,905**	**–**	**–**	**(1,666)**	**21,240**	**(1,666)**
Cost of Sales	2,982	549	–	–	3,531	549
Gross Profit	**19,923**	**(549)**	**–**	**(1,666)**	**17,709**	**(2,215)**
Sales & Marketing	7,568	–	138	–	7,706	138
Research & Dev.	4,477	(432)	34	–	4,078	(398)
General & Admin.	3,191	(117)	53	–	3,127	(64)
Total Oprg. Exps.	15,236	(549)	224	–	14,911	(325)
Operating Profit	**4,687**	**–**	**(224)**	**(1,666)**	**2,797**	**(1,890)**

Explanatory Notes:

1. GAAP results reflect fully burdened Cost of Sales, not just direct expenses. (Adjustments should net to zero in each period.)

2. GAAP results include compensation expense attributed to stock options.

3. GAAP results reflect revenues per GAAP documentation; Internal results are revenues reported in incentive compensation plans. (Adjustments should net to zero in over time.)

REPORT 12-1:   VASTCo, Comparison of 2006 Internal and GAAP Income Statements

The report design is the Functional P&L that you've seen in many exhibits in the book,[7] and the left-hand column ("Internal 2006 Total") reports VASTCo's operating results for all of 2006. VASTCo's GAAP income statement is the column second-from-right. The three "Adjustments" columns in the middle of the report are used to reconcile the differences between the Internal Functional P&L and the GAAP income statement. The "COS" column reconciles two different approaches to accounting for Cost of Sales, and the "Options" and "Rev Rec." columns reflect the kinds of adjustments required by GAAP and discussed in this chapter. The "Explanatory Notes" at the bottom are essential for helping *all* readers (not just the GAAP *cognoscenti*) to understand the differences in the accounting methodologies underlying the two reports.

I want to emphasize that Report 12-1 is a report that can be designed in myriad ways, depending on the reports you are trying to reconcile. It's an important report for the reasons we've discussed, but there are no particular rules about the right way to design it. As I have said many times, you have choices, but when making a report like this, it's important to know what exactly your readers will need to understand about the GAAP numbers your company generates, and the other financials you are presenting.

In this chapter, we discussed a reporting area that is critically important but gets very little attention elsewhere in this book: financial statements prepared in accordance with generally accepted accounting principles (GAAP). We don't focus on GAAP in *Painting with Numbers*, but note that the GAAP financial statements could not be produced without the support of all the other quantation that businesses and other organizations use to manage their operations. So it's important to understand how that quantation relates to and interacts with the GAAP statements, and vice versa.

In recent years there has been considerable debate and controversy surrounding GAAP. Some of the debate has been tactically focused on specific issues like the software revenue recognition and stock option accounting discussed in this chapter. Some of the debate has focused on whether it is important to establish worldwide accounting standards. And some of the debate has focused on how to use technology to make the financial information provided to the SEC and other regulatory bodies easier to access and to understand. Still, much of the debate has also focused on the philosophical foundations of quantation. In particular, there has been an extended debate about whether rules-based or principles-based reporting systems are preferable, and about the possibly destructive impact of the increasing complexity of GAAP compliance.

One of my goals in *Painting with Numbers* is to get you thinking about just why it is that you are presenting numbers and what that means for *how* you present them. The debate about GAAP illustrates why this goal has a real, practical, and high-stakes importance.

APPENDIX 12 A

Some Notes on GAAP

Many readers of *Painting with Numbers* will be professionally involved with preparing or interpreting the financial statements of publicly traded companies, or of other organizations required to report their financial results in accordance with generally accepted accounting principles (GAAP). For those who aren't, this Appendix is intended to provide enough background on GAAP that the topics discussed in Chapter 12 will make sense to all readers. And please understand that while I've had extensive experience with the accounting issues discussed in this chapter, I am neither a CPA by training nor a GAAP expert. So while I believe the discussions in this chapter are factually accurate, they are nonetheless simplifications of complex topics and should be understood as such.

What Is GAAP?

Generally accepted accounting principles (GAAP) is the set of rules that governs all aspects of the financial statements that companies publicly traded in the United States are required to provide to their stockholders. The GAAP documentation is the most revered canon of the accounting profession, at least in the United States. It is not terse: it consists of approximately 25,000 densely worded pages,[8] and those pages are dwarfed by the volume of further explanations and clarifications generated by accounting firms and by academics. This "feature" of GAAP has exposed it to a fair amount of ridicule (some of it good-natured), but GAAP is a set of rules that enables the financial statements of U.S. businesses and other organizations to serve a number of valuable purposes, including:

- Ensuring that a company's financial statements can be meaningfully compared to those of competitors and other companies, and to those of prior time periods

- Providing guidance for extremely complex situations, where the proper accounting treatment from an economic perspective isn't obvious
- Providing an objective, codified basis for government regulation and law enforcement with respect to accounting practices

Stock Options

A *stock option* is the right to buy stock at some time in the future at a purchase price that is fixed at the time the option is granted or created. There are numerous different types of options; the variety is limited only by the imagination of the people entering into the agreement. Some options where the underlying stock is publicly traded are traded on exchanges in much the same way the underlying shares are traded.

The specific type of stock options at the center of the accounting debate discussed in this chapter were options granted to founders and other employees of early-stage companies (typically in high technology), and especially companies that had not yet gone public. These options *vest* over a time period (four years is a typical vesting period), which means that the employee's right to buy the shares at the option price accrues gradually over the vesting period. If the employee leaves the company, he or she has a fixed period of time (typically 90 days) to purchase the vested shares of (or *exercise*) the option, and the employee forfeits the right to buy the unvested shares. The advantages of stock options for companies in this situation are:

- Cash-strapped startups can use options to attract and retain employees, by using the options as a substitute for the higher salaries and cash incentives larger, more well-established companies can more easily offer. To the venture capitalists and other investors in early-stage companies, the cost of granting stock options becomes material only if the enterprise turns out to be successful, either through a public stock offering or by being acquired by a larger company.
- Especially for very early-stage companies that don't yet have much to show for their efforts besides a well-crafted business plan and an intriguing product demonstration, the fair market value used to set the purchase (exercise) price of the options can be an attractively low price compared to what the shares will fetch if the venture becomes successful.
- For the fortunate (but relatively few) folks who have gone to work for the next Intel or Microsoft or eBay or Amazon or Google, options offer them the potential for something much more lucrative than the cash compensation they passed up to come to work for an uncertain venture.
- The vesting provisions of stock options are a powerful employee retention tool for a company whose future prospects are looking good.

Just like the publicly traded options mentioned earlier, these employee stock options have an economic value that can be estimated with mathematical models that take into consideration factors such as the number of shares, the volatility of the underlying stock, the period during which the option can be exercised, and the vesting provisions.[9]

Revenue Recognition

Central to proper accounting for any business is understanding when that business can record revenue (or have *revenue recognition*) for a transaction, consistent with the rules of GAAP. This is usually pretty simple if you are manufacturing and selling, say, trucks. A truck costs a lot of money to build and ship, so you don't want to hand the truck over to a customer unless that customer has made a clearly binding commitment to pay for that truck, and the customer is credit worthy or you have other assurances that you will get paid. The same is true if you are selling services, such as a housecleaning business. As the employer, if you are going to pay an employee for every hour he or she works, you won't send that employee off to clean someone's house until you have certainty that you will get paid for the hours worked.

A second aspect of revenue recognition is that it is a *binary* event: either you have revenue or you don't. If you've sold a $20,000 truck but received only a $5,000 down payment up-front, from an accounting perspective you have to decide whether you have $20,000 in revenue—for which you have $5,000 in cash plus a binding obligation to pay you the other $15,000 at some time in the future—or you have zero in revenue. If you are the truck's manufacturer and you've shipped the truck to an independent dealer, you *can* take revenue if the dealer is obliged to pay you regardless of when or even whether he finds a customer for that truck, but you *can't* take revenue if the dealer has the right to return unsold inventory.

NOTES

1. Recall from Chapter 3 that *to expense* is a verb form with a specific meaning: that an outlay is treated as an expense in the income (or profit & loss) statement. By comparison, for example, the *expenditure* for a capital asset (such as a car or piece of manufacturing equipment) is *not* reflected immediately in the income statement. Instead, that outlay is recorded as an asset, and the *depreciation* of that asset over its useful life is what's treated as the expense that flows through the income statement. (See the Appendix to Chapter 11, or better yet a book about accounting, for further discussion of this accounting process.)

2. This is a rather technical argument, but arguably a correct one. For several decades, companies had already been required to factor the impact of the possible exercise of outstanding stock options into their earnings-per-share calculation, using an approach called the *treasury stock method*. Moreover, during that same time, companies had also been required to disclose a number of further details about their stock option grants in the footnotes to their financial

statements, including shares granted, vested, exercised, and canceled, and the range of prices at which option grants were made. Although this approach does not mean that stock options are reported as an expense in any way, some argue that the information available is sufficient for investors to factor stock options into their analysis as they see fit.

3. But please note that while these benefits are still stock related, there the similarity to stock options ends. From the perspective of motivating employees or tying compensation to overall corporate success, they are radically different instruments. But that is a subject for another book.

4. This observation highlights the difference between *measurement* and *disclosure*. As we discussed earlier, some argued that FAS 123 was unnecessary because the existing accounting rules already gave investors enough information to fully understand the compensation implications of stock options, if they chose to do that analysis. Look at it this way: whether a statement like, "There are 18 horses in that field," is more correct than, "There are 72 horses' hooves in that field," is a debate about *measurement*. Whether either of these statements is more appropriate than, "There may be some horses in that field," is a debate about *disclosure*. The Enron saga is a real-life example of this distinction: the most fraudulent aspect of Enron's financial statements was their failure to include on the balance sheet the debt obligations held by the special-purpose entities. This was a *disclosure* choice, and a choice that was much more consequential than any issues about how to *measure* the exact size of the debt. The accounting profession has at times been criticized for focusing excessively on measurement issues at the cost of attention to disclosure issues.

5. Please note that from an accounting perspective, this outcome is neither good nor bad. There is virtually nothing in the GAAP "rule-book" stating that companies should choose more conservative accounting practices. The object of accounting is to get the numbers *right*, and it is no more blessed to report numbers that are too conservative than too aggressive. That, of course, is what the accounting rules say; in real life, every CFO knows that it's virtually impossible to get sued for *under*reporting revenues or profits, and that is not true for the inverse.

6. This can happen even if the vendor has received payment for the unrecognized revenue. In such cases, the portion collected but not recognized appears on the company's balance sheet in a liability usually called *deferred revenues*. As a result, investors can at least look to the balance sheet to get a sense of how much software the company has sold but not recognized as revenue; this is an example of the distinction between measurement and disclosure discussed in an earlier note in this chapter.

7. The eight design characteristics discussed in Chapter 11 apply principally to the design of the Natural P&L report, but characteristic #8 applies equally to the ability to compare *any* two different ways of reporting on the enterprise. In fact, it is much more apt to compare the GAAP statements to the Functional P&L, because the line items in the Functional P&L translate better than those in the Natural P&L to the line items in the GAAP income statement.

8. By comparison, the GAAP documentation is about 50% longer than the *Talmud*, the fundamental text of Judaism, which includes stunningly extensive discussions of the religion's law, ethics, philosophy, customs, and history. The fact that it has taken only 70 years to generate this much GAAP literature while the *Talmud* was written over a period of more than 1,000 years suggests an ominous trend.

9. The best-known of these mathematical models is the Black-Scholes model, named after Fischer Black and Myron Scholes, who developed it in the early 1970s. In fact, Scholes was one of the recipients of the 1997 Nobel Prize in Economics for his work in this area. (Black had died in 1995, and was therefore ineligible for the award.)

CHAPTER 13

Quantation: It's Not Just for Business Anymore

A billion here, a billion there, and pretty soon you're talking real money.

—Attributed to Sen. Everett M. Dirksen (R-Ill) (1896–1969)

Most of the examples and discussion in *Painting with Numbers* focus on business. But there are plenty of other areas in life where clear, meaningful quantation is essential to decision making. The arenas of politics and public policy top this list, in such critical areas as fiscal management, taxation, healthcare, education, public safety, and national security. Because good quantation skills are critical in *every* place where numbers are presented, this chapter will focus on how good quantation can affect an audience's understanding of the underlying issues in public policy.

The specific topic we will examine is individual income taxes: how they're calculated, who pays them, and the extent to which things have changed in recent years. Income taxes are relevant and important to everyone, and effective quantation can be a huge help in understanding the issues and the facts behind taxation. We will be using publicly available data, and focusing on how the rules and techniques we've discussed so far apply in this area, just as they do to business reporting. Some of the quantation skills we'll touch on include:

- Putting numbers on the page so that they are easy to understand and organized to make intuitive sense (see Chapters 1 and 2)

- Making sure that the *words* included in the presentation are concise, clear, and free of ambiguity or emotional content (see Chapter 3)

- Striking the right balance between a complete, exhaustive presentation and one that's easily and quickly understandable by your *audience* (see Chapter 4), especially when so much raw data is available

- Using *graphs* effectively when (a) the quantity of data is too large to be absorbed if presented in tables and (b) there are trends and patterns the audience can grasp intuitively when they are presented visually (see Chapter 7)

- Using *key indicators* (that is, ratios) to give context and meaning to raw numbers when (a) the ideas are complex and (b) the magnitudes of the numbers are hard for an audience to grasp (see Chapter 10)

- Using approaches that not only present the underlying information coherently, but organize the information and attract the audience's attention in a way that demonstrates a *grasp and mastery* of the subject matter and the issues involved (see Chapter 9)

As you read this chapter, try *not* to focus on whether the presentations in this chapter confirm or challenge your personal opinions. Instead, focus on whether the information is comprehensible and organized, and whether it raises other questions you'd like to explore. I will consider this chapter a success if it simply helps you take an organized, balanced, rhetoric-free view of a complex, emotional, and critically important public policy issue.

One Taxpayer at a Time

Let's start with a real-life example of your tax dollars at work producing quantation. Almost every taxpayer is intimately familiar with tables that look just like Report 13-1, which is a copy of Schedule X from the IRS website. What do you think of this as quantation?

I consider this a solid piece of work. It's easy to read and understand, and the level of precision is appropriate for the table's intended purpose—that is, to figure out an individual's income tax. Still, it does use more white space than necessary, which makes the table physically larger than needed and makes it harder on the viewer to sight along a single row. Also, I would have grouped the columns differently: I would have grouped the first two columns ("Over–" and "But not over–") together, and I would have moved the percentage number of the "The tax is" column farther from the dollars column and closer to the "of the amount over–" column. (See Chapter 2 about how looks and layout affect readability.)

It's not a bad report, but I'll stress that the Schedule X shown in Report 13-1 is well-designed *for its intended purpose*, which is to help one taxpayer (who usually has a very clear idea of his or her own taxable income) to calculate his or her income tax. It's *not* a useful or well-designed report if

---

Report 13-1
Example of an IRS Tax Table
(Individual Income Taxes, 2010 Tax Rate Schedules)

Schedule X—If your filing status is **Single**

If your taxable income is: Over—	But not over—	The tax is:	of the amount over—
$0	$8,375	.... 10%	$0
8,375	34,000	$837.50 + 15%	8,375
34,000	82,400	4,681.25 + 25%	34,000
82,400	171,850	16,781.25 + 28%	82,400
171,850	373,650	41,827.25 + 33%	171,850
373,650	....	108,421.25 + 35%	373,650

Source: http://www.irs.gov/pub/irs-pdf/i1040tt.pdf (p. 98)

REPORT 13-1: Example of an IRS Tax Table (Individual Income Taxes, 2010 Tax Rate Schedules)

the reader is more interested in getting a general sense of how much tax is owed at various levels of income. This is because the large gaps of varying size make it difficult to pick out a specific income level, and because the tax rates shown are *marginal* rates—that is, they are the rates applicable *to the next dollar of income*—and don't provide a sense of a taxpayer's *total* tax burden in relation to his income.

Report 13-2 provides an example of how the basic information in Schedule X could be presented if total taxes and effective rates at various income levels were the reader's principal interest. The numbers in the Income Tax column are calculated from only the information in Schedule X. The Marginal Tax Rate is the tax rate that would apply to the taxpayer's next dollar of income, and is, again, taken directly from that schedule. But note the addition of the Effective Tax Rate, which is the kind of *key indicator* we discussed in Chapter 10. Adding the Effective Tax Rate metric is important, because a person with Taxable Income of $200,000 is said to be "in the 33% tax bracket" (the Marginal Tax Rate), but that person's Income Tax of $51,117 is actually 25.6% (the Effective Tax Rate) of his or her $200,000 of Taxable Income.

This topic of income tax rates also happens to lend itself nicely to a graphical presentation. Report 13-3 is an example. This graph gives the reader a visual sense of how the Effective Tax Rate changes with income. In fact, this graph illustrates an example of what is a *progressive* tax. A progressive tax is one where the share of the total tax bill paid by the top X% of income earners is *greater* than that particular group's share of the total income generated.[1] The issue of how progressive our taxation system is, and how progressive it *should be*, is central

| Report 13-2 | | | |
| 2010 Income Tax (single taxpayer) | | | |
Taxable Income ($)	Income Tax ($)	Marginal Tax Rate	Effective Tax Rate
–	–	10%	10.0%
20,000	2,581	15%	12.9%
40,000	6,181	25%	15.5%
60,000	11,181	25%	18.6%
80,000	16,181	25%	20.2%
100,000	21,709	28%	21.7%
120,000	27,309	28%	22.8%
140,000	32,909	28%	23.5%
160,000	38,509	28%	24.1%
180,000	44,517	33%	24.7%
200,000	51,117	33%	25.6%
220,000	57,717	33%	26.2%
240,000	64,317	33%	26.8%
260,000	70,917	33%	27.3%
280,000	77,517	33%	27.7%
300,000	84,117	33%	28.0%
320,000	90,717	33%	28.3%
340,000	97,317	33%	28.6%
360,000	103,917	33%	28.9%
380,000	110,644	35%	29.1%
400,000	117,644	35%	29.4%
420,000	124,644	35%	29.7%
440,000	131,644	35%	29.9%
460,000	138,644	35%	30.1%
480,000	145,644	35%	30.3%
500,000	152,644	35%	30.5%

REPORT 13-2:   2010 Income Tax (Single Taxpayer)

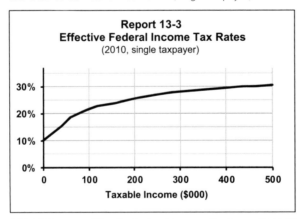

REPORT 13-3:   Effective Federal Income Tax Rates (2010, Single Taxpayer)

to the searching fiscal debate taking place in the United States and in many other countries at the time of this writing. In any debate it's a wise idea to start with a clear and honest look at the facts and the numbers, so let's do that next.

All the Taxpayers at Once

So far, we've looked at taxation only for an *individual* taxpayer. But what if you wanted to get a sense of where *all* of the federal income tax dollars in the United States come from? It turns out that this information is directly available from the IRS (as well as from private organizations that focus on public policy issues). Let's look at some of that information from the standpoint of effective quantation, and what we might want to do differently. Report 13-4 is a report generated by the Tax Foundation, one of those well-respected private organizations. (The print is smaller than ideal, since I've reproduced it exactly as it appears on the Foundation's website. Don't worry about that for now.) The squiggles denote the omission of several years of data from this exhibit for space reasons. The data underlying this report ranks taxpayers by income, where the specific income metric is Adjusted Gross Income (AGI), a line item that appears on every year's income tax form. At the left, the Total column shows the *total* individual income tax liability of U.S. taxpayers in $ millions. The columns to the right of the Total show how much of that Total tax bill is owed by taxpayers at different income levels. For example, in 1980, the income tax liability of the 1% of taxpayers with the highest AGI (i.e., the "Top 1%") was $47,456 million, out of a total U.S. income tax liability of $249,077 million.

This is an excellent and incredibly informative report. Even so, Report 13-5 shows my own spin on how I would choose to present exactly the same information.[2]

What are the principle quantation differences between Reports 13-4 and 13-5? First, let's look at the differences from the standpoint of how the information is presented to the reader:

- Report 13-5 shows the numbers in $ billions and Report 13-4 in $ millions. Even with the one decimal place (i.e., to the nearest $100 million) in Report 13-5, each number is two digits shorter than in Report 13-4. This choice not only removes two digits that I would say are unimportant to most readers, but also helps ensure I can fit this report onto one page and thereby avoid committing Deadly Sin #9! (See Chapter 1, on the precision of numbers, and Chapter 4, on respect for your audience's time.)

- Over the entire 1980–2008 time horizon, the IRS data used by the Tax Foundation categorized taxpayers into the Top 1% and the Top 5% categories. Beginning in 2001, though, the IRS also reported on the Top 0.1% and the Top 2%, 3%, and 4% categories. I've chosen to ignore these additional categories in the interest of being able to compare data over the entire 29-year time horizon, and to stay away from Deadly Sin #9. (See Chapter 2, on times when white space is and is not your friend, as well as Chapter 4.)

Report 13-4
Income Taxes Data, from the Tax Foundation

Total Income Tax after Credits, 1980-2008 ($ Millions)

Year	Total	Top 0.1%	Between .1% & 1%	Top 1%	Between 1% & 2%	Top 2%	Between 2% & 3%	Top 3%	Between 3% & 4%	Top 4%	Between 4% & 5%	Top 5%	Between 5% & 10%	Top 10%	Between 10% & 25%	Top 25%	Between 25% & 50%	Top 50%	Bottom 50%
1980	249,077										44,307	91,763	30,991	122,754	59,125	181,879	49,646	231,525	17,552
1981	282,298										49,344	98,966	36,428	135,394	68,674	204,068	57,195	261,263	21,035
1982	276,076										47,227	99,753	34,383	134,136	66,022	200,158	55,635	255,793	20,283
1983	271,645										46,033	101,228	33,804	135,032	63,535	198,567	53,600	252,167	19,478
1984	297,376										50,153	112,947	37,418	150,365	68,172	218,537	56,970	275,507	21,869
1985	321,916										54,641	124,850	40,802	165,652	72,767	238,419	60,423	298,842	23,074
1986	366,979										61,749	156,240	44,463	200,703	78,273	278,976	64,313	343,289	23,690
Tax Reform Act of 1986 changed the definition of AGI, so data above and below this line not strictly comparable																			
1987	369,046			91,559							68,083	159,642	45,588	205,230	78,627	283,857	62,798	346,655	22,391
2000	980,521			366,929							186,741	553,670	106,480	660,150	163,556	823,706	118,473	942,179	38,342
2001	887,882	142,616	158,282	300,898	65,953	366,851	43,318	410,169	33,906	444,075	28,748	472,823	103,340	576,163	159,890	736,053	116,589	852,642	35,240
2002	796,862	122,975	145,633	268,608	61,026	329,634	40,136	369,770	31,892	401,662	27,018	428,680	95,132	523,812	144,746	668,558	100,405	768,963	27,899
2003	747,939	117,275	139,065	256,340	58,281	314,621	37,623	352,244	29,472	381,716	24,881	406,597	85,855	492,452	134,928	627,380	94,647	722,027	25,912
2004	831,890	145,118	161,784	306,902	67,070	373,972	42,416	416,388	32,134	448,522	26,702	475,224	92,049	567,273	138,642	705,915	98,556	804,471	27,419
2005	934,703	180,008	188,124	368,132	76,878	445,010	47,997	493,007	35,785	528,792	28,967	557,759	99,326	657,085	146,687	803,772	102,256	906,028	28,675
2006	1,023,739	200,281	208,088	408,369	84,176	492,545	52,008	544,553	39,180	583,733	31,947	615,680	109,060	724,740	158,413	883,153	110,023	993,176	30,563
2007	1,115,760	225,239	225,687	450,926	92,121	543,047	56,512	599,559	42,050	641,609	34,684	676,293	118,139	794,432	171,443	965,875	117,624	1,083,499	32,261
2008	1,031,512	190,498	201,651	392,149	85,143	477,292	53,577	530,869	40,870	571,739	33,979	605,718	115,703	721,421	169,193	890,614	113,025	1,003,639	27,873

Source: IRS (http://www.irs.gov/taxstats/indtaxstats/article/0,,id=133521,00.html)

Tax Foundation source: http://www.taxfoundation.org/publications/show/23408.html

TAX FOUNDATION

REPORT 13-4: Income Taxes Data from the Tax Foundation

Report 13-5
Income Tax after Credits, 1980-2008 ($ Billions)

Year	Total	By AGI Percentile Bracket						Cumulative AGI Brackets					
		Top 1%	1-5%	5-10	10-25	25-50	Bottom 50%	Top 1%	Top 5%	Top 10%	Top 25%	Top 50%	All 100%
1980	249.1	47.5	44.3	31.0	59.1	49.6	17.6	47.5	91.8	122.8	181.9	231.5	249.1
1981	282.3	49.6	49.3	36.4	68.7	57.2	21.0	49.6	99.0	135.4	204.1	261.3	282.3
1982	276.1	52.5	47.2	34.4	66.0	55.6	20.3	52.5	99.8	134.1	200.2	255.8	276.1
1983	271.6	55.2	46.0	33.8	63.5	53.6	19.5	55.2	101.2	135.0	198.6	252.2	271.6
1984	297.4	62.8	50.2	37.4	68.2	57.0	21.9	62.8	112.9	150.4	218.5	275.5	297.4
1985	321.9	70.2	54.6	40.8	72.8	60.4	23.1	70.2	124.9	165.7	238.4	298.8	321.9
1986	367.0	94.5	61.7	44.5	78.3	64.3	23.7	94.5	156.2	200.7	279.0	343.3	367.0
1987	369.0	91.6	68.1	45.6	78.6	62.8	22.4	91.6	159.6	205.2	283.9	346.7	369.0
1988	412.8	113.8	74.5	48.1	84.9	67.8	23.6	113.8	188.3	236.4	321.3	389.1	412.8
1989	432.8	109.3	80.9	51.3	92.8	73.3	25.2	109.3	190.2	241.5	334.3	407.6	432.8
1990	447.1	112.3	82.8	52.4	96.8	76.7	26.0	112.3	195.1	247.5	344.3	421.1	447.1
1991	448.3	111.3	83.2	55.8	96.2	77.2	24.6	111.3	194.5	250.3	346.5	423.8	448.3
1992	476.2	131.2	87.3	57.7	97.5	78.4	24.1	131.2	218.5	276.2	373.7	452.1	476.2
1993	502.7	145.8	92.2	59.7	100.7	80.0	24.2	145.8	238.1	297.8	398.5	478.6	502.7
1994	534.8	154.3	99.8	63.8	107.5	83.9	25.5	154.3	254.1	317.9	425.4	509.3	534.8
1995	588.3	178.0	109.7	69.7	115.4	88.4	27.1	178.0	287.7	357.4	472.8	561.2	588.3
1996	658.1	212.6	122.8	76.0	123.8	94.5	28.4	212.6	335.4	411.4	535.2	629.7	658.1
1997	727.3	241.2	136.0	82.4	134.4	102.2	31.1	241.2	377.2	459.6	594.0	696.2	727.3
1998	788.5	274.0	150.5	88.3	139.1	103.3	33.2	274.0	424.5	512.8	652.0	755.2	788.5
1999	877.3	317.4	169.0	96.5	149.9	109.3	35.1	317.4	486.5	583.0	732.9	842.2	877.3
2000	980.5	366.9	186.7	106.5	163.6	118.5	38.3	366.9	553.7	660.2	823.7	942.2	980.5
2001	887.9	300.9	171.9	103.3	159.9	116.6	35.2	300.9	472.8	576.2	736.1	852.6	887.9
2002	796.9	268.6	160.1	95.1	144.7	100.4	27.9	268.6	428.7	523.8	668.6	769.0	796.9
2003	747.9	256.3	150.3	85.9	134.9	94.6	25.9	256.3	406.6	492.5	627.4	722.0	747.9
2004	831.9	306.9	168.3	92.0	138.6	98.6	27.4	306.9	475.2	567.3	705.9	804.5	831.9
2005	934.7	368.1	189.6	99.3	146.7	102.3	28.7	368.1	557.8	657.1	803.8	906.0	934.7
2006	1,023.7	408.4	207.3	109.1	158.4	110.0	30.6	408.4	615.7	724.7	883.2	993.2	1,023.7
2007	1,115.8	450.9	225.4	118.1	171.4	117.6	32.3	450.9	676.3	794.4	965.9	1,083.5	1,115.8
2008	1,031.5	392.1	213.6	115.7	169.2	113.0	27.9	392.1	605.7	721.4	890.6	1,003.6	1,031.5

NOTE: Tax Reform Act of 1986 changed definition of Adjusted Gross Income (AGI),
   so data for 1980-86 are not strictly comparable with data for 1987-2008

REPORT 13-5:   Income Tax after Credits, 1980–2008 ($ Billions)

- Report 13-4 intersperses the columns for the "By AGI Percentile Bracket" group (i.e., Top 1%, 1–5%, 5–10%, etc.) with the columns for the "Cumulative AGI Brackets" group (i.e., Top 1%, Top 5%, Top 10%, etc.), while Report 13-5 puts them into two groups of columns. This was a judgment call on my part, but my sense was that the layout of Report 13-5 is a more intuitive and natural way to group the columns. (See Chapter 11 on the intuitive organization of the line items in a report (design characteristic #4).)

- Report 13-5 has different wording for some of the column headings, and additional wording for the column groups. (See Chapter 3 on the importance of concise yet clear and accurate wording.)

- In Report 13-5, note that the rightmost column (the "All 100%" column of the "Cumulative AGI Brackets" group) is identical to the Total column at the left of the report, and in that sense is unnecessary. Including it was another judgment call on my part, because omitting it might have seemed strange to the reader. First, the "Cumulative AGI Brackets" group has the same number of columns as the "By AGI Percentile Bracket" group, and second, this last column acts as a sort of validity check on the numbers in this portion of the report.

Now let's look at Report 13-5 from the standpoint of efficient and effective spreadsheet design:

- The formulas and the computation logic of the "By AGI Percentile Bracket" columns are fundamentally similar to each other, as are the formulas and computation logic of the "Cumulative AGI Brackets" columns. So not only does this organization of columns make sense from the *reader's* perspective, it makes good *spreadsheet design* sense. (See Chapter 5, Instant Payoff Tip #7—organize data for easy computation.)

- The text inserted between the rows for the years 1986 and 1987 in Report 13-4 may be useful from the perspective of informing the reader about differences in methodology between the years above and below the text, but it's poor spreadsheet design, because it breaks the spreadsheet into two groups of noncontiguous cells. (Again, see Instant Payoff Tip #7.) Also, I moved the advisory note to the bottom of the spreadsheet and created a visual separation by widening the rows for 1986 and 1987 (and using a double-lined cell border between those two years).

Now that we've got a report design that presents all this important information and takes advantage of the design principles discussed in this book, let's see whether we can get some actual *meaning* from these numbers. There are a lot of numbers in Report 13-5, but let's focus mostly on the rows for 1980 and 2008. Here are a few takeaways from a review of that report:

- Total income taxes more than quadrupled, from $249.1B in 1980 to $1,031.5B in 2008.

- Over the same period, income taxes of the Top 1% grew from $47.5B to $392.1B, *nearly a tenfold* increase.

- By comparison, the income taxes paid by the 25–50% bracket went from $49.6B to $113.0B, "only" roughly doubling. And the taxes of the Bottom 50% *less than* doubled, from $17.6B to $27.9B.

- A quick look at each of the columns in the report shows numbers generally increasing over the 29-year time horizon, with a few ups and downs. In particular, there was a "local peak"[3] in the amounts in every column in the year 2000, and the *highest* amount in each column occurred in 2007 (except 25–50% and Bottom 50%).

At the highest level, these results are not surprising. The U.S. gross domestic product (GDP) increased significantly from 1980 to 2008, partly due to increased real output and partly due to inflation, and whereas significant tax reform legislation was enacted in both 1986 and 2001, the overall federal income tax structure did not change radically. As far as the peaks in 2000 and 2007 are concerned, this is also not surprising, since both 2001 and 2008 were recession years. Moreover, the stock market peaked in the year 2000, so it would be a year in which capital gains taxes (which generally play a relatively larger role in the tax returns of taxpayers in the higher income brackets) were especially high.

Beyond this high-level analysis it's hard to get much meaning out of Report 13-5 without exhaustive analysis. The numbers are large and there are lots and lots of them. *This is where key indicators can play a role.* To understand this, consider Report 13-6.

Report 13-6
Income Tax after Credits, 1980-2008 (as % of Total Income Taxes)

		By AGI Percentile Bracket						Cumulative AGI Brackets					
Year	Total ($B)	Top 1%	1-5%	5-10	10-25	25-50	Bottom 50%	Top 1%	Top 5%	Top 10%	Top 25%	Top 50%	All 100%
1980	249.1	19.1%	17.8%	12.4%	23.7%	19.9%	7.0%	19.1%	36.8%	49.3%	73.0%	93.0%	100.0%
1981	282.3	17.6%	17.5%	12.9%	24.3%	20.3%	7.5%	17.6%	35.1%	48.0%	72.3%	92.5%	100.0%
1982	276.1	19.0%	17.1%	12.5%	23.9%	20.2%	7.3%	19.0%	36.1%	48.6%	72.5%	92.7%	100.0%
1983	271.6	20.3%	16.9%	12.4%	23.4%	19.7%	7.2%	20.3%	37.3%	49.7%	73.1%	92.8%	100.0%
1984	297.4	21.1%	16.9%	12.6%	22.9%	19.2%	7.4%	21.1%	38.0%	50.6%	73.5%	92.6%	100.0%
1985	321.9	21.8%	17.0%	12.7%	22.6%	18.8%	7.2%	21.8%	38.8%	51.5%	74.1%	92.8%	100.0%
1986	367.0	25.7%	16.8%	12.1%	21.3%	17.5%	6.5%	25.7%	42.6%	54.7%	76.0%	93.5%	100.0%
1987	369.0	24.8%	18.4%	12.4%	21.3%	17.0%	6.1%	24.8%	43.3%	55.6%	76.9%	93.9%	100.0%
1988	412.8	27.6%	18.0%	11.7%	20.6%	16.4%	5.7%	27.6%	45.6%	57.3%	77.8%	94.3%	100.0%
1989	432.8	25.2%	18.7%	11.8%	21.4%	16.9%	5.8%	25.2%	43.9%	55.8%	77.2%	94.2%	100.0%
1990	447.1	25.1%	18.5%	11.7%	21.7%	17.2%	5.8%	25.1%	43.6%	55.4%	77.0%	94.2%	100.0%
1991	448.3	24.8%	18.6%	12.4%	21.5%	17.2%	5.5%	24.8%	43.4%	55.8%	77.3%	94.5%	100.0%
1992	476.2	27.5%	18.3%	12.1%	20.5%	16.5%	5.1%	27.5%	45.9%	58.0%	78.5%	94.9%	100.0%
1993	502.7	29.0%	18.3%	11.9%	20.0%	15.9%	4.8%	29.0%	47.4%	59.2%	79.3%	95.2%	100.0%
1994	534.8	28.9%	18.7%	11.9%	20.1%	15.7%	4.8%	28.9%	47.5%	59.4%	79.6%	95.2%	100.0%
1995	588.3	30.3%	18.6%	11.8%	19.6%	15.0%	4.6%	30.3%	48.9%	60.7%	80.4%	95.4%	100.0%
1996	658.1	32.3%	18.7%	11.5%	18.8%	14.4%	4.3%	32.3%	51.0%	62.5%	81.3%	95.7%	100.0%
1997	727.3	33.2%	18.7%	11.3%	18.5%	14.0%	4.3%	33.2%	51.9%	63.2%	81.7%	95.7%	100.0%
1998	788.5	34.8%	19.1%	11.2%	17.6%	13.1%	4.2%	34.8%	53.8%	65.0%	82.7%	95.8%	100.0%
1999	877.3	36.2%	19.3%	11.0%	17.1%	12.5%	4.0%	36.2%	55.5%	66.5%	83.5%	96.0%	100.0%
2000	980.5	37.4%	19.0%	10.9%	16.7%	12.1%	3.9%	37.4%	56.5%	67.3%	84.0%	96.1%	100.0%
2001	887.9	33.9%	19.4%	11.6%	18.0%	13.1%	4.0%	33.9%	53.3%	64.9%	82.9%	96.0%	100.0%
2002	796.9	33.7%	20.1%	11.9%	18.2%	12.6%	3.5%	33.7%	53.8%	65.7%	83.9%	96.5%	100.0%
2003	747.9	34.3%	20.1%	11.5%	18.0%	12.7%	3.5%	34.3%	54.4%	65.8%	83.9%	96.5%	100.0%
2004	831.9	36.9%	20.2%	11.1%	16.7%	11.8%	3.3%	36.9%	57.1%	68.2%	84.9%	96.7%	100.0%
2005	934.7	39.4%	20.3%	10.6%	15.7%	10.9%	3.1%	39.4%	59.7%	70.3%	86.0%	96.9%	100.0%
2006	1,023.7	39.9%	20.3%	10.7%	15.5%	10.7%	3.0%	39.9%	60.1%	70.8%	86.3%	97.0%	100.0%
2007	1,115.8	40.4%	20.2%	10.6%	15.4%	10.5%	2.9%	40.4%	60.6%	71.2%	86.6%	97.1%	100.0%
2008	1,031.5	38.0%	20.7%	11.2%	16.4%	11.0%	2.7%	38.0%	58.7%	69.9%	86.3%	97.3%	100.0%

NOTE: Tax Reform Act of 1986 changed definition of Adjusted Gross Income (AGI),
so data for 1980-86 are not strictly comparable with data for 1987-2008

REPORT 13-6:   Income Tax after Credits, 1980–2008 (as % of Total Income Taxes)

This report has the same layout and uses the same underlying data as Report 13-5, except that the numbers for each percentile and cumulative bracket are presented *as a percentage of that year's total income taxes*, rather than in dollars.[4] (Recall that a KI is usually nothing more than a ratio of two raw numbers, and in this case it's the ratio of the dollar value in that column from Report 13-5 to the value in the Total column for that year.)

A table like Report 13-6 gives us some context, by enabling us to separate the impact on total income taxes due simply to growth in the U.S. economy from the impact due to changes in how the tax burden was distributed among different income groups. We can now see, for example, that:

- The share of the income tax bill paid by the Top 1% doubled, from 19.1% in 1980 to 38.0% in 2008.

- The share for the next three brackets changed moderately over the same time horizon, increasing from 17.8% to 20.7% for the 1–5% bracket, decreasing slightly from 12.4% to 11.2% for the 5–10% bracket, and dropping from 23.7% to 16.4% for the 10–25% bracket.

- The bottom two brackets saw declines from 1980 to 2008 that were significant by almost any standards—the share of income taxes paid by the 25–50% dropped by nearly one-half, from 19.9% to 11.0%. And the share of the Bottom 50% dropped even more—on a relative basis, if not an absolute basis—from 7.0% to 2.7%. This combined "Bottom 75%" group saw its share of the income tax burden go from 27.0% to 13.7% (that number equals 100% minus the value in the Top 25% column).

Now we're starting to learn something! But we also still have a whole lot of numbers to analyze and digest. At this point in the analysis, a graph might provide useful visual clues to what's going on (see Report 13-7). Report 13-7 graphs the values in the "Cumulative AGI Bracket" columns for the years 1980 (the blue curve) and 2008 (the orange curve). Adding curves for all of the intervening years would make the graph awfully busy (if not downright unreadable), but I did include a curve for a "midpoint" year (1995, the green curve) to give the reader a sense of whether there's a trend.[5] I've also included a straight line labeled "Flat Distrib.," which is what the curve would look like if every taxpayer had the same tax liability. For a graph like this, the visual cue is that the more uneven the distribution of the income tax liability, the more convex the curve will be (i.e., the more it bulges out above the "Flat Distrib." line). The trend that we saw emerging in Report 13-6 is more visually evident in Report 13-7.

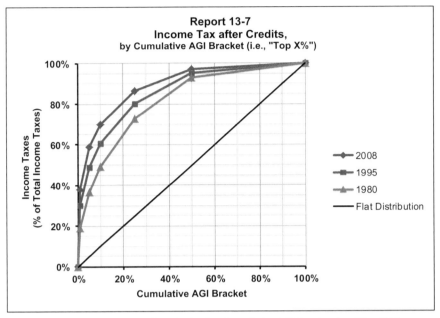

REPORT 13-7:   Income Tax after Credits by Cumulative AGI Bracket (i.e., "Top X%")

What's *Really* Going on Here?

Now that we've identified a trend, are we done with this analysis? *Not so fast!* Whereas introducing a key indicator has enabled us to separate the impact of the growth in the *total* U.S. income tax bill from other factors affecting how much tax was paid by each income bracket, we still don't know *why* the tax burden is shifting so significantly toward taxpayers in the upper income brackets. Have the tax laws changed? Or has the distribution of *income* changed, and as a result the distribution of the taxes based on that income? What's going on?

To consider this question, we need one more table, showing how *income* is distributed among taxpayers. Fortunately, the Tax Foundation has once again done the legwork for us, extracting from data maintained by the IRS. Report 13-8 is identical in both layout and design to the Report 13-6 that we've already reviewed, *except* that Report 13-8 looks at the distribution of Adjusted Gross Income[6] (AGI) rather than the distribution of income taxes. As with Report 13-6, the Total column at the left is the total AGI of all taxpayers, but all of the other numbers show the total AGI of various brackets as a percentage of Total.

I hope I haven't induced "digit fatigue," but we're almost done![7] A look at the table shows trends in AGI similar to the one we've seen for income taxes, including:

- Significant growth in the Total AGI—in fact, a greater growth in AGI than we saw for income taxes—from 1980 to 2008 (from \$1,626.6B to \$8,426.6B)

Report 13-8
Adjusted Gross Income (AGI), 1980-2008 (as % of Total AGI)

Year	Total ($B)	By AGI Percentile Bracket						Cumulative AGI Brackets					
		Top 1%	1-5%	5-10	10-25	25-50	Bottom 50%	Top 1%	Top 5%	Top 10%	Top 25%	Top 50%	All 100%
1980	1,626.6	8.5%	12.5%	11.1%	24.6%	25.6%	17.7%	8.5%	21.0%	32.1%	56.7%	82.3%	100.0%
1981	1,791.1	8.3%	12.5%	11.2%	24.7%	25.6%	17.7%	8.3%	20.8%	32.0%	56.7%	82.3%	100.0%
1982	1,875.9	8.9%	12.3%	11.0%	24.5%	25.5%	17.7%	8.9%	21.2%	32.3%	56.8%	82.3%	100.0%
1983	1,969.6	9.3%	12.5%	11.0%	24.4%	25.3%	17.5%	9.3%	21.7%	32.8%	57.2%	82.5%	100.0%
1984	2,173.2	9.7%	12.5%	11.1%	24.3%	25.0%	17.4%	9.7%	22.2%	33.2%	57.6%	82.6%	100.0%
1985	2,344.0	10.0%	12.6%	11.1%	24.2%	24.8%	17.3%	10.0%	22.7%	33.8%	58.0%	82.7%	100.0%
1986	2,524.1	11.3%	12.8%	11.0%	23.9%	24.3%	16.7%	11.3%	24.1%	35.1%	59.0%	83.3%	100.0%
1987	2,813.7	12.3%	13.3%	11.2%	23.9%	23.6%	15.6%	12.3%	25.7%	36.9%	60.8%	84.4%	100.0%
1988	3,124.2	15.2%	13.4%	10.9%	23.0%	22.6%	14.9%	15.2%	28.5%	39.5%	62.4%	85.1%	100.0%
1989	3,298.9	14.2%	13.7%	11.2%	23.3%	22.8%	15.0%	14.2%	27.8%	39.0%	62.3%	85.0%	100.0%
1990	3,451.2	14.0%	13.6%	11.1%	23.4%	22.8%	15.0%	14.0%	27.6%	38.8%	62.1%	85.0%	100.0%
1991	3,516.1	13.0%	13.8%	11.4%	23.6%	23.0%	15.1%	13.0%	26.8%	38.2%	61.9%	84.9%	100.0%
1992	3,680.6	14.2%	13.8%	11.2%	23.2%	22.6%	14.9%	14.2%	28.0%	39.2%	62.5%	85.1%	100.0%
1993	3,775.6	13.8%	14.0%	11.3%	23.4%	22.6%	14.9%	13.8%	27.8%	39.1%	62.5%	85.1%	100.0%
1994	3,961.1	13.8%	14.0%	11.3%	23.4%	22.5%	14.9%	13.8%	27.8%	39.2%	62.6%	85.1%	100.0%
1995	4,244.6	14.6%	14.2%	11.4%	23.2%	22.1%	14.5%	14.6%	28.8%	40.2%	63.4%	85.5%	100.0%
1996	4,590.5	16.0%	14.3%	11.2%	22.7%	21.6%	14.1%	16.0%	30.4%	41.6%	64.3%	85.9%	100.0%
1997	5,023.5	17.4%	14.4%	11.0%	22.2%	21.1%	13.8%	17.4%	31.8%	42.8%	65.0%	86.2%	100.0%
1998	5,469.2	18.5%	14.4%	10.9%	21.9%	20.7%	13.7%	18.5%	32.9%	43.8%	65.6%	86.3%	100.0%
1999	5,909.3	19.5%	14.5%	10.8%	21.6%	20.3%	13.3%	19.5%	34.0%	44.9%	66.5%	86.7%	100.0%
2000	6,424.0	20.8%	14.5%	10.7%	21.1%	19.9%	13.0%	20.8%	35.3%	46.0%	67.2%	87.0%	100.0%
2001	6,241.0	17.5%	14.5%	11.1%	22.1%	21.0%	13.8%	17.5%	32.0%	43.1%	65.2%	86.2%	100.0%
2002	6,113.8	16.1%	14.4%	11.2%	22.6%	21.4%	14.2%	16.1%	30.6%	41.8%	64.4%	85.8%	100.0%
2003	6,287.6	16.8%	14.4%	11.2%	22.5%	21.1%	14.0%	16.8%	31.2%	42.4%	64.9%	86.0%	100.0%
2004	6,875.1	19.0%	14.4%	10.9%	21.8%	20.5%	13.4%	19.0%	33.4%	44.4%	66.1%	86.6%	100.0%
2005	7,508.0	21.2%	14.5%	10.7%	21.1%	19.7%	12.8%	21.2%	35.7%	46.4%	67.5%	87.2%	100.0%
2006	8,122.0	22.1%	14.6%	10.7%	20.8%	19.3%	12.5%	22.1%	36.7%	47.3%	68.2%	87.5%	100.0%
2007	8,798.5	22.8%	14.6%	10.6%	20.7%	19.0%	12.3%	22.8%	37.4%	48.1%	68.7%	87.7%	100.0%
2008	8,426.6	20.0%	14.7%	11.0%	21.6%	19.9%	12.8%	20.0%	34.7%	45.8%	67.4%	87.2%	100.0%

NOTE: Tax Reform Act of 1986 changed definition of Adjusted Gross Income (AGI),
so data for 1980-86 are not strictly comparable with data for 1987-2008.

REPORT 13-8   Adjusted Gross Income (AGI), 1980–2008 (as % of Total AGI)

- A significant increase in the Top 1% bracket's share of Total AGI, from 8.5% in 1980 to 20.0% in 2008

- A decline in the last two brackets—from 25.6% to 19.9% for the 25–50% bracket and from 17.7% to 12.8% for the Bottom 50%—over the 29-year time horizon

From this report we see that the shift in the distribution of the income tax burden between 1980 and 2008 corresponds to a shift in the distribution of income (as measured by AGI). To understand this visually, first look at Report 13-9, a graph similar to the one we saw in Report 13-7. The solid blue curve again shows how income taxes were distributed across taxpayers in 2008. The broken blue curve shows the corresponding distribution of Adjusted Gross Income for the same year. Note that the income taxes curve sits *above* the AGI

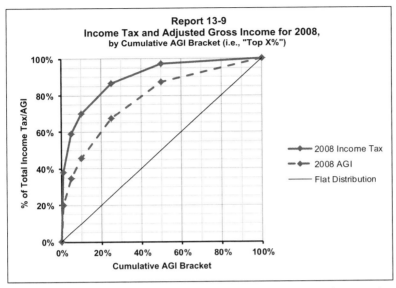

REPORT 13-9: Income Tax and Adjusted Gross Income for 2008 by Cumulative AGI Bracket (i.e., "Top X%")

curve, from which we infer that the tax burden was more heavily skewed toward higher earners than the distribution of the underlying income. In other words, harking back to the discussion of *progressive* income taxes earlier in this chapter, this graph tells us that in 2008 the federal income tax system was progressive.

Next, let's add the same pair of curves for another year. Report 13-10 also graphs the corresponding distribution of income taxes and AGI for 1980 (the orange curves).

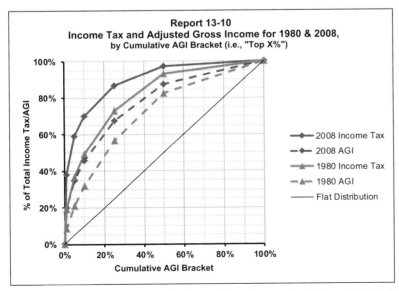

REPORT 13-10: Income Tax and Adjusted Gross Income for 1980 and 2008 by Cumulative AGI Bracket (i.e., "Top X%")

As you can see, both pairs of curves—the two AGI curves (the broken lines) and the two income taxes curves (the solid lines)—shifted upward from 1980 to 2008. This supports the earlier hypothesis that the increasingly uneven distribution of AGI contributed to the increasingly uneven distribution of the income tax burden.[8]

Let's stop here. We've seen a lot of exhibits and a lot of numbers. And while I consider Report 13-10 to be the simplest way to present this particular analysis, it was comparing the distributions of AGI and income taxes for only *two* years. Imagine how that graph would have looked if it had included more than just two years! Feel free to review these reports and consider how quantation can help answer key questions in public policy and beyond.

I hope the discussion in this chapter has shown that if you apply the basic techniques of good quantation, it is possible to generate reports that are as meaningful to the area of understanding taxation as we have come to demand in the business world. And the same goes for fiscal management, healthcare, education, and so many other important areas of public policy.

If you took the position that those responsible for delivering management reports and financial statements for businesses have it much easier than those who provide information on public policy issues, you would have a point. In business there is a profit motive, which drives how business reports are designed. There are also established, formal standards for investor reporting prescribed by generally accepted accounting principles (GAAP), as discussed in Chapter 12, and the combination of the profit motive and the ultimate need to report to investors contribute to the existence of widely understood templates and best practices for management reporting. Those standards aren't nearly as clear in the public policy arena. More important, the *end objectives* are not always clear in the public policy arena and they are often hotly debated. This makes the task of delivering meaningful quantation about public policy issues especially challenging. But that also means that doing quantation *well* plays a key role in bringing the critical issues into focus, making it especially worthwhile.

NOTES

1. The specific value for "X" is open to discussion, but as a practical matter in most progressive taxation systems, the total share of the tax bill will exceed the total share of income regardless of the value chosen for "X."

2. The Tax Foundation provides a remarkable public service, and the information in the tables they provide is intended to meet the needs of as many potential users as possible. My focus is a little different. Also, one of the principal services the Tax Foundation provides is that they organize the information obtained from the Internal Revenue Service, and considering the condition that data from most government agencies arrives in, that is a valuable service indeed!

3. A *local* maximum (or minimum) is a value that is the largest (or smallest) value among nearby data points—such as the few years immediately preceding or following that data point—but is not necessarily the largest (or smallest) value across the entire range of data points.

4. The one exception column is the Total column at the left, which I'm still presenting in dollars. I made that choice to give readers a sense of the scale of the overall numbers, and to give readers who were interested the ability to convert the percentage numbers in the rest of the table back into dollars. Also note the inclusion of the "($B)" in the column heading to identify the unit of measure, one of the identification methods discussed in Chapter 1.

5. It's a small thing, but note that the legend to the right of the graph lists the curves in the same position as they appear visually on the graph. This is a design choice I made; you can choose the order the series appear in the legend. In this case, I think it makes the graph a little easier to read.

6. Adjusted Gross Income is a taxpayer's total income, less reductions for items such as pension plan contributions, certain healthcare costs, alimony, and some professional expenses. It is a reasonable measure of total household income, and is the most meaningful and consistent measure of income available from tax returns filed.

7. Recall that Report 13-6 was preceded by Report 13-5, which showed income taxes in total dollars. For the corresponding information on AGI distribution I've skipped that step in the interests of space and an effort to minimize "digit fatigue."

8. I'm relegating this comment to a note, because we're focusing on presenting rather than analyzing the raw information. However, one use of a graph showing the distribution of both income and taxes for the same year is that it can give you a visual sense of how progressive a taxation system is: the farther the tax curve sits above the income curve, the more progressive the tax (or, for that matter, if the tax curve sits *below* the income curve, how *regressive* that tax is). A close visual inspection of the AGI and income taxes curves for 2008 (the blue curves) indicates that they sit farther apart from each other than the two corresponding curves for 1980 (the orange curves), suggesting that federal income taxes became more progressive over that time period. Probably the largest contributors to this change were the tax reform acts passed in 1986 and 2001.

CHAPTER 14

Quantation in Ordinary Life

A little simplification would be the first step toward rational living, I think.

—Eleanor Roosevelt

In this chapter, we'll discuss a few quantation examples that are a little off the beaten track. Still, they are excellent examples of the relevance of quantation to our daily lives, and provide further examples of how the rules and best practices we discuss can be applied. The topics we'll visit include:

- **Models**—a particular type of quantation that makes decisions clearer in all kinds of situations by making processes and interrelationships easier to understand.

- **The meaning of words**—a few examples from the newspapers, showing the importance of how we *characterize* numerical things.

- **That quiz I promised.** Way back in the Introduction, I showed you a table of numbers and said that by the end of this book you would be able to identify its flaws. Let's see how you do.

Models

In the world of quantation, a *model* is a method of describing a process that can be quantified in a way that enables you to understand the dynamics of that process. In a business context, models also help estimate the impact of key uncertain variables on critical outcomes like profits or revenues. You could think of a model as a *simulation*.[1] You can create a model on a sheet of paper, or a whiteboard, or a cocktail napkin, but the most effective way to create a model is with a spreadsheet, so you have a helping hand with the arithmetic as your underlying assumptions change. A simple example of a model is the pricing models for the Gutenberg Printing Company we first saw in Chapter 2, where the inputs were variables driven by the customer (image size, number of copies, paper quality, and color versus black and white) and the output is the price quoted to the customer.

The purpose of a model is *to help someone make a decision.* You or I might want to build a model to help us make an important decision we face in our personal life, such as:

- What kind of mortgage loan to apply for where there are choices about terms such as maturity (30 years, 15 years, etc.), fixed versus variable rate, and paying points to reduce the interest rate
- What type of health insurance to buy where the choices include PPO versus HMO versus Health Savings Account, amount of deductible, and many other factors

Business situations that lend themselves to modeling include:

- How much to charge for a complex product (like Gutenberg's printing services)
- How much expense to budget for a sales organization, depending on market demand and sales productivity assumptions

In order for a model to work properly, it must do two things: (1) clearly characterize the model environment, and (2) clearly characterize the logical relationship between the inputs (i.e., the uncertain variables) and the outputs (i.e., the objectives to be maximized). Because a model is designed to help you make an informed choice, comprehensible layout and organization are essential. To see how important this is, consider Report 14-1, a real-life model that I actually built for myself to help me decide whether to seek a publisher for *Painting with Numbers* or whether to self-publish.[2]

First, a little background: With the advent of (1) increasingly powerful software tools for book design and layout and the availability of print-on-demand services, and (2) online bookstores and increasingly powerful websites with easily implementable methods of electronic commerce, self-publishing is no longer an alternative available only to the rich and vain. The dramatic increases each year in the number of self-published books attest to that. Economically, the choice boils down to whether bearing *all* of the fixed costs of bringing a book to market is justified by the greater revenue per book (minus the printing and fulfillment costs you must bear), as compared to the royalties the publisher will share with an author. What this means is that if the book doesn't sell many copies,

Report 14-1
Analysis of Decision to Self-Publish vs. Use a Publisher

Editorial/Design Costs		Self-Pub.	Publisher
Book coach	3,000	100%	100%
Development ed	15,000	100%	70%
Copy/proofread	1,500	100%	0%
Layout/cover	1,500	100%	0%
		21,000	13,500

Other Out-of-Pocket Costs			
Publicist	20,000	100%	70%
Website	5,000	100%	100%
		46,000	32,500

Revenue Factors	
List price	$29.95

Self-Publish		
Avg. sale discount	48%	($15.57 net price)
Fulfillment/unit	$2.50	

Use a Publisher	
Royalty from publisher (% of List)	10%
Agent Fee (% of royalties)	15%

Considerations not quantified:

P 1. Value of publisher's "name" (beyond volume uplift)
P 2. Publisher advance (i.e., cash flow)
S 3. Time-to-market
S 4. Control over content & design
P 5. Effort involved if I self-publish

P = Advantage goes to Use a Publisher
S = Advantage goes to Self-Publish

SCENARIOS

Basic Units	Self-Publish Print/Copy	Net $$	Use a Publisher (with % volume uplift scenarios)								
			+ 0%	Net $$	Diff. $$	+ 25%	Net $$	Diff. $$	+ 50%	Net $$	Diff. $$
500	$11.00	(44,963)	500	(31,227)	(13,736)	625	(30,909)	(14,054)	750	(30,591)	(14,372)
1,000	$10.50	(43,426)	1,000	(29,954)	(13,472)	1,250	(29,318)	(14,108)	1,500	(28,681)	(14,745)
2,500	$10.00	(38,315)	2,500	(26,136)	(12,179)	3,125	(24,545)	(13,770)	3,750	(22,953)	(15,362)
5,000	$9.50	(28,130)	5,000	(19,771)	(8,359)	6,250	(16,589)	(11,541)	7,500	(13,407)	(14,723)
10,000	$9.00	(5,260)	10,000	(7,043)	1,783	12,500	(678)	(4,582)	15,000	5,686	(10,946)
25,000	$8.50	68,350	25,000	31,144	37,206	31,250	47,055	21,295	37,500	62,966	5,384
50,000	$8.00	207,700	50,000	94,788	112,913	62,500	126,609	81,091	75,000	158,431	49,269
Breakeven Units:		~9,121		~12,656			~20,054				

REPORT 14-1:   Analysis of Decision to Self-Publish versus Use a Publisher

you may be better off using a publisher, since the publisher will bear many of the fixed costs; but if the book sells well, the greater per-copy net revenues may ultimately more than cover the fixed costs you have to bear yourself. However, one additional factor to consider is the possibility that the credibility of having a well-known publisher and its access to larger distribution channels may mean higher sales than you would get by self-publishing.

With this in mind, here's how to read Report 14-1:

- The **assumptions regarding out-of-pocket expenses**—editing, book design, and marketing costs—associated with producing a book are grouped together at the top-left of the worksheet. Just below them is the **revenue assumptions**—the list price of the book, the self-publishing assumptions (the average discount from list price and fulfillment cost per copy), and the assumptions if you use a publisher (the per-copy royalty and the fee to an agent).

- The two largest uncertainties surrounding this decision are (a) the **number of copies** the book will sell, and (b) the **uplift in the number of copies** that will result from using a well-known and reputable publisher. I've chosen to define *uplift* as the percentage increase in unit sales that will result from using a publisher. So, at the bottom of the worksheet is a table showing the net result of self-publishing and using a publisher under various possible scenarios for (a) and (b).

- Throughout the worksheet, only the **shaded boldface** cells are **values that the modeler can change.** All other cells are either values that do not change, intermediate calculations, or critical metrics. In particular, note that:

  - I presume that if I were to self-publish, I would bear 100% of all out-of-pocket costs. If I used a publisher, the publisher would bear all of the costs of copyediting, proofreading, layout, and cover design, and only some of the other costs—developmental editing, publicity, and website management.

  - Note that there is only one value for the list price—I presume that the price will be the same whether I self-publish or use a publisher.

  - Since there are printing economies of scale, it's important to model a declining per-copy cost of printing as the number of copies increases (see the "Print/Copy" column in the "Self-Publish" scenario).

  - In the "Use a Publisher (with % volume uplift scenarios)" area, I model three possible volume uplift scenarios: 0% (i.e., the same number of copies is sold under either alternative) is a default that is always there, but I have also chosen to consider publisher volume uplifts of 25% and 50%, where 50% is the largest uplift I believe I can reasonably expect from using a publisher. The "Basic Units" column shows the number of copies sold if I self-publish, and the percentage columns (0%, 25%, and 50%) show the corresponding number of copies sold if I use a publisher.

- The "Diff. $$" column shows the **difference in net dollar outcome** between self-publishing and using a publisher. As you can see, as the number of copies increases, this number gradually shifts from a negative number (self-publishing is less lucrative than using a publisher) to a positive number.

- The **Breakeven Units row,** shown at the bottom of the report, is an estimate of the number of copies that would have to be sold under the self-publishing alternative before self-publishing becomes more lucrative than using a publisher.

Getting to this Breakeven Units number was the entire object of this exercise. The number of copies that will ultimately be sold is highly uncertain, as is an estimate of how many more copies will be sold because a publisher is involved (i.e., the volume uplift). But with this model, I can now make a statement like, "If using a publisher will increase my volume by 25% or more, then if I self-publish *Painting with Numbers* I will have to sell at least 12,656 copies to come out ahead of using a publisher." Although I may not know exactly how many copies will get sold, I might have a good sense of whether 12,656 copies is likely or unlikely.

A model is a different type of report from the ones we've looked at previously, but nevertheless the lessons of this book apply just as strongly. Here are some examples of quantation principles applied in this example:

- There is a logical flow of thought about the economics of this issue that mirrors the process of producing a book, from the initial costs (Editorial/Design Costs), to later out-of-pocket fixed costs (Publicist and Website), to the parameters of the revenue model (Revenue Factors), to the actual financial results (Scenarios), so that's how the model is laid out on the page. (See Chapter 3, about the intuitive ordering of words, and a similar discussion in Chapter 11.)

- Making the assumptions that can be changed visually distinct from all the other cells (the **shaded boldface** cells) in the worksheet makes it much easier to understand the model's logic. (See Long-Term Payoff Tip #7—on making different types of cells visually distinguishable and physically separate—from Chapter 6.)

- The Breakeven Units metric is an example of a *key indicator* that is calculated from other numbers in the same report. In this case, not only does it add context and meaning to the raw numbers (see Chapter 10), *understanding this breakeven point is actually the ultimate objective of this model.*

- In a blank area of the worksheet, I've added the "Considerations not quantified." While none of the five considerations listed has any impact on the model calculations, it's useful to have them available to the model's user. Some of these considerations might be tiebreakers if the Breakeven Units result were very close to what actual sales are expected to be. (See Chapter 3 on the use of appropriately placed comments to clarify and enhance.)

- Note the relatively free-form layout of this particular model. It doesn't resemble any of the other reports we've looked at in this book and its design is really driven by how we would logically organize our thoughts. (My assertion that *you have choices* is expressed frequently throughout this book.)

If you were to look closely at the spreadsheet that generated Report 14-1, you would see a few formulas that take a small amount of math skill,[3] but not many. The *real* value of a model lies not in the convenience of having your arithmetic done for you, but in the exercise of organizing your thinking. The value *to me* of the model shown in Report 14-1 is that it made me think clearly about my costs of producing a book under the two alternatives, the revenue economics of selling a book myself versus using a publisher, and what the decision was really going to come down to—that is, how many copies of *Painting with Numbers* I would have to sell to justify the expense and hassle of doing the work myself. You'll be surprised at how valuable an exercise like this can be in helping you understand important processes and decisions in your own life.

The Meaning of Words

Let's talk about *words* instead of numbers for a moment. As we've discussed, especially in Chapter 3, numbers mean nothing without a bunch of words around them. Taking this one step further, sometimes words mean nothing without a few numbers mixed in. For example: "I can afford to take a nicer vacation this year because I got a 25% raise." Or, "We're batting Kreitzmeyer leadoff and Zwick in the #7 slot, even though Zwick is batting .297 and Kreitzmeyer .243, because Kreitzmeyer's on-base percentage is .357 and he's stolen 40 bases." My point is that sometimes quantation does not involve any tables or graphs, but any time quantation is not done properly, the results can be confusing. In this section, we'll discuss a few examples of this taken from today's press and broadcast media.

"Tax Rates." As I write this, one of the most contentious debates in Washington is about tax rates, with much rhetoric on both sides of the aisle about the need to "rationalize" and "simplify" the federal income tax code, and "reduce tax rates" in the process. The intention of many proponents of this approach, though, is also to *increase tax revenues* in the process. Now how can that be? How can you reduce tax rates and increase tax revenues?

The answer lies in the kind of "rate" the speaker is talking about. Consider a very simple example, of a household with total gross income of $80,000 that currently pays taxes at a 20% rate, with deductions and other income reductions totaling $30,000. Let's suppose a proposed "rationalization" of taxes would reduce those deductions to $16,000, but also lower the tax "rate" to 18%. Report 14-2 shows how the two scenarios would look. Because the household's lower tax "rate" under the proposed scheme (18% versus 20%) gets applied to Taxable Income that is $14,000 higher, the income tax bill ends up $1,520 higher, so the *effective* tax rate—that is, Income Tax divided by Gross Income, which most of us think of as the way to calculate our "tax rate"—has actually gone *up*, from 12.5% to 14.4%.[4]

Report 14-2
Current vs. Proposed Tax Schemes

(in $$, except %s)	Current Scheme	Proposed "Lower Rate"
Gross Income	80,000	80,000
Deductions, etc.	(30,000)	(16,000)
Taxable Income	50,000	64,000
Published Tax Rate	20.0%	18.0%
Income Tax	10,000	11,520
Effective Tax Rate	12.5%	14.4%

REPORT 14-2: Current versus Proposed Tax Schemes

In other words, the question of whether tax rates have gone up or down depends on which rate you are talking about. The problem is that many of the politicians making the news (with some noble exceptions) would rather we focus on "lower tax rates" than "higher tax revenues," and the people reporting the news don't seem to feel that point is worth clarifying.[5]

"Gazillions in Savings." For the past few years, there has been a disturbing trend toward unhooking dollar amounts from time periods, especially by legislators and public servants. You will hear statements like, "This program will cost [or save] taxpayers $53 billion." What they're *not* always telling you is that the $53 billion is the cost [or savings] *over the next ten years*. Even when they do provide the time horizon, is the total given for a ten-year period a number

you can relate to? One of the strangest examples I've ever seen was in the *New York Times*, which ran a story about a piece of New Jersey legislation that "will save local and state governments $132 billion over the next 30 years...."[6] Huh? Thirty years? What does that mean? Why not $264 billion over the next 60 years? Or $396 billion over the next 90 years?

But that still leaves some questions unanswered, such as: Are the costs [or savings] evenly distributed over the 30 years, or are they heavily front- or back-loaded? And what happens at the end of the 30 years? Do the costs [or savings] continue or just drop off a cliff? Considering all these concerns about a number that is confusing in the first place, what we have here is a variant of Deadly Sin #7—presenting numbers with no context whatsoever. When you don't provide a time period over which a dollar amount applies, the audience has no context for the amount. And even if you *do* provide a time period, but the horizon is a nonstandard period of time, there's *still* no context.

On this particular point, there is a ray of hope. As I write this, the Great Debt Ceiling Debate of 2011 is climaxing. Numbers are being thrown around like confetti, but many politicians and the journalists seem fairly diligent about specifying when numbers are for a 10-year period. And maybe we'll just have to get used to the decade as a timeframe for numbers, just as we've gotten used to year, quarter, month, week, and day. At least when 10 years is the time horizon, we can translate to a per-year number just by moving the decimal point over one place. I just pray that we don't start citing numbers over 7 years, or 18 years, or some other hard-to-grasp number.

"Grew." A recent news item said, "April 2011 U.S. auto sales of 1,144,868 units grew 17.7% over the April 2010 figure of 972,615." Is *grew* the right word to describe what's happening? Well, that depends. Suppose, for example, that sales in the intervening months were as shown in Report 14-3, which we'll call "Model 1" of the sales trend.[7]

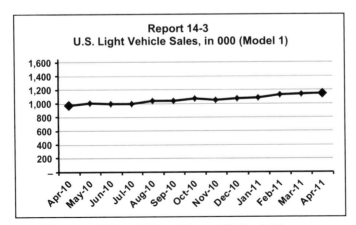

REPORT 14-3: U.S. Light Vehicle Sales, in 000 (Model 1)

The graph in Report 14-3 shows a fairly steady, generally upward movement from 973,000 units in April 2010 to 1,145,000 units in April 2011. In this scenario, it's reasonable to say that sales "grew" by 17.7% year-over-year, because there does appear to be a clear, steady trend.

However, suppose the results in the intervening months were something completely different, like the hypothetical results shown in Report 14-4 ("Model 2").

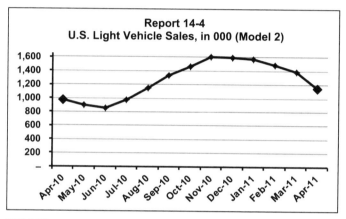

REPORT 14-4:   U.S. Light Vehicle Sales, in 000 (Model 2)

What we have here is a situation where sales dropped fairly significantly in the two months following April 2010, rose dramatically for the next five months, and then showed an increasingly steep slide downward in the five months ending April 2011. Does "growth" seem like the right characterization of what's happening here?

The problem is that when we speak of *growth*, our natural inclination is to think of that process over contiguous periods of time. It makes complete sense to think of a positive change between the results for *all of* 2010 and *all of* 2011 as growth. It also makes sense to us when the time periods are not contiguous but the period-to-period change is steady. A good example of this perspective is the U.S. population, which per the Census was about 281 million in 2000 and 309 million in 2010. It makes complete sense to us to characterize that difference of 9.7% as growth, because it's hard to imagine that there was anything but a steady trend over those ten years. The population of a country with hundreds of millions of people just doesn't flop around year-to-year or month-to-month like the revenues of a startup software company.

The descriptions we see and hear in our daily lives are just loaded with imprecise uses of the language. But when just words are involved, most of us who are literate instantly recognize imprecise or misleading uses of the language. This is less true when numbers are cited. Moreover, as I've noted before, when numbers are involved it often means that *the stakes are higher*—what you are reading or hearing is particularly important, perhaps even to you personally. I'm encouraging you to be a diligent member of the audience, and when the quantation you hear or read is unclear, speak up and demand clarity.

That Quiz I Promised

Way back in the Introduction, we looked at a real-life example of quantation that had many flaws, and I promised those flaws would become apparent to you in the course of *Painting with Numbers*. Here it is again, as Report 14-5. See whether you can spot the quantation flaws.

Report 14-5
Item Taped to Table in County Clerk's Office

MASS CONVERSION FOR METERS TO FEET

Divide the amount of meters by .3048 to get
the proper feet

Meters	Feet
1,524	5'
1,5494	5'1"
1,5748	5'2"
1,6002	5'3"
1,6256	5'4"
1,651	5'5"
1,6764	5'6"
1,7018	5'7"
1,7272	5'8"
1,7526	5'9"
1,778	5'10"
1,8034	5'11"
1,8288	6'
1,8542	6'1"
1,8796	6'2"
1,905	6'3"
1,9304	6'4"

REPORT 14-5: Item Taped to Table in County Clerk's Office

Here's my list (although you might have some others):

- **Column order.** I presume that the table is for converting feet to meters, because the meters numbers are taken out to four decimal places. (Why would you have a table to help you convert *from*, say, 1.8288 meters *into* feet, which by coincidence happens to turn out to be exactly 6 feet?) We read from left to right, so if we're thinking of converting *from* feet *to* meters, the Feet column should precede (i.e., be to the left of) the Meters column.

- **Layout.** The two columns are unnecessarily far apart, making it hard to read along a single row. Just because white space is available doesn't mean you must use it.

- **Precision.** The meters measurement needs only two decimal places, at least for any purpose worth presenting in a county clerk's office in the United States.[8] Moreover, a centimeter (i.e., 0.01 meter) is the metric "inch." We rarely think in fractions of an inch (at least as far as a person's height is concerned), so why would we think in *hundredths* of a centimeter?

- **The words #1.** The instruction at the top—to divide the meters by .3048 to calculate the feet— is a little strange when the meters are being converted into feet *and inches*. And if the table is for converting feet into meters and not the other way around (as I speculate above), why is this statement there at all?

- **The words #2.** What the heck is a "mass conversion"? Some sort of religious ceremony? And isn't mass a unit of weight, not length, anyway? And what are "proper feet"? Nicely shaped, aristocratic ones? Oh, and the "inches" are probably feeling left out.

- **Tiny details.** And some minor points:
  - In a column of numbers, it's customary to show each number to the same number of decimal places, which the Meters column does not do.
  - In the United States, we use periods as the decimal point, not commas.
  - In my opinion, centering the numbers in the Feet column makes those values a little hard to read. It makes more sense to line up the values for the feet, as you'll see in Report 14-6.[9]

Report 14-6 shows my own version of this report, which took me only about 15 minutes to generate. Now we have a table that is easier to read, is linguistically accurate, and—in less space than Report 14-5 takes up—can be used to convert from feet/inches to meters, *and* from meters to feet/inches.[10]

This example reflects the fact that quantation is like air: it is all around us, for all kinds of uses to which we don't give a second thought. Think about all the little ways you see numbers constantly in your daily life: credit card receipts, the pricing information beneath every item in the grocery store, sports box scores, your monthly bank and credit card statements, the readouts on your car's dashboard, to name just a few. Take a look at them. Some are clear and comprehensible, some not. And have you ever gotten a hospital bill or an "explanation of benefits" statement from your insurance provider that actually made sense to you? How would you present the information differently? If any of the information was time-consuming to absorb or flat-out confusing or misleading,

Report 14-6 Converting between Feet/Inches and Meters			
from Ft./In.	to Meters	from Meters	to Ft./In.
5'	1.52	1.52	5'
5' 1"	1.55	1.54	5' 1"
5' 2"	1.57	1.56	5' 1"
5' 3"	1.60	1.58	5' 2"
5' 4"	1.63	1.60	5' 3"
5' 5"	1.65	1.62	5' 4"
5' 6"	1.68	1.64	5' 5"
5' 7"	1.70	1.66	5' 5"
5' 8"	1.73	1.68	5' 6"
5' 9"	1.75	1.70	5' 7"
5' 10"	1.78	1.72	5' 8"
5' 11"	1.80	1.74	5' 9"
6'	1.83	1.76	5' 9"
6' 1"	1.85	1.78	5' 10"
6' 2"	1.88	1.80	5' 11"
6' 3"	1.91	1.82	6'
6' 4"	1.93	1.84	6'
6' 5"	1.96	1.86	6' 1"
6' 6"	1.98	1.88	6' 2"
6' 7"	2.01	1.90	6' 3"
6' 8"	2.03	1.92	6' 4"

REPORT 14-6:   Converting between Feet/Inches and Meters

did you complain? Did you suggest improvements? If you did neither, then I have a prediction: *nothing is going to change.*

I feel a little self-conscious about picking on something as mundane and trivial as a metric conversion table in a county clerk's office. But the value of that quantation can be significantly enhanced by just a little attention to detail. That attention isn't time-consuming at all, if you give serious thought to what you're actually trying to do for your audience, and if you make the clear, thoughtful presentation of numbers a *habit*. And to audiences weary of being presented with incomprehensible, meaningless numbers, that attention to detail will be a much-appreciated breath of fresh air.

Quantation is ubiquitous and it creeps into our lives in many ways. When we think about the craft of writing, we usually think about the important things that we write and read—memos, position papers, legal documents, works of fiction. But the volume of all that is dwarfed by all the other written material that shows up in our lives—e-mail messages, notes to ourselves, thank-you notes, text messages, birthday and holiday cards, written tests, shopping lists, and so on. The same is true of quantation. It's natural to think first of the annual, quarterly, or monthly financial statements, or reporting packages that must be prepared for board of directors meetings, but there is lots more.

With all of the quantation around us, you have a wonderful opportunity to sharpen your skills at presenting numbers. If you are in the audience for the information, learn from what seems to work and what doesn't, and *speak up* if you see opportunities for improvement. If you are generating the information, you can give yourself lots of practice for those times when the stakes really *are* high. If we all did this, the world would be a better-run, less confusing place. I will once again quote Shaquille O'Neal quoting Aristotle, who said, "Excellence is not a singular act, but a habit."

NOTES

1. Although the word *model* is widely used in this context, both as a noun and as a verb, I could not find an intelligible dictionary definition, so I made up my own. If it's *still* not intelligible, keep reading and you'll get it from the context.

2. I am not kidding—I actually did use this model. However, in order to stay on the right side of my publisher, the underlying assumptions presented here are fictionalized.

3. I said in the Introduction that this book is *not* about numbers—it's about *presenting* numbers—so the math in Report 14-1 is of little interest here. In case you *are* interested, though, the formulas in the Net $$ columns do arithmetic based on the cost and revenue parameters, and the Breakeven Units formula uses linear interpolation to calculate the point at which the Diff. $$ number switches from negative to positive. Other than that, the formulas use no math other than simple addition and multiplication. I might add that the Breakeven Units formula takes advantage of Lookup & Reference functions—see Instant Payoff Tip #6 from Chapter 5.

4. This discussion gets even more complicated with graduated tax rates, like the rates shown in Schedule X (Report 13-1) at the beginning of Chapter 13. Recall that we discussed the difference between the marginal tax rate and the effective tax rate. Well, there are really *two* effective tax rates: the rate calculated using Taxable Income as the numerator (as we do in Report 14-2), and the one calculated using Gross Income (or Adjusted Gross Income, the measure used in the exhibits in Chapter 13) as the denominator. The difference between these two *effective* tax rates is driven by the difference between Gross Income (or AGI) and Taxable Income, which equals the amount of itemized deductions, credits, and other adjustments permitted. So, in this more complex but more real-life scenario, we are really considering *three* different tax rates.

5. Please don't think I'm on a soapbox here. I am using this debate merely to raise the matter of what we mean when we say *tax rate*. The numerous proponents of reforming the U.S. tax system by eliminating many deductions and credits and at the same time lowering rates argue that the U.S. economy would be better off after such reform, even if total tax revenues increase or stay about the same. Not everyone agrees with that, but their logic is worthy of discussion.

6. From the *New York Times*, June 23, 2011. Strangely, this number was cited by the administration of Gov. Chris Christie, who has developed a rather positive reputation for straight talk. And depressingly, but unfortunately *not* strangely, when I Googled the above-quoted phrase *verbatim*, I got 164,000 hits! I guess many journalists are satisfied just to repeat the news rather than write their own stories.

7. The April 2010 and April 2011 figures are the actual numbers as reported, but the numbers for the intervening months are pretend numbers.

8. I confess that I have absolutely no idea why a table like this contains information that would be useful in a county clerk's office, let alone important enough to be taped to a tabletop in the lobby. If you can explain this, please let me know.

9. For more on the question of aligning unusual types of numbers in a column, see the discussion of Deadly Sin #1 in the Appendix.

10. There are various ways to present a distance in feet and inches (e.g., 5 feet 7 inches as 5′ 8″) in Excel. The method I used was to start with the raw number of inches, calculating the number of feet using the ROUND() function (INT() also works) and the number of remaining inches using the MOD() function. Then I used the CONCATENATE() function to join the feet and inches into a single string of characters.

PART IV

WRAP-UP

CHAPTER 15

Speaking Truth to Power

"I paint what I see, child."

—*Gahan Wilson, American cartoonist.*

A few years ago, I would not have considered this chapter appropriate, let alone necessary. Over the past few years, though, public perceptions have hardened about the motivation of people who present numbers. With respect to corporate financial results, there have been a few spectacular cases of accounting fraud, such as Enron, HealthSouth, and MCI WorldCom. The aftermath of the Global Financial Crisis of 2007–08 has included many allegations of fraudulent presenting of numbers. And even though the high-technology bubble of the late 1990s provoked very few criminal complaints, it still led many people to believe that those who present financial information are interested in following the rules only for the sake of compliance, and not to provide clear, comprehensible information about their businesses.

And the perceptions of those in the public policy arena aren't any kinder. With respect to the numbers we're given on important public policy issues like fiscal policy, taxation, and healthcare all too many people—both presenters and audiences—look at the numbers through the filter of partisan politics.

These perceptions are a real shame, and it's the wrong way to look at the craft of quantation. In this chapter, we will examine the topic of honesty in the presentation of numbers. Why is honesty important? Does dishonesty pay, or is it just too hard to get away with? What accounts for all those negative perceptions? How often are numbers presentations *intentionally* dishonest? Where does the responsibility lie for making sure that information is clear and properly understood? These questions are an interesting place to start.

My "Tell the Truth" Syllogism

I'm going to give it to you straight. As much as I'd like to preserve my reputation as a pragmatic, unsentimental, and businesslike provider of financial and other information, there is one inflexible rule for presenting numbers: *you must tell the truth*. To understand why this is so, I have constructed a cascading list of five reasons why honesty is so essential:

1. It's the right thing to do.
2. It's in your employer's interest.
3. It's in *your* interest.
4. You *will* get caught.
5. It's the "gotcha" of this book.

Reasons #1 through #4 are evident to most people, but I list them all for the sake of Jesuitical (or perhaps Talmudic) completeness. Permit me to elaborate on each one.

Reason #1 for Telling the Truth: It's the Right Thing to Do

It just is.

Reason #2: It's in Your Employer's Interest

Perhaps your parents and teachers never gave you reason #1. If so, you might find it tempting to fudge some numbers and ignore others to make your employer, or your department, or maybe just your boss look good. Avoid the temptation. First, you are overlooking one of the fundamental characteristics of double-entry bookkeeping, the accounting methodology that has been with us for the past thousand years or so: that the *total* financial results over an extended period of time are very difficult to mess with. Any upward adjustment to, say, revenues in the current accounting period has to mean a correspondingly lower result at some point in the future. Not only that, in a management and investment environment that focuses intensively on period-to-period comparisons, by beefing up your current-period results you may be setting an impossible standard for results in future periods.

Moreover, when questionable accounting or reporting practices are discovered, the overall result is very likely to be more negative than the positive impact of those practices on the current period. Put another way, the downside is likely to be more "down" than the upside is "up." Recall the discussion of Bolten's Law and its corollaries from Chapter 4. Your audience may form conclusions about you, or at least about your employer, even from seemingly innocent behaviors like omissions. And those conclusions may be harsh. And the harsher the conclusion, the less likely you are to be aware that your audience has formed those conclusions about you or your employer. You do not want to be in this bind. It's always better to put the best face you can on obviously bad results than to alter those results.

Reason #3: It's in *Your* Interest

Perhaps you have somehow gotten past reason #2, and still believe that your employer's numbers would actually benefit from a bit of, how shall I put this, "nudging the ball out of the rough." If so, stop for a quick conversation with a mirror. Leave questions of conscience aside, and ask yourself if this is a good thing for *you* to do. First, just as it is true for your employer, the downside of these actions is almost certain to be more down for you than your upside is up. Moreover, if that downside scenario materializes, your company will act in *its* interest, not yours. Regardless of the appreciation initially showered on you for saving the day, the organization will look for someone to throw under the bus.

 Note

A real-life parable: One of the most spectacular accounting fraud cases of recent years was HealthSouth. The CEO, Richard Scrushy, and several senior finance executives were indicted for accounting fraud and/or securities law violations. Each finance executive was convicted of (or pled guilty to) something, and all testified against the CEO. Even so, Scrushy claimed that he was an innocent dupe of his underlings, and was acquitted on all counts. Now, I know finance executives; most of us are not the kind of people who freelance this sort of thing. The odds that an innocent, well-meaning CEO would get bamboozled by a long string of fraud-inclined financial officers are comparable to the odds that you will be struck by a meteor the day the Chicago Cubs win the World Series. So, as to the question of who—you or your superior—would win in a dispute over who committed the fraud, you may want to consider the evidence.[1]

Reason #4: You *Will* Get Caught

Even if you have managed to zigzag your way past reasons #1, #2, and #3, you are now about to run up against the harsh, pitiless reality of double-entry bookkeeping, and its fundamental premise: *the accounting for every transaction has two sides.* For example, if you sell 50 widgets to somebody for $1,300, you record $1,300 in revenue from that sale in your accounting records. But you also receive something of value in exchange for that sale (cash, or a promise to pay cash in the future, or the forgiveness of a debt that you owe, or an equally valuable asset in exchange), and that also must be recorded in your accounting books.

From the standpoint of ensuring ethical conduct and telling the truth with your accounting information, this mathematical model of double-entry bookkeeping is a very powerful thing, because in order to preserve an accounting fiction, *you have to lie about two things, not just one.* Suppose the above 50-widget sale were a complete fiction that you were trying to slip past everyone. Your first lie is in your sales revenue records, but the all-important second lie relates to what you received of value in exchange for the sale. Obviously, if you haven't received the $1,300 in cash, you won't get any support from the bank account records. Instead, you record an outstanding receivable, and then someone making a simple phone call to the purported customer ("Hello? When are you going to pay the thirteen hundred dollars for the fifty widgets you bought?") can cook your goose. And it's even worse for you if it's your *auditors* who figure all this out.[2]

To support my assertion that it's extremely difficult to get away with accounting fraud, I offer this fact for consideration: there are *very few* examples of sustained accounting fraud. Even Enron, whose accounting fraud was perpetrated by "the smartest guys in the room," took less than two years to unravel completely, at least from the time that the principal fraud in question became material to Enron's overall results. In fact, the record of successful accounting frauds is so skimpy that one has to wonder why they were even attempted in the first place. Then again, how often do we learn of examples of all sorts of criminal, immoral, or otherwise inappropriate behavior, and our first reaction is to scratch our heads and wonder what the perpetrators were thinking when they thought they could get away with it?

 Note

A notable sidebar to this discussion is the **Bernie Madoff case**. Although a few renegades asserted that his astonishing investment returns simply weren't possible, his fraud went generally undetected for nearly 20 years. It now appears that audits were never actually performed by the auditing firm that provided the auditor's opinion letter that accompanied Madoff's annual financial statements. Madoff's fraud (really nothing more than a Ponzi scheme) was so simple that a proper audit would have uncovered it immediately. Even failing that, a peer review of the auditor's work (which for hard-to-swallow reasons was never performed) would have instantly uncovered the flaws in the auditor's work. This episode highlights the reliance we place on supposedly credible individuals and institutions, and **the importance of properly conducted audits** to our entire financial system.

Reason #5: It's the "Gotcha" of This Book

Not all deception is deliberate. In fact, when it comes to presenting numbers, I can identify three types of deception:

1. You deceive *yourself*, and therefore publish deceptive information.
2. You deceive *your audience*, unintentionally.
3. You deceive your audience, *intentionally*.

Instances of the first two types of deception outnumber instances of the third, and overwhelmingly so. I know this not just from experience, but from the observation that few people have the combination of skill, venality, nerve, and stupidity necessary to attempt deception. But even more than that, *the rules and practices suggested in this book make each of the above three situations less likely to lead to tragedy.* In other words, good quantation leads to less deception. Permit me to elaborate.

You Deceive **Yourself, *and Therefore Publish Deceptive Information.*** Think of yourself as the most important member of your audience. You are certainly the *first* one to see your information. You are the person most familiar with the subject matter of your reports and probably the person who cares the most about their accuracy. If you can't understand your own quantation, go back and improve your report designs until you do. Once you can understand it, and you have produced reports that are succinct, clear, and meaningful *to you*, you will find that you are much less likely to deliver reports that either have errors or are prone to being misunderstood.

You Deceive **Your Audience, *Unintentionally.*** Being your own editor does not work 100% of the time. You will, from time to time, deliver erroneous or confusing information. This happens, but the only thing more painful than sending out erroneous or confusing information *is to send it out and have it go undetected for too long*, because then you might get blamed for sloppy work, or worse. In other words, in a perfect world, your audience finds your mistakes *quickly*. Your best protection is to deliver high-quality quantation that your audience knows how to read and can provoke good questions, so flaws will get smoked out quickly. If nothing else, if you deliver good reports, then at least there is a much better chance that your audience will actually *read* them!

You Deceive Your Audience, **Intentionally.** Ironically, it's *good* quantation that brings out the questions and skepticism in people. As I said in Chapter 9, you should view this as a *good* thing if your intentions are benevolent. (If your intentions are malevolent, that's another issue.) Probing questions will often smoke out numbers that are too good to be true, or pierce the veil of information that is deliberately confusing. In this way, good quantation leads to more astute audiences, which is a complex process of influence that we'll discuss ahead. So, regardless of whether your intentions are honorable, the fact remains that following the rules and practices of effective quantation reduces the chance of misunderstandings between you and your audience. And that's a good thing.

Don't Be So Smug, You Civil Servants and Elected Officials!

Presenting and understanding numbers in the public policy arena is of enormous importance in areas like fiscal management, taxation, healthcare, and environmental issues, among others. Unfortunately, the quality of quantation and the professional standards for presenting numbers that most of us see in politics (and the public policy arena in general) are *worse* than they are for business management and financial reporting. Here's why:

- The "metrics" and objectives in public policy areas like fiscal management, taxation, and health care are poorly defined and selectively chosen. There are few unarguable metrics like good-ol' revenue and profits, and it's much more difficult to design reports when you don't know what the most important numbers are or why they're important.
- The audiences for business numbers have a clear and vested interest in accurate, comprehensible information. This linkage is much less clear regarding public policy, and the audiences are far less likely to demand more clarity, especially from politicians and administrators *they support*.
- Senior corporate leaders, especially CEOs and CFOs, thoroughly understand the consequences of missteps. That awareness doesn't always prevent bad behavior, but it's definitely a deterrent.

There is an immense wealth of data generated by professional, unbiased organizations. This information is often hard to find, poorly organized, and presented in ways confusing to all but the *cognoscenti* and not easily downloadable into usable spreadsheets.

I mention this because a critical driving force that can convince our civil servants and elected officials to upgrade the quality and availability of all this great information and present the numbers clearly and ethically is—you guessed it—the audience! Do you vote? Do you pay taxes? The cycle of improvement where better quantation leads to more knowledgeable audiences, which leads to better presenters and better quantation, applies to public policy just as it applies to business reporting. So feel free to start training your presenters!

Your Audience Has a Role, Too

Clear, competent quantation makes it much easier for the audience to read and understand the numbers, and it helps them grasp the subject matter well enough to ask intelligent, probing questions. I cannot stress this enough. But there's more going on here than meets the eye. People are famously afraid of numbers, and they are often unwilling to learn more about how to understand them, partly because they don't realize that understanding numbers is a literacy skill, just like reading *words* is a literacy skill. Numerical literacy is a skill that must be taught and then practiced; it is not an innate aptitude that only a few are blessed with. It's a shame that so many people fail to recognize this and just throw their hands up at the first sight of a few numbers. Moreover, it's a lot easier to practice numerical literacy if you start with numbers that are presented competently. After all, no matter how literate you are, you won't understand a memo if the writer can't construct an English sentence, and you won't be able to get anything out of an oral presentation if the speaker is incoherent.

In any kind of communication, there must be a feedback loop. The presenter writes, or speaks, and the audience reads, or listens. If the audience doesn't understand, they speak up, and the presenter uses the feedback to improve the way the information is presented. With quantation, this feedback loop is all too often broken—the audience doesn't speak up, presuming that they're simply not gifted enough or smart enough to understand the numbers. If the *real* problem is that the numbers aren't being presented in a way that any reasonably competent audience member can understand them, the presenter never learns, and, sadly, the quantation never improves.

 Note

The **Enron fiasco** is a case in point. Information that could have provoked searching questions (and perhaps unraveled the inappropriate accounting practices) was presented to board members, auditors, outside legal counsel, securities analysts, and many others. So few of them spoke up that the ones who did speak up weren't taken seriously. The record shows that some of those who didn't speak up *acknowledged* that they didn't understand the information they were looking at, and stayed silent because they didn't feel competent or knowledgeable enough to understand the information, or out of a misplaced trust in the presenters.

We can cite other culpable examples as well: the investors who were clueless about the lending risks they were investing in during the 2008 financial industries meltdown; the homeowners who, in the period leading up to that meltdown, signed up for financial commitments they didn't understand; and regulators at the Securities and Exchange Commission who failed, in spite of numerous complaints, to observe that Bernie Madoff's investments were completely fictitious. Tragedies like this can be avoided by information competently presented to an audience that takes its review responsibilities seriously and does not make decisions if it doesn't understand the information presented.

Note

At a recent "Directors' College," a three-day event held for public company directors by Stanford University and other universities, I heard Professor Roman Weil[3] deliver this admonition/plea to a roomful of high-powered corporate directors: "If you don't remember anything else I say today, *please* remember this: **never vote *yes* on any board proposition that you don't understand**."

If *directors of Fortune 50 corporations* need to be encouraged to do this, we all do. Permit me to broaden this encouragement to assert that presenters need to train their audiences, and audiences need to train the presenters.

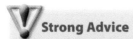

Strong Advice

Tell your audience that you expect them to **read your reports** and that you expect them to **ask questions** when they don't understand and to **suggest improvements**. If they do this for you, your commitment to them is that you will **respond** to their questions, you will **help them understand** the reports, and you will provide continually **clearer and better** information.

As long as people have been around other people, it has been possible to be inundated by *words*. But the twin revolutions of computing and communications have made numbers much easier to produce and disseminate, and as such, *anyone* can generate numbers and *everyone* has access to them. In previous periods in history, quantation was generated for people who had a particular reason for being deeply interested in the numbers, by people who contributed significant effort and possessed specialized skills. But those days are gone. Today, we have access to volumes of numerical information and our responsibility to know how to present numbers *and* to understand them is now an obligation of the modern age.

While there are of course examples of quantation that are *meant* to deceive, all too often the deception is unintended. What too many people take as dishonesty is nothing more than incoherence, and that is easily remedied by understanding the rules and practices described in *Painting with Numbers*. But take heart! Quantation is a literacy skill, no harder or easier to master than writing or reading. And if audiences took the perspective that they *ought* to be able to understand the numbers, they would be more likely to demand clearer information from the presenters, rather than question their own intelligence or assume that most numbers presenters are untrustworthy.

NOTES

1. Scrushy has not gotten off scot-free. In 2009, in a civil trial related to the issues raised in the criminal trial, he was ordered to pay $2.9 billion in damages. And he was convicted of bribing the governor of Alabama in a completely different, but still HealthSouth-related, matter, for which he began serving a prison term in 2007.

2. Many people not intimately familiar with accounting methodology react with raised eyebrows when they hear the term *double-entry bookkeeping*, because to them it conjures up images of "two sets of books," a practice that is sometimes (but by no means always) highly unethical. Considering that the double-entry feature of accounting is what makes financial statements so reliable and so hard to fiddle with, I find this perception ironic.

3. As of this writing, Professor Weil is professor of Accounting, Taxation, and Business Law at New York University's business school. He has numerous other teaching, writing, and executive education credentials, including an affiliation of 45 years with the University of Chicago's business school. Perhaps most important for this book and for me personally, he is the co-author of *Accounting: The Language of Business*, a book, which is now in its 11th edition, that makes common sense of a complex discipline.

CHAPTER 16

Now, What's the *First* Thing You Do?

Well begun is half done.

—Aristotle

As we conclude this review of the craft (and art) of quantation, I'd like to share a personal anecdote: Early in my career as a CFO at a software startup company, I participated in a large meeting where we were addressing a pressing and complex financial issue. All of us around the table were looking at a rather elaborate spreadsheet intended to analyze and summarize the issue we were discussing. At one point in the discussion, I started to provide an explanation of the spreadsheet logic, remarking that I was the one who had built the spreadsheet. One of the participants, an investor and a partner at a venture capital firm, looked across the table at me and said, "I know you did, Randy. I recognize the work." The remark stunned me. I didn't interpret the partner's comment as praise for the spreadsheet—although I *hope* he thought it was good work! No, what struck me was that he was observing that he could tell *who* had prepared a report by looking at it.

When we read a few paragraphs of an article or hear a few bars of a song, we can often tell who the writer or the artist was. But what is it that makes the work so recognizable? The style? The delivery? The attention to detail? The technical skill? The creativity of expression? The answer could be a combination of any of those factors, but having your work of art be recognizable as yours is *usually* a good thing and something to be proud of. Until this investor's remark it had never occurred to me that the same could be true of *quantation*. But it is.

My Last, Best Tip

The notion of quantation as both a craft and an art is a central premise of this book. So is the idea expressed above, that quantation is a personal expression that reflects your own abilities to think and organize and your skill at understanding your audience. In this vein, it seems only fitting that we end *Painting with Numbers* with a suggestion about what to do *first* when you're asked to design and deliver new quantation:

> **Strong Advice**
>
> When developing a report or a complete reporting package, the *first* thing you should do is **lay out the final summary page.**

Not only is this the *first* thing you should do, but it is the single most valuable tip out of the hundreds of suggestions in these pages.

Your job is to provide information that is useful and meaningful to your enterprise, so you should *start* by designing the report that will achieve this objective. Focus first on your audience's needs and on how they will best understand your information. Do *not* focus on what data you have in your accounting system (or other database) or how it's organized. And if you are designing a *package* of several reports, take the same approach within the package: start with the *big kahuna*: the "executive summary," the one page your audience will read first and the one page they will read if they read only one page. Once you've done that, work backward from there: lay out the supporting reports, and *only then* focus on figuring out how to derive the report numbers from the raw numbers out there in the accounting system or other data sources.

Not only is this suggestion good quantation design, but if you start with the end report, you will get insight into whether your systems can provide the needed information. If they *can't*, the right approach is to make the system changes necessary to ensure that you *can* collect the right information. Even if that process will take some time, early awareness and setting expectations accordingly is better than having to say, "*Uhhh*, sorry—we don't know how to get that information," after you've handed out the reports.

It's Just a Skill

You've just completed a long course in quantation, and you should feel both energized with your new knowledge and pleasantly surprised that you understood it all (especially if you don't consider yourself a "numbers person"). In other words, you don't have to be good at math to be good at quantation. You are not *born* with the ability to do quantation—you *learn* it.

Many career counseling and personal testing agencies distinguish between skills and aptitudes. A *skill* is a learned or acquired ability, like typing quickly or being able to construct a grammatically correct sentence. An *aptitude* is an innate component of our makeup, like the ability to reason mathematically, having perfect pitch, or the ability to envision a building in three dimensions from glancing at a blueprint. Aptitudes are something we are born with. Skills are something most of us can master if we work at them.

I draw this distinction because I feel strongly that the abilities to present numbers clearly and to understand properly presented numbers are skills no harder or easier to learn than other abilities associated with literacy, like writing, reading, and speaking. To reinforce this point, frequently throughout *Painting with Numbers*, I've made analogies between the various quantation skills and the skills of writing and speaking. All too often people see the abilities to generate and to understand quantation as aptitudes that only a few are born with and that cannot be developed by those who aren't. This is a total fallacy. It's also a shame because when people see quantation skills as aptitudes that can't be learned, they don't try to learn them, and because they don't *try* to learn them, they *don't* learn them, and poor quantation continues to proliferate.

Where We Have Been

Let's review what you've learned and where we've been. We started *Painting with Numbers* in a very tactical way, with a close look at using the Arabic numeral system to your advantage. We then examined how the way your quantation *looks* affects its clarity and usefulness, and the importance of the *words* as well as the numbers. We discussed how to take into account the way your particular *audience* sees the world, and how to factor that into your quantation. We reviewed how to use software tools to develop spreadsheets, graphs, and slideshows in order to save time and make your quantation more efficient and effective. Our final area of tactical focus covered how *key indicators* provide your audience with additional context and meaning, and how reports like the Natural P&L address the management needs of a specific business or other organization. I sincerely hope that you've come away from your reading well-armed with useful tips and tricks.

I like to think of this quantation journey as a pathway to mastering a real skill. There is a progression of ability as you develop that skill. Being a real virtuoso, whether as a musician, a writer, or a creator of quantation, requires *three* levels of mastery:

1. Knowing and understanding the **rules and best practices**
2. Understanding your **audience**
3. Being expert in the **subject matter**

Mastering each level depends on having mastered the previous level(s). You can't perform at all unless you have basic skill in the craft. You can't perform *for a particular audience* unless you have a deep awareness of whom you are performing for. And you can't communicate and display your *expertise* to that audience unless you can demonstrate a true grasp of the subject matter.

The Rules and Best Practices.   Every craft has its basic knowledge. In writing, you can't write a coherent, comprehensible sentence until you learn grammar and have a large enough vocabulary to choose the right words. In speaking, you can't be an effective speaker until you learn how to project your voice, and keep the *ums*, *ers*, and *y'knows* out of your speech. In music, you can't play in an orchestra until you know the scales, can read music, and know how to transpose to another key. Every skill has its rules and best practices, and quantation is no exception. The specific areas we touched on for quantation include:

- Putting numerals and numbers on the page properly (Chapter 1)
- Organizing information so that it's *visually* comprehensible and meaningful (Chapter 2)
- Using words economically, yet clearly, precisely, and in a way that makes the *numbers* as meaningful as possible (Chapter 3)
- Using emphasis and providing context to make your quantation logic easy to follow (Chapter 4)
- Using Excel and other spreadsheet software skillfully and efficiently to enhance your ability to deliver great quantation (Chapters 5 and 6)
- Designing graphs so that they are not only visually meaningful but comprehensible (Chapter 7)
- Understanding the limitations of PowerPoint and other presentation software so that the quantation in your slideshows is as effective as possible (Chapter 8)
- Understanding the delicate quantation balances and trade-offs involved in the War of the Adjectives (Chapter 9)
- Presenting key indicators for maximum effect and in a way that your audience understands how they were calculated (Chapter 10)
- Designing management reports useful for your specific organization (Chapter 11)

Your Audience.   Understanding and respecting your audience is just as important with quantation as it is with any other communication skill. In some ways, it's more important, because so many people display a lack of confidence or even fear when confronted with numbers, and some even express a mistrust of the presenter merely because quantation is involved. Chapter 4 was focused extensively on understanding this dynamic, and offered a number of specific tips and guidelines. Sprinkled throughout the rest of the book were discussions of how the way you present numbers affects your relationship with your audience. The Deadly Sins are so categorized because of their effect on that personal audience relationship. As I've said before, it is no accident that nearly half of the Deadly Sins presented in *Painting with Numbers* are introduced in Chapter 4.

The Subject Matter.   You've learned the rules about how to put the numbers on the page, and you know your audience (you know what their information needs are, how they process information, and their general level of technical awareness). All of this is essential, but one more important requirement of having deep skills is to be as knowledgeable about your organization's business as your audience.

 Note

One of my favorite childhood books was *The Peterkin Papers*,[1] a collection of short stories written by Lucrecia P. Hale in the 1800s. The stories were about the Peterkins, a delightful, earnest family a little short on brains and common sense. In one of the stories, "The Peterkins Try to Become Wise," the family concludes that the main thing that distinguishes wise folks from others is having written a book, so they set about to achieve that. They collect all the necessary materials, and the story concludes as they gather round to write the book:

"So Solomon John sat down, and the family all sat round the table looking at him. He had his pen, his ink, and his paper. He dipped his pen into the ink and held it over the paper, and thought a minute, and then said, 'But I haven't got anything to say.'"

Don't be a Peterkin. In "Part III: Real Mastery" we discussed using subject matter expertise to help deliver really effective quantation, with topics that included:

- The overall importance of being just as much of an expert in your organization's operations as the people for whom you are preparing quantation (Chapter 9)
- Using key indicators to provide context for the raw report numbers and as metrics for determining and measuring success (Chapter 10)[2]
- Designing a management income statement (or P&L) that is truly useful and meaningful to your particular organization (Chapter 11)
- Understanding the interaction between the financial statements produced to comply with generally accepted accounting principles (GAAP), and the more free-form quantation that is really the subject of *Painting with Numbers* (Chapter 12)
- Using quantation to deliver useful information in the public policy arena and in other walks of life besides business reporting (Chapters 13 and 14)

As I was writing *Painting with Numbers*, I talked with many people about what the book was about. The reactions were largely positive and I got lots of useful suggestions. One suggestion that I have resisted, though, was to have the book provide templates for specific reports and spreadsheets, or include a CD with such items that the reader could upload to his or her computer. I've resisted this suggestion because every organization's information needs are different, and every audience has different characteristics. Moreover, the truly immense range of choices you have as a presenter of numbers, and the opportunities you have to put your own personal stamp on the way you present numbers, make relying on someone else's templates a poor idea that will prevent you from taking full advantage of the medium. It's just not possible for there to *be* a quantation cookbook. After all, I am not aware of any books titled *Eloquent Rhetoric for Idiots,* or *Jazz Composition for Dummies.*[3]

I like to think of *Painting with Numbers* as one giant pep-talk. Many people think of *presenting* numbers as some sort of alchemy practiced only by the "numbers guys." And a similar number of people see *understanding* numbers as an equally black art. Both perspectives are just plain wrong. Presenting numbers effectively is nothing of the sort: it is a *communication* skill much like clear and coherent writing and eloquent speaking are communication skills. I hope I've demystified this art by laying out the rules and best practices of quantation and helping you understand how your audience processes this particular type of communication.

You can do this! Now, go forth and quantate!

NOTES

1. See Lucrecia P. Hale, *The Peterkin Papers*, New York Review Children's Collection, 2006.
2. Chapter 10 has enough presentation and layout suggestions that it could easily have been one of the chapters in "Part I: The Tools," but I chose to include it in "Part III: Real Mastery" because the real art of presenting key indicators lies in creating and presenting those metrics and ratios that are the ones that are meaningful to your particular organization and audience.
3. I note with some chagrin that my publisher, John Wiley & Sons, does publish a book titled *Thermodynamics for Dummies.* I have not read it yet. If Wiley comes out with *Non-Euclidian String Theory for Dummies*, I am going to throw in the towel on this point.

APPENDIX

Jazz Meets Theology

Punctuation to the writer is like anatomy to the artist: He learns the rules so he can knowledgeably and controllédly depart from them as art requires.

—Lynne Truss, in *Eats, Shoots & Leaves: The Zero Tolerance Approach to Punctuation,* quoting Thomas McCormack, in *The Fiction Writer, the Novel, and the Novelist*

Here, we revisit *all* of the Deadly Sins introduced throughout *Painting with Numbers*. We discuss why they are organized the way they are, and consider some specific situations where it might actually be permissible to (gasp) commit them.

What do a great jazz musician and a great presenter of numbers have in common? Well, for starters, ask a jazz musician about his or her training and background. You'll be hard-pressed to find a good one that doesn't have years of classical (or at least formal) training and a solid grounding in music theory. And yet, great jazz is all about breaking the rules, and not only that, breaking the rules on the spur of the moment and in an improvised way. It takes tremendous skill to play jazz well. You have to know which rules you can break (and when), and you often have to do it in real time.

Presenting financials and other numbers is like playing music: to do it well you have to know the rules, because following the rules makes the quantation understandable (and the music sound good). When a jazz musician *breaks* the rules, the audience doesn't notice as long as it makes the music enjoyable or interesting to listen to. Similarly, in quantation, occasionally breaking the rules makes it easier for your audience to see the truth. What I mean here is that one aspect of good quantation is its ability to reveal the truth. I don't mean *truth* in a moral sense; I mean it in an objective sense. The Deadly Sins are practices and behaviors that get in the way of revealing that truth, either by making your information hard to understand or by making your audience question your professionalism or your credibility.

Revisitation

Let's start with a recap of the Deadly Sins. First, consider the *original* Seven Deadly Sins from Christian theology. They are often grouped into the "warm-hearted" sins that are committed in a fit of passion on the spur of the moment (lust, gluttony, and anger) and the "coldhearted" or "slow-burning" sins that eat at a person's insides over a long time (greed, sloth, and envy). (We'll get to pride, the remaining Deadly Sin, later.) Similarly, we can classify the Deadly Sins of Presenting Numbers into the Sins of Presentation and the Sins of Behavior. In that spirit, here are all the sins introduced in *Painting with Numbers* (with original chapter references in parentheses):

The Sins of Presentation

1. **Not right-justifying** a column of numbers (Ch. 1)
2. Basing column width or row height on the **length of the caption** (Chs. 2, 8)
3. Using visual effects for any reason **other than clarifying, distinguishing, or adding meaning** to information (Chs. 2, 7, 8)
4. **Unclear, imprecise**, or (worst of all) **incorrect** row and column captions (Ch. 3)
5. **No title or timestamp** (date *and* time) on printed spreadsheets (Chs. 3, 4)
6. In a package with more than one multiple-time-period report, presenting **some reports in forward and some in reverse chronological order** (Ch. 4)
7. Presenting numbers with **no context** whatsoever—no comparison to prior periods, to plan/budget, to competitors, or to anything else (Ch. 4)
8. **Omitting totals** where they would be appropriate or **presenting totals** where they aren't appropriate (Ch. 4)
9. **Shrinking font size** in order to fit a report onto a single page, or creating a "single page" **with the help of Scotch tape** (Ch. 4)
10. Using a **pie chart**—period (Ch. 7)

The Sins of Behavior

11. Publishing a spreadsheet with a **basic error** that should have been **easy to detect** (Ch. 6)

12. To print the finished report, requiring your audience to **do more than just click the "Print" icon** (Ch. 4)

13. "Well, I can see why you reached that conclusion, but that's because you didn't review the whole package." (Ch. 4)

14. "Oh, is *that* what you wanted? We have all that information—all you had to do was ask." (Ch. 9)

15. "Gee, no one has ever had a problem with this report before." (Ch. 9)

16. "I never intended for anyone else to use this spreadsheet." (Ch. 5)

17. "I know most of you can't read the numbers on this slide, but . . ." (Ch. 8)

The distinction between these two categories is important: the Sins of Presentation are errors related to how you put numbers on the page and how your quantation looks. The Sins of Behavior are acts or utterances that reflect your professional attitude toward your audience and your work.

So, in the spirit of jazz musicians and theology, let's review each of these Deadly Sins in a little more detail and talk about when it actually might be OK to commit them. Some of these sins are hard to justify under any circumstances, but in the interests of completeness, I'll provide at least one excuse for every one—even if a few of the excuses are pretty flimsy.

The Sins of Presentation

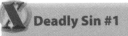

Deadly Sin #1

Not right-justifying a column of numbers

Recall from Chapter 1 that right-justifying a column of numbers makes it easier for your audience to grasp the magnitudes of the numbers in that column at a glance. But sometimes, *size does not matter*. If you are presenting a column of numbers where there is no meaning associated with the arithmetic value of the numbers, the normally important feature of right-justification isn't so important. In fact, you may even find it useful *not* to right-justify the numbers, just to send a signal to your audience that the information should be processed like words rather than numbers. Consider, for example, dates presented in the "mm-dd-yy" notation commonly used in the United States. Report A-1 is a list of people's birthdates.

```
┌─────────────────────────────┐
│       Report A-1            │
│       Birthdates            │
│                             │
│   Frank        1-5-62       │
│   Mary        12-31-58      │
│   Louis       10-6-79       │
│   Ed           5-1-83       │
│   Jane        10-11-67      │
│   Marcel       5-30-52      │
└─────────────────────────────┘
```

REPORT A-1:   Birthdates

In this case, *centering* the numbers doesn't look too bad. If you *really* wanted the dates to be used as numbers, with sorting and ranking easier (for example, you wanted it to be easier to find the oldest or the youngest people on the list), it would make more sense to use the "yy-mm-dd" notation.[1]

Here's another example—a list of product identification numbers—where the numbers have some "intelligence." In this case, the first digit identifies the product category and the remaining digits complete the ID number. Report A-2 is the alphabetical list of products.

```
┌─────────────────────────────┐
│       Report A-2            │
│    Product ID Numbers       │
│                             │
│   chaise lounge    4100     │
│   fertilizer        609     │
│   hedge clipper     316     │
│   lawn mower       3602     │
│   patio table       495     │
│   shovel           3100     │
│   tomato seeds     6222     │
└─────────────────────────────┘
```

REPORT A-2:   Product ID Numbers

In this numbering scheme, the category code is the leftmost digit: *3* for gardening tools, *4* for outdoor furniture, and *6* for plants and materials. A more specific identification is in the two *or three* digits after the category code. In this case, *left-justifying* makes more sense, because it makes it easier to recognize the category for each product name.[2]

Finally, consider a list of international telephone numbers. Note that international phone numbers have a one-, two-, or three-digit country code, and the length and format of each country's in-country numbers differ widely. Report A-3 is a list of people's complete phone numbers, including both country code and local number.

Report A-3 Telephone Numbers		
Omar al-Saud	+966	2468-3073
Anton Chekov	+7	06 08 09 27 38
Marcel Duchamp	+33	03 121698476
Pierluigi Indelicato	+39	5 333 709 622
Ed Jones	+1	(650) 465.9999
Chuck Mountbatten	+44	007 2953-6060
Sean O'Halloran	+353	64.73.82
John Smith	+1	(212) 555.4343

REPORT A-3:   Telephone Numbers

In this example, we've chosen to *right-justify* the country code (that's the digits at the left, right after the "+"). As a result, the local numbers that follow (which have completely different formats, with different numbers of digits, from country to country) are left-justified. This makes it a little easier to make visual groupings by country, but at the same time it's also easier to pick out where the local number begins.[3,4] This might be useful if you don't *need* the country code to call a given phone number—for example, if you are already in that country and want to dial what is now a local number.

 Deadly Sin #2

Basing column width or row height on the **length of the caption**

You may occasionally be presenting information where it's essential to present exactly worded row or column headings, and no paraphrasing or summarizing will do. An example might be documents where the legal requirements prescribe exact wording.

 Deadly Sin #3

Using visual effects for any reason **other than clarifying, distinguishing, or adding meaning to** information

This is a presentation tactic that is both a Deadly Sin *and* takes extra effort to execute, but everyone is entitled to some fun once in a while. If your purpose for the additional "unnecessary" visual effects is to entertain, amuse, or just simply get your audience's attention, then go right ahead. Just because you're presenting numbers doesn't mean you can't display a little showmanship, as long as your showmanship is not actually *destructive* to your audience's ability to understand your quantation.

Of course, if the style guidelines set by your organization call for it, you may need to comply with those guidelines (rather than be blamed for an act of insubordination).

Deadly Sin #4
Unclear, imprecise, or (worst of all) **incorrect** row and column captions

Clarity and precision are not essential when you are merely trying to get a *concept* across. Consider the following example in Report A-4, which is a graph illustrating basic approaches to incentive compensation. The graph charts incentive compensation (defined as a percentage of target compensation) as a function of performance (scored as a percentage of the employee's objectives). In all cases, both overachievement (i.e., scoring above 100%) and underachievement are possible. The three types of employees are:

1. **Sales representatives.** Their plans (the solid line in Report A-4) are frequently intended to motivate reps to hit home runs. Underachievement (performance below 100% of objectives) is penalized, but overachievement is heavily rewarded: in the graph shown, a sales rep performing at 150% earns 225% of target compensation.

2. **Professional services staff.** Their plans (broken line) provide incentive compensation directly in proportion to performance. So this graph is a straight line starting at the origin and passing through the point showing 100% of target compensation earned at 100% performance.

3. **General line management.** Often called MBO (management by objective) plans, their plans (dotted line) reward performance against a set of goals that is frequently highly subjective. As in school, 60% is considered a passing grade, so no bonus is paid for scores below that. And payouts above 100% of target, regardless of performance, don't occur. For example, if one of the MBO goals is to start all meetings on time, there's no extra bonus for starting all meetings five minutes early![5]

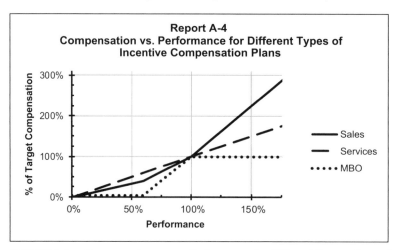

REPORT A-4: Compensation versus Performance for Different Types of Incentive Compensation Plans

The purpose of Report A-4 is to illustrate different *approaches* to incentive compensation (not how a particular incentive actually pays out in specific dollars). In an example like this, there is no reason to use terms more specific than "Performance" or "% of Target Compensation." Using more specific terms than that might actually defocus the reader from the fundamental principles the graph is intended to illustrate.

 Deadly Sin #5

No title or timestamp (date *and* time) on printed spreadsheets

First, let's remember why this is a sin: the timestamp enables your audience to have some sense of when the report was run, which can be useful or even critical information for many reasons.

However, sometimes the timeliness of the report isn't important. If the report supports an analysis that is valid at any time and isn't dependent on current information, you might want to omit the timestamp. In fact, omitting the timestamp can be a signal to your audience that this report *isn't* time dependent. Some examples:

- The impact of price discounts on gross margin, given the cost of sales as a percentage of list price on one axis, and the amount of the discount on the other. This can be a handy cheat-sheet for salespeople trying to decide which products the company can afford to discount and how much; the logic in the table is totally unaffected by what the prices and margins are for any specific product.

- An analysis of the impact on an individual's net worth, given various personal financial planning decisions, such as the amount of income put into retirement plans, current individual tax rates and possible future rates, expected return on the investments, and so on.

Information like this reveals fundamental truths that haven't changed in the past and won't in the future. No need to tell them *when* you clicked the "Print" icon.

As far as omitting the *title* of a report, I am at a loss for an excuse.[6]

 Deadly Sin #6

In a package with more than one multiple-time-period report, presenting **some reports in forward and some in reverse chronological order**

This Deadly Sin usually occurs only when you are delivering a package with reports that were generated by various people. I'm presuming that you would *never* commit this error all by yourself. So when you are faced with this particular Deadly Sin, and (1) you are pressed for time and (2) the author of this particular report is not you, *and that fact is absolutely clear to the audience*, go ahead and present the report as is.

If, however, you've received a spreadsheet for inclusion in a package that is in the opposite chronological order from the other reports in the package and you'd like to fix it, don't panic. Here's a handy-dandy spreadsheet procedure for getting the columns in the right order:

1. In an unused row of the worksheet, enter the numbers 1 through *n* consecutively in the columns you need to reorder (where *n* is the number of columns involved).
2. Highlight the columns you've numbered.
3. Using the Data/Sort command sequence, re-sort the columns using the row you created in step #1 as the "Sort By" row.
4. Before you move on to the next item on your to-do list:
    - Make sure the additional row isn't in your Print_Area.
    - Make sure you don't need to make any cosmetic format corrections needed as a result of reversing the column order.
    - Make sure nothing strange happened with your cell formulas as a result of the sort.

While we're on the subject of Deadly Sin #6, note that occasionally you will have one influential, autocratic person in the organization (often a corporate director) who insists on reverse chronological order. This is a good opportunity to practice standing your ground or to enlist the support of other senior managers or corporate directors. Producing reports in *both* chronological orders is a pointless, time-consuming activity. Moreover, nothing good ever comes from having two different reports floating around containing identical information merely formatted differently.

 Deadly Sin #7

Presenting numbers with **no context** whatsoever—no comparison to prior periods, to plan/budget, to competitors, or to anything else

Once in a while your audience actually *does* have "photographic memory," or at least they're sophisticated enough or familiar enough with the subject matter that the numbers will make sense even *without* other numbers to compare them to. If this is the case, *and* the information needs to be presented so that it can be quickly digested and acted upon, then committing this Deadly Sin isn't quite so awful.

Deadly Sin #8

Omitting totals where they would be appropriate or **presenting totals** where they aren't appropriate

As I mentioned in the introduction of this Deadly Sin in Chapter 4, omitting totals is subtler and less destructive than the other Deadly Sins, and it is one of the sins your audience is least likely to notice. Accordingly, if your report has a lot of rows and you are faced with a choice between omitting a few rows and either committing Deadly Sin #8 or committing Deadly Sin #9 (shrinking font size or using Scotch tape), good-ol' #9 is the more noticeable and annoying sin.

The sin of presenting totals when they *aren't* appropriate is subtler still. Go ahead if you think that for some reason those totals *might* actually be useful to your audience, or if the presence of totals can somehow act as a built-in validity check on the report numbers.[7]

Deadly Sin #9

Shrinking font size in order to fit a report onto a single page, or creating a "single page" **with the help of Scotch tape**

This is a bad habit that leads down the slippery slope to sloppy quantation, so I'm reluctant to give aid and comfort here. Moreover (and please note that I am watching out for your best interests), this Deadly Sin is a bad habit because seniority is often highly correlated with age, *as is difficulty reading tiny print*. Consider yourself warned.

However, committing the Deadly Sin of shrinking font size is more permissible if the particular report you are shrinking is *backup* material that you have included for completeness, while the essential report(s) remain(s) regulation size. Also, if you are confident that the report is most likely to be read on a computer screen (rather than in hardcopy) by people who know how to use the "zoom" capabilities, this sin is somewhat less likely to do harm.

Moving on to the Scotch-tape portion of this sin, I will acknowledge that once in a while:

- The report is addressing a really complicated process or situation.
- The audience includes primarily sophisticated consumers of this type of information, who are willing to spend lots of time understanding the information.
- The audience actually likes reports with Scotch tape all over them.

If at least two of these conditions are present, go with the Scotch tape. Otherwise, do yourself a favor and present the information per the admonitions in this book, because Scotch tape will certainly annoy many of the people in your audience, and it's the kind of tactic that people associate with junior and un-skilled administrators. Put yourself in a different category.

Deadly Sin #10
Using a **pie chart**—period

Although some might find a few of my Deadly Sins a bit *picky*, Deadly Sin #10 is the only Sin of Presentation that actually seems to be *controversial* to some. Some people just *looooooove* their pie charts. For that reason, I was sorely tempted to embellish on the theological undertone of this chapter and go papal on you by issuing an encyclical banning pie charts. But I concluded that such an approach would work about as well for me as it does for His Holiness. So instead, I will acknowledge that situations acceptable for using a pie chart *might* include:

▪ You have an unsophisticated audience to whom you are trying to give a rough sense of the magnitude of an issue. (A *very* unsophisticated audience. And a *very* rough sense of the magnitude of the issue.)

▪ You have a direct order from a superior officer.

Oh, wait. . . There actually is *one* type of visual impression where pie charts are effective, and I have Stephen Few to thank for pointing it out.[8] That impression is when you are trying to compare the sums of individual components. Say, for example, you have four components—we'll call them A, B, C, and D—and you want to compare A + B to C + D. Report A-5 is one of the relatively rare real-life examples of such a situation.

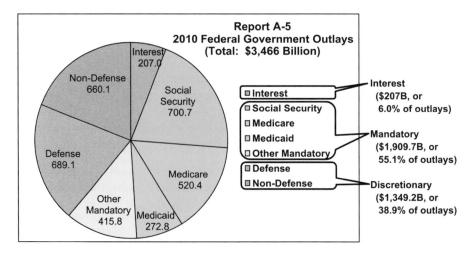

REPORT A-5:   2010 Federal Government Outlays (Total: $3,466 Billion)

Report A-5 shows your federal tax dollars[9] at work in 2010,[10] broken out by type of outlay. Note the use of the color shading to separate the outlays into three main categories:

1. **Mandatory** (yellowish wedges)—money the government must spend by law, which cannot be altered in the annual appropriations process
2. **Discretionary** (bluish wedges)—money that is allocated through the annual appropriations process
3. **Interest** (pink wedge)—the interest on the federal debt

Although each of the individual wedges is a significant component of federal spending (the smallest one is $207 billion!), the most important purpose of this graph is to give the viewer a sense of how much of federal outlays cannot be controlled by Congress through the appropriations process. You can get this sense by comparing the Interest (pink wedge) combined with the Mandatory outlays (yellowish wedges), to the Discretionary outlays (bluish wedges). As you can see, well over half (6.0% for Interest plus 55.1% for Mandatory, or 61.1%, to be exact) of federal spending is on autopilot. Only 38.9% of federal outlays— about half defense related and half not—can be controlled by congressional appropriations, and that's visually apparent from seeing the combined size of the two bluish wedges.

The Sins of Behavior

It's generally hard to defend yourself against (or receive absolution from) the Sins of Behavior. Because these sins relate to your *conduct* and not what your reports look like, it's hard to identify situations where committing them is even remotely technically appropriate. Moreover, whereas it is often possible to atone for a Sin of Presentation simply by fixing your report, atoning is much harder when the sin is more about your attitude than about what your numbers look like. As I've said frequently, one of the problems with these sins is that *you may never learn about the impression you created*. Recall from the discussion of Bolten's Law and its corollaries.

 **The Laws of Quantation**

Corollary #3 (general form) to Bolten's Law: The likelihood that your audience will express their concern about your motives for presenting information poorly is inversely proportional to the harshness of the conclusion they are in the process of forming.

So, rather than identifying when the Sins of Behavior are permissible, in some of the cases I'll focus on how you might act *instead*. And if you enjoy a little office dogfight now and then, I'll also offer a few suggestions on when these sins might be exactly what you *do* want to do. As they say, "A true gentleman never hurts someone else's feelings unintentionally." In other words, since the Sins of Behavior are sins mainly because of the impact they have on your audience, if that's the impact you're going to have on them, please make sure you mean it!

 Deadly Sin #11

Publishing a spreadsheet with a **basic error** that should have been **easy to detect**

Obviously, it is hard to imagine that you would ever deliberately deliver a report with errors. But let's not ignore reality, either. When you are in the business of generating and packaging information under time pressure, you will always find yourself facing the War of the Adjectives (see Chapter 9), which may mean you must trade off the time you spend ensuring that what you have is accurate for the time spent enhancing or clarifying your information. Sometimes it is wiser to choose the latter.

If you are concerned that you might have errors because you had to prepare the report hastily, one tactic is to enlist the audience's help. You can offer a humble and team-oriented remark like, "Folks, this is the first time we've had anyone review this package, and we'd appreciate your help in making sure we've got it right." (Obviously, you should consider your audience first. A remark like that is not exactly career-enhancing at a board of directors meeting!)

 Note

An anecdote from the olden days: Many years ago, I attended a presentation skills workshop. The basic lessons about oral presentations were just as true then as they are now, but the technology at the time of this workshop consisted of writing the slides on paper flipcharts with a large felt-tip pen. The instructor told us that some experienced presenters, when presenting numbers, would *deliberately* create occasional easy-to-find arithmetic errors. Since there's almost always someone in the audience checking the arithmetic in his or her head, that person would call the error to the presenter's attention. The presenter would offer profuse thanks for finding the error, and correct it immediately (with that felt-tip pen, of course—life was so simple back then). This was one tactic the presenter had for getting the audience more involved in the presentation experience. Unfortunately, this trick doesn't play as well when the numbers are computer-generated.

 Deadly Sin #12

To print the finished report, requiring your audience to **do more than just click the "Print" icon**

I've asked hundreds of people about their reaction when hitting the "Print" icon doesn't result in the intended report being printed out, and either irritation or anger is the unanimous reply. Even so, keeping your audience from being annoyed can be a challenge, especially when different people in your audience need to see different portions of the document or different levels of detail. For example, if your worksheet contains both summary information and backup detail, some people will need just the summary, some the detail, and some both. Or if your spreadsheet contains monthly, quarterly, and annual results (and maybe over several years, to boot), you might actually *want* your audience to have some flexibility about which portion gets printed out.

For this particular Deadly Sin, let's focus instead on successful strategies when you're confronted with a spreadsheet that just can't have one single Print_Area range. Here are some possible approaches:

- **Named ranges.** Create named ranges with sensible, intuitive names for each of the possible ranges the audience might want to print. See Long-Term Payoff Tip #4 ("Use Named Ranges") in Chapter 6 for more detail and an example.

- **Multiple worksheets.** If, for example, your document includes monthly, quarterly, and annual information, you might create each of the three reports in its own worksheet. You can assure that all the reports will be consistent with each other by making the annual and quarterly worksheet cells be formulas using the monthly cells. It's also helpful to use informative worksheet names in the tabs at the bottom of the Excel window ("Sheet1," "Sheet2," and "Sheet3" rarely cut it).

- **Macros.** When a workbook's range and variety of print alternatives is truly large, writing a macro to help users select what they want printed can be a huge labor saver. See the "Command Macros" discussion in Long-Term Payoff Tip #5 ("Use Named Formulas or Macros") in Chapter 6 for more detail and an example.

 Note

A digression/suggestion regarding print macros: This approach can be an extremely effective and impressive visual tool when you're presenting at a meeting where your information is being reviewed in real time. Rather than actually print the reports, have the macro execute the Print Preview function. That way, the audience can see the report on the screen or monitor and then just hit Escape to exit without printing. This method is especially powerful when you're presenting a business model with easily changeable assumptions; just change the assumptions, and then run the macro again.

Deadly Sin #13

"Well, I can see why you reached that conclusion, but that's because you didn't review the whole package."

In some subject areas, there will be reporting packages where the audience actually does have to review the reports carefully. These situations are rare, but if the situation (or the organization's culture) requires a high level of audience preparation, you might as well point that out to the slackers (that is, if they don't outrank you by too much).

Also—and this is an even rarer situation—you may be delivering a package with a "gotcha" in it. Sometimes pointing that out to the reader doesn't have to be a criticism of the reader's diligence, merely an observation that things aren't always what they seem to be. In such a situation this comment can be instructive rather than antagonistic.

 Deadly Sin #14

"Oh, is *that* what you wanted? We have all that information—all you had to do was ask."

Like the other Sins of Behavior, this remark often has nothing to do with the information itself, but rather with the message you're sending to the audience. Just because a comment is accurate doesn't always mean it's a good idea to make it (see Chapter 9); instead, it's usually best merely to thank the audience for the suggestion and ask them to keep the feedback coming.

Of course, once in a while you'll get an audience that actually *doesn't* understand what they should be asking for, and has given you no previous guidance in spite of your numerous requests. We can't all be spineless wimps all of the time, and sometimes blunt candor is a public service. I have stressed that delivering effective quantation depends on active audience participation and feedback (see Chapters 9 and 15 for a discussion of this specific point), so once in a while it is appropriate for you to speak up and tell your audience to do *their* job.

 Deadly Sin #15

"Gee, no one has ever had a problem with this report before."

Recall that this comment is a Deadly Sin because it sends so many different negative messages about you *and* your audience (see Chapter 9). So, harking back to my comment about gentlemanly behavior, make this comment to your audience only if you really mean it, that is, if you *intend* to disparage your audience (and you are not worried about the comments you might be making about yourself).

Deadly Sin #16

"I never intended for anyone else to use this spreadsheet."

Let me reintroduce this reminder: if you take the lessons of this book to heart, you will rarely need to utter these words in defense of sloppy work. If every time you tell yourself that the spreadsheet you're about to develop is going to be included in a package for the board of directors, you'll turn out great work every time. *And if you use these skills all the time, you'll be good enough and fast enough that it won't even be time consuming!*

But you can also use this statement to suggest both humility and an extremely high level of competence. If, in spite of your product's ad-hoc character, you sense that your audience is impressed by your quantation, a mildly worded suggestion that you set high standards for even the most ordinary tasks might make you seem more humble—much the same way your grandmother might say, "Oh, this old thing? It's just something I put on," when she wanted to express her modesty when complimented on her outfit.

Deadly Sin #17

"I know most of you can't read the numbers on this slide, but . . ."

This is an ugly one! This particular Deadly Sin is so annoying to so many people that I have given it the place of honor at the end of the list even though it wasn't the last one introduced in these pages. The only legitimate justification for this one is if you really *don't* care that your audience can't read the numbers. For example, the unreadable numbers might simply be supporting data for your presentation, and not central to your message. If you do this, though, be sure to make it clear to the audience that the information is being included only for purposes of completeness, and that they can review it at their leisure after your presentation (which they can do only if you're also distributing hard copy or electronic copy, of course).

The Deadliest Sin of All

I've had so much fun with the Deadly Sins that I can't resist adding just one more, even if it's only here in the Appendix. Picking up the thread of our theological discussion, I'll observe that the *deadliest* of the Seven Deadly Sins (on the Christian theology list, that is) is *pride*. Why is pride the deadliest Deadly Sin? Because it is the sin of feeling superior to everyone else because you are not guilty of the other six Deadly Sins. It's forgivable to be a sinner, especially if you acknowledge that fact occasionally, but to suggest that you are completely without sin puts you in a totally different theological league, and not one that is good.

In this spirit, I am pleased to announce the final, and *deadliest*, of the Deadly Sins of Presenting Numbers:

Deadly Sin #18

"I'm more focused on content than on presentation."

Please, *never* say this to your audience. With this statement, you are sending a message like the one that pride sends: that you are without sin because you are focused on the worthy pursuit of *content*, while others have yet to put away their childish, cosmetic concerns about how it all *looks* (which they have allowed to get in the way of understanding your excellent work).

I'll wrap up this discussion with the following true anecdote:

Note

At a board of directors meeting of a large oil company, a division manager was trying to explain a report to the board. After the first explanation, board members said they didn't understand the report, so he went through the explanation a second time. When the manager got that reaction again from the board after his second explanation, in frustration he said to them, "Look, I can *explain* it to you again, but I can't *understand* it for you."

One can only wonder how high this fellow bounced when he was thrown out the window into the parking lot.[11]

In conclusion, the art of quantation and the art of jazz are indeed very similar. In both communication forms, you need to understand the rules before you can break them, and you must break the rules in a way that will lead the audience to a greater understanding of some deeper truth. The epigraph to this Appendix, comparing the relationship between painting and anatomy, makes this point about a skill as mundane and persnickety as punctuation, for goodness sake. And if this understanding is critical to *punctuation*, then it's critical to *all* communication skills. The Deadly Sins of Presenting Numbers are a lighthearted way of looking at the rules of quantation that ultimately guide you to do the right thing: they guide you in the mechanics of how to put numbers on the page, and they tell you what to say and do to reflect a professional attitude toward your audience and your work. When and how you decide to break these rules is up to you, but break them only when you know *why* these rules work, and why breaking them is a better choice in any particular moment.

NOTES

1. For example, when using dates in your filenames, as discussed in Long-Term Payoff Tip #1 in Chapter 6.

2. A thoughtful reader might notice that the numbers in Report A-2 are intended to be read in the same way that a column of words might be read, for the same reasons. As we scan down a list of words, the length of the word is usually of little relevance. Instead, we look for a word by its first letter, and then by its second letter, and so on. Doing this visually is most efficient if the words are left-justified

3. There's a useful little trick here: in most computer fonts, each of the numerals 0 through 9 takes up the same amount of space on the page, and that amount is exactly equal to hitting the "space" key twice. This means that we could create the above table with a left-hand tab, and then type "space" twice before numbers with a two-digit country code, and four times before numbers with a one-digit country code.

   Computer fonts are cleverly designed this way to make sure that in columns of numbers, sighting down the page the numerals aren't ragged. And (this is true only for numerals and not for letters) the width of the boldface character is exactly the same as the width of the unbolded character. This means that columns of numbers won't look ragged even if some of the numbers are in boldface and some aren't. Check it out!

4. Report A-3 reflects an approach to presenting numbers you often see in scientific documents. It is considered proper scientific method to show only the number of significant digits appropriate for the measurement method. If a measuring device is considered accurate to four significant digits, regardless of the scale of the measured result, you should present only four digits in your report, with the decimal points lined up in the column. For example:

   4.305
   85.62
   0.1135
   308.1

   In business documents, you would almost never present such a "ragged" column of numbers. Instead, all numbers are shown with the same unit of measure (i.e., thousands of dollars, dollars, pennies, etc.) and precision. But when presenting scientific data it's a requirement, because the number of significant digits is important information.

5. One reason MBO plan payouts are so often capped at 100% is that objectives chosen are hard to quantify and score, and therefore subject to abuse. This is a shame, and often short-changes general line managers. Clear, meaningful quantation can play a significant role in well-thought-out compensation plans, but that is a subject for another book.

6. A famous bridge player was once asked by another player how he should have played a particular hand, and the famous player replied, "Under an assumed name." I guess some quantation reports might be like that.

7. See Long-Term Payoff Tip #9 in Chapter 6 for more discussion of built-in error-checking tactics.

8. See Few's paper, "Save the Pies for Dessert," on his website, www.perceptualedge.com, which I first cited in Chapter 7.

9. Plus about $1.5 trillion Uncle Sam borrowed to cover the deficit.

10. On a matter that takes us back to Chapter 1, note my choice to present the total as "$3,466 Billion" in the report title, rather than "$3.466 Trillion" or "$3.5 Trillion." I made that choice because all the numbers in the graph itself are presented in $ billions, and it seemed appropriate to use the same scale in presenting the title.

11. Actually, I'm told that this presenter's relationship by marriage to one of the corporate directors helped him avoid serious bodily harm.

About the Author

Randall Bolten grew up in Washington, D.C., the son of a CIA intelligence officer and a history professor. A Princeton University economics graduate, he headed west to earn an MBA at Stanford University. Falling in love with the west, he stayed and has spent his career in Silicon Valley. He is a seasoned financial executive, with many years directing the financial and other operations of high-technology companies. His 30-year career includes nearly 20 years as chief financial officer for both public companies and startups. Bolten has served as CFO for BroadVision, Phoenix Technologies, Arcot Systems, BioCAD, and Teknekron, and has also held senior financial management positions at Oracle and Tandem Computers. He now runs Lucidity, a consulting practice in Menlo Park, California, focused on short engagements with specific deliverables including business models, reporting packages, and incentive compensation plans. He divides his work time between Silicon Valley and Washington, D.C. When not working, he relaxes in Glenbrook, Nevada, in the tranquility of the Sierras. Most of all he is extremely proud of his two daughters. For more information, please visit www.painting-with-numbers.com.

Index